Communicating for Results in Government

James L. Garnett

FOREWORD BY DWIGHT WALDO

Communicating
for Results in
Government

A STRATEGIC APPROACH
FOR PUBLIC MANAGERS

Jossey-Bass Publishers · San Francisco

Substantial discounts on bulk quantities of Jossey-Bass books are available to corporations, professional associations, and other organizations. For details and discount information, contact the special sales department at Jossey-Bass Inc., Publishers. (415) 433-1740; Fax (415) 433-0499.

For international orders, please contact your local Paramount Publishing International office.

Library of Congress Cataloging-in-Publication Data

Garnett, James L.
  Communicating for results in government : a strategic approach for public managers / James L. Garnett. — 1st ed.
    p.   cm.—(The Jossey-Bass public administration series)
  Includes bibliographical references and index.
  ISBN 1-55542-405-8
  ISBN 0-7879-0000-1 (paperback)
  1. Communication in public administration.   I. Title.
  II. Series.
  JF1525.C59G37   1992
  350.007—dc20   91-29727
                                                                          CIP

FIRST EDITION
HB Printing   10 9 8 7 6 5 4 3 2 1   Code 9210
PB Printing   10 9 8 7 6 5 4 3 2 1   Code 9480

The Jossey-Bass
Public Administration Series

CONTENTS

**Part Three: Crucial Issues
in Government Communication**

FOREWORD

Communicating for Results in Government is a major undertaking on a significant but neglected topic. The book ought to prove valuable for government practitioners and academics alike. Once again, the author displays the talents that made his *Reorganizing State Government: The Executive Branch* a significant work of synthesis and innovation. But whereas in *Reorganizing* the task was to take a fresh look at traditional interests and activities, in this case the task has been one of drawing together diverse concepts, techniques, and experiences and focusing them on and in the interests of public management.

This work is better described as road building than as pathbreaking. Many paths have been opened over the years between the field of communications and the field of public management. After all, as Garnett reminds us, *reporting* was the R in Luther Gulick's 1937 mnemonic POSDCORB, a summary categorization of the tasks of public management. Indeed, the book makes the point that Gulick and other public administration pathbreakers were influential in shaping government administration and policy because they emphasized communication, an emphasis that later was lacking. This can justly be characterized as a road-building work because Garnett has brought together knowledge from many sources, integrated that knowledge by crafting a working model of government communication, and created a major synthesis. I predict that this work heralds, and will itself help to promote, a significant increase in the attention paid to communication as a crucial aspect of governance.

Gareth Morgan, in his widely noted review of metaphors through which an organization can be understood (*Images of Organization*), develops the metaphor of the "Organization as Brain." Of the several metaphors he explores, this is, I judge, the one most appropriate for "placing" this work: an organization's communication system altogether—its two-way messages, data storing and processing, decision making, and so forth—certainly has remarkable parallels in the brain and the nervous system generally.

But exploring a metaphor is not Garnett's central purpose. Rather, *Communicating for Results in Government* stresses purpose, application, results. The reader's expectation that the work will give guidance in solving problems and getting results is warranted. There is much useful advice about communicating to citizens and clients, to peers, to administrative subordinates and superiors, to elected officials—and about communicating during crisis situations. The advice is interspersed with vignettes, research findings, and case examples in a highly readable fashion. However, this is not merely a how-to book of simple rules that are guaranteed to be effective. Instead, Garnett conceptualizes government communication as an exercise in strategic contingency management. The book acquaints readers with pertinent concepts and variables in the communication process and shows how to diagnose relevant variables in a particular situation that require communication. Managers are however still required to exercise their knowledge and judgment: the book offers aid, but no automatic answers.

In essence, this is a book both of relevant theory *and* of guidance and advice. The theory is drawn from a wide range of sources (a listing of the disciplines and categories of theory would be long), but it is not presented as "hard science" that gives unfailing instruction for action. Suggestions are given, to be sure. And the author draws judiciously on his personal experience in public management. But this is emphatically *not* a book that ignores the complex reality of government today.

In short, *Communicating for Results in Government* builds a two-way road, which in one direction branches out into a multitude of disciplines and concepts and in the other branches out into all significant aspects of government and all reaches of society. The result may well be to make communication not just another "interest" but a major focus of instruction, inquiry, and practice in public management.

January 1992   Dwight Waldo
                                           Professor emeritus
                                           Syracuse University

To
Jenny Anderson, Raymond L. Garnett, Mabel Holmes,
John R. Gosney, Charles H. Levine, David R. Powers,
Donna E. Shalala, Jay A. Sigler, William C. Garrow,
David B. Walker, Alexander Kouzmin, Barry L. Van Lare,
James Rowley, Bryant Mays Kirkland,
George Kuykendall, Daniel Hammond Barfield,
Helen Berwald, Ralph Fjelstad, Gayle Walker,
Milton Shaw, John Sabaka, Annmarie Hauck Walsh,
D. Stephen Cupps, Charles A. Morrison,
Robert H. Davis, Jr., George Hallett,
and other effective communicators
I have known

PREFACE

Public administrators at all levels of government communicate daily with superiors, subordinates, peers, clients, and others. This in itself makes communication a subject worth learning more about. Moreover, communication is the critical management process that makes or breaks our other administrative efforts. Good plans sloppily written, sound budgets poorly presented, and performance appraisals that do more harm than good illustrate the way that faulty communication can hinder managerial effectiveness.

Background and Audience

The idea for this book came from my early experience in government. As a new public servant I quickly discovered that I was required to write reports, brief superiors, answer letters, and perform other communication tasks, some of which I had little training to handle. My greatest "need to know" was about communicating rather than about analyzing policy, devising public budgets, and other tasks for which I had been better prepared in graduate school. At that time, few books on public administration dealt with communication in enough depth or breadth to help me, and virtually no courses in government administrative communication existed. Even today most graduate and undergraduate programs in public administration or public policy offer no courses in government communication. While the number of programs that do offer communication training is increasing, a number of schools rely on the

English department to teach administrative writing and on the speech department to teach public speaking. Although such courses often provide solid technical training, many lack the managerial focus that public administrators need. As a former government practitioner and now professor of government communication for fourteen years, I am convinced that a sizable gap exists between what government practitioners and students need to know about communicating and what training and reading are available to them. *Communicating for Results in Government* is therefore targeted at two groups: practicing managers and other professionals in government, education, and nonprofit organizations, and master's degree students in public administration, management, political science, business administration with public sector tracks, education or educational administration, nonprofit management, and similar graduate programs. This book concentrates on communication within and between government agencies rather than on political rhetoric, campaign communication, and the like. The skills and knowledge covered are relevant for public managers and staff professionals in the administrative, legislative, and judicial branches of federal, state, and local governments.

How This Book Is Different

Even though several books on public sector communication now exist, there is still a need for a book that applies research and conceptual knowledge to realistic public management situations. *Communicating for Results in Government* differs from the few other books on public sector communication in that it draws extensively upon research findings in the behavioral and social sciences; in the fields of communication, organization theory, and management; and in other bodies of knowledge. This grounding in research is used to help inform and guide public administrators' communication in government rather than as an end in itself. *Communicating for Results in Government* also is the only book on public sector communication that develops and consistently applies a conceptual model: a *strategic contingency model for government communication*. Strategic planning and strategic management have become important government tools. Communication itself is vital to developing and implementing management strategy—identifying organizational strengths, weaknesses, threats, and opportunities; developing alternatives; and conveying a strategy to employees, clients, and others. Communication can also be conceived of as involving a strategic process. The model holds that effective *communication strategy* is *contingent* on a set of factors that need to be assessed and acted on if communication is to succeed. It assumes that there is no single right or best way to communicate in all government situations but rather that appropriate ways to communicate depend upon the *audience, sender, management situation, objectives for communicating, medium,* and *message.*

Communicating strategically involves:

- Systematically integrating knowledge of human behavior, communication technology, managerial and organizational politics, communication skills, and social and behavioral sciences, along with knowledge of public management and the technical subjects communicated
- Recognizing that communication in government is more than a technical process of adhering to the mechanics of grammar, style, and so on, and therefore that administrative, political, legal, economic, and other factors must be taken into account
- Analyzing the objectives for communicating, the audience, the sender, and the management situation, as well as the public manager's own skills and preferences as a communicator
- Devising strategy appropriate to the total communication situation rather than always communicating in the same manner or slavishly following some ideal, "proper" method

A third difference between this book and others is its greater emphasis on audiences and receiving skills. Most communication books and courses emphasize the sending skills—writing, speaking, body language—and the public manager's role as sender. This book is consistent with current research showing that how the receivers of a message interpret that message is the most important element in communication. *Communicating for Results in Government* therefore stresses the public manager's role as a receiver and the importance of knowing audiences and the receiving process before a message can be intelligently crafted and sent. Indeed, a major section of this book concerns the public administrator's major audiences: superiors and elected officials, subordinates, colleagues in the same and other agencies, and government's multiple publics.

A fourth major difference in this book's approach is its emphasis on the importance of lateral and informal communication to enhance managerial and organizational learning and problem solving. I emphasize the value of subformal and personal communication as an aid to accuracy and openness, even for conveying messages upward and downward in government. Communication is presented more as a crucial means of learning and adapting than as a means of maintaining strict managerial control.

Overview of the Contents

Part One provides an overview of government communication. Chapter One describes several situations in public management that demonstrate how crucial effective communication is to government success. The chapter also discusses how government communication differs from other types of communication and is more challenging. Chapter Two examines major communication barriers that one must avoid or overcome to communicate successfully in government. Chapter Three presents and explains the strategic contingency model for government communication previously described.

Part Two applies the strategic approach to communicating with key audiences: superiors (Chapter Four), subordinates (Chapter Five), colleagues and those in other agencies (Chapter Six), and multiple publics (Chapter Seven). These chapters stress the role of communication in the performance of essential public management tasks, such as setting goals, motivating others, appraising individual and group performance, reporting progress, gleaning intelligence inside and outside an agency, and the like. Clearly, these management purposes apply to multiple audiences. Administrators, for example, need to motivate citizens, superiors, and peers as well as subordinates. Instead of discussing each management task in relation to every audience, I have attempted to cut down on repetition by addressing each task in the chapter about the audience to which it most closely applies (for example, the management tasks of motivating and appraising performance in general are discussed in the chapter about communicating with subordinates, Chapter Five). Readers should transfer key ideas about these and other management tasks to other relevant audiences while recognizing that important adjustments must be made for communicating with different audiences.

Part Three addresses salient issues in government communication: communicating during crises (Chapter Eight), communicating ethically (Chapter Nine), and improving communication skills (Chapter Ten).

Because the literature on government communication per se is woefully inadequate, I have deliberately tried to draw from a wide range of sources in the literature of other fields that relate to communication. I have also attempted to illustrate government communication within diverse levels and functions of government. In an effort to include current and relevant examples of government communication, I have drawn widely on newspaper articles and reports. Where possible, I have tried to confirm the accuracy of those reports. Readers should recognize, however, that news coverage sometimes fails to capture all sides of an issue and sometimes must be amended because of subsequent developments. News reports constitute a vital form of communication and a valuable source of information about government communicating, but readers need to bear in mind that new facts and interpretations will emerge. In addition to synthesizing a broad range of published knowledge, I base much of the advice in this book on interviews with and observations of government practitioners and on my more than twenty years of experience in government agencies, public schools, universities, and other public organizations.

Camden, New Jersey   James L. Garnett
January 1992

ACKNOWLEDGMENTS

I gratefully acknowledge the help of many people in making this book become a reality. Hal G. Rainey, James L. Perry, Richard W. Campbell, and anonymous reviewers contributed valuable insights that strengthened it significantly. Colleague Jon Van Til supplied advice, useful information, and support. Mary F. Powers taught me much about the Jossey-Bass audience and how to write for professionals. Ann Sostrom, Barbara Wallace, and Douglas Draper contributed valuable knowledge in key areas. The following graduate students conscientiously uncovered useful sources and examples: Cynthia Atanda, Paula Selzer, James A. Hoyer, Madhuri Sarin, and Katherine Todd. Mario and Sara Impagliazzo, William and Carmen Harris, and Sandra Cheeseman provided invaluable logistical and moral support. Gary Golden, James Nettleman, Susan Beck, Theo Haynes, Jean Crescenzi, Elaine Navarra, Debra Gross, Mary Anne Chaney, and other Rutgers University librarians greatly aided my search. Surgeons Charles Butler and Frederick Ballet patched me up so that I could finish writing. My wife, Petra, and daughter, Erin, deserve appreciation for, in turn, doing without me and putting up with me. Alan R. Shrader has been a paragon of editorship, displaying encouragement, patience, and a critical eye for what managers find useful. Marie Enders did a first-rate job of editing the manuscript, and I am grateful to the staff at Jossey-Bass for providing editorial and production expertise.

THE AUTHOR

James L. Garnett is associate professor of public administration and policy in the Graduate Department of Public Policy and Administration, Rutgers University, Camden. He received his B.A. degree (1967) in government from Carleton College and his M.P.A. (1971) and Ph.D. (1978) degrees in public administration from the Maxwell School, Syracuse University.

Garnett's research has focused on public management, government communication, administrative reorganization and reform, intergovernmental relations, and government strategy formulation and implementation. Garnett's books include *Reorganizing State Government: The Executive Branch* (1980)—for which he won the Published Scholar's Award, School of Government and Public Administration, American University—*Handbook of Administrative Communication* (ed., forthcoming), and *Administrative Communication in Government* (forthcoming). His articles have appeared in *Public Administration Review, Administration and Society, State Government, International Journal of Public Administration,* and *Urban Interest.*

Garnett has served as program assistant to the governor of New York (1971), research associate for the New York State Study Commission for New York City (1971–1973), and research associate for the New York Charter Revision Commission (1973–1974); has taught on air force and navy bases overseas (1980–1981); and has served as faculty development coordinator for the West Virginia

Board of Regents (1986–1988). He has also served as a consultant with federal, state, and local governments on executive reorganization and on improving administrative communication.

Communicating
for Results in
Government

PART ONE

Understanding Communication in Public Management

1

Why Communication Is So Crucial to Government Success

A large part (perhaps all) of an executive's job has to do with giving and receiving communications. Managers are nerve centers in the organizational communication network; they receive, process and transmit all sorts of memoranda, letters, policy statements, instructions, reports, face-to-face communications and what not. Perhaps nothing is more important to successful administration than successful communication.
—*Robert S. Lorch, 1978, p. 174*

Greater Consequences of Government Communications

Government administrators and staff professionals spend most of their time communicating—with superiors, subordinates, peers in the same and other agencies and with members of government's various publics. Speaking, writing, reading, listening, gesturing, transmitting data, and other forms of communication so pervade government that they are often taken for granted. And yet communication often makes the difference between government success and failure, sometimes between life and death. Consider the following events.

The Gulf War: Communication Successes and Failures

Like all major events, the Persian Gulf War of 1991 was a mixture of tragedy and triumph, both personal and organizational. That well over a hundred thousand people lost their lives in a war that could possibly have been avoided was a tragedy. That unprecedented resources that could have gone for other purposes were expended was a tragedy. That brutal aggression was confronted and defeated was a triumph. That the United States military and its allies in Operation Desert Storm could perform with such intelligence and precision during a war shortened by this thoroughgoing competence was a triumph. That this enormous administrative military machine could then be harnessed to spearhead recovery and rescue efforts afterward was a triumph. In fact, the United States military performed so well throughout this event that this military triumph has restored considerable confidence in the United States and in government's ability to get the job done. Columnist Robert Samuelson (1991, p. 31) noted that "national pride now derives not only from victory but also from a sense that the 'can do' spirit is once again alive and well. You already hear comparisons to the moon landing and to World War II." Much of this success resulted from competence displayed from top to bottom in the chain of command. A crucial competence involved communication—among leaders, among soldiers, and through high-tech systems. Consider the following communication successes and failures, keeping in mind that Persian Gulf policies and events are still controversial and that more information about these events continues to emerge. It is instructive, however, to highlight some of the roles communication played before and during the war.

- After the Iraqi invasion of Kuwait on August 2, 1990, President Bush and top officials from the Department of Defense, the Department of State, and the National Security Council decided it was necessary to persuade Saudi Arabia's King Fahd that his country might be attacked unless American troops were invited there to deter aggression. Persuading King Fahd was thought to be a monumental task. It was unprecedented for Saudi Arabia to ask the United States for forces. King Fahd was regarded as a "master of indecision," and Saudi deliberations were known to be contentious and lengthy (Woodward, 1991b). A group led by Secretary of Defense Richard Cheney arrived in Saudi Arabia on August 6 to meet with King Fahd and other Saudi leaders. On the flight there, Secretary Cheney insisted on thinking through their presentation. The presentation's parts and sequence were planned and rehearsed. On the basis of this practice, Secretary Cheney canceled a highly technical briefing explaining intelligence photographs. "Cheney realized the [Central Intelligence] agency man's presentation was not going to set the world on fire. Act One of the New World Order shouldn't begin with a technician demonstrating his prowess at reading tea leaves from overhead photography. It was not a presentation that would impress King Fahd" (Woodward, 1991b, p. 7). Secretary Cheney and General Norman Schwarzkopf, commander of U.S. forces in the Persian Gulf, included intelligence highlights in their remarks. The team's presentation was smooth and convincing, persuading but not overselling the Saudis about a possible attack and assuring them that the United States would supply forces and then withdraw them after the danger had passed. After a short, animated discussion, King Fahd overturned precedent and agreed to American cooperation.

- After getting Saudi agreement to host U.S. armed forces, President Bush, Secretary of State James Baker, and others embarked on a massive effort to gain support for this policy in Congress and from other nations around the world. Numerous hearings, press statements, private meetings, diplomatic missions, and other forms of communication ensued. The fact that these efforts succeeded in garnering the necessary support from Congress and in assembling and maintaining an international coalition that almost totally isolated Iraq is a testament to convincing communication.
- The allied high command viewed communication as such a strategic military asset that a strike to sever Saddam Hussein's communications with forces in southern Iraq and Kuwait was the allied force's priority at the start of the war.
- Bomber squadron leaders were flown to Desert Storm headquar-

ters to discuss bombing missions. There they met with commanders and strategy planners and were allowed to react to bombing plans from the perspective of those who actually had to implement the bombing. Plans became refined through such give-and-take, and the bombing missions were successful from a military standpoint. The Defense Department, the stereotypical hierarchy, made effective use of participative decision making and interrank communication.

- Before the ground war, allied forces made numerous statements about the importance of Operation Imminent Thunder involving an amphibious assault. They also used nonverbal communication—deployment of troops near the Kuwaiti border and rehearsals of massive amphibious landings—to convince the Iraqis that the major offensive would attack their strength head-on from both directions. After the Iraqis had bunched their forces to meet direct attack, and after the allies had eliminated Iraqi reconnaissance planes that could communicate allied troop positions to Iraqi forces, the allies moved their forces secretly, swept around the Iraqi forces, and surrounded them. This war-ending maneuver involved communicating to deceive the enemy while coordinating precision movements of allied troops.

As with any historical event involving so many people and nations, some communication failures occurred. Probably the greatest failure stemmed from the misunderstanding of Iraqi leader Saddam Hussein—his misunderstanding of others and their misunderstanding of him. Misunderstanding of Hussein's intentions by many U.S. officials, other world leaders, and even Hussein's fellow Arabs, such as Hosni Mubarak of Egypt and Saudi Arabian leaders, certainly hindered efforts to prevent war. Despite intelligence reports showing a massive Iraqi troop buildup near the Kuwaiti border, a perception prevailed that Hussein was posturing, bluffing. According to one U.S. official, " 'We were guilty of a kind of mind-set or a framework' about Iraq. 'It might even be cultural. The idea that a country would march up to the border, put 100,000 troops there, go in and do what they've done; I don't think anybody here thought they'd do it' " (Oberdorfer, 1991, p. 10). Hussein likewise misunderstood United States resolve to protect its interests in the Persian Gulf. Despite formal statements and personal messages delivered by envoys—some of them perhaps conveying messages Hussein could interpret as precluding American action—Hussein was clearly unprepared for the scale of U.S. opposition and later worldwide opposition. Fearing limited opposition, he attacked. Misunderstandings on both sides contributed to going to war.

Communication and miscommunication played a role in many other facets of diplomatic efforts, military operations, and news media efforts to cover these events. As more information and insight become available, we will appreciate even more the vital role communication played in both successes and failures in the Gulf.

Space Shuttle Challenger: *Communication Breakdowns Contributing to a Safety Breakdown*

On January 28, 1986, the space shuttle *Challenger* exploded seventy-three seconds after liftoff. The worst space disaster in history killed seven people, caused worldwide grief, destroyed and postponed important scientific experiments, ruined equipment costing millions of dollars, cost a contractor severe penalities, and immeasurably damaged the reputation of NASA and the U.S. space program. After intensive investigations and scrutiny of flight films, the Presidential Commission on the Space Shuttle Challenger Accident concluded that the primary cause was failure of a small pressure seal in the right solid rocket motor. This seal leaked, thus allowing exhaust gas to escape, which caused a series of explosions that expanded into an enormous fireball. Seal failure was the technical cause of this disaster, but a lengthy series of communications gaps and breakdowns contributed to the technical failure. The presidential commission uncovered the following information.

• The failed part was upgraded to criticality 1 in 1982, meaning that no dependable backup system could be assumed. Failure of this part could result in "loss of mission, vehicle and crew due to metal erosion, burn through, and probable case bursting resulting in fire and deflagration," according to the Space Shuttle Program Requirements Document. Despite requirements that the top level of NASA (level 1) review and approve this list of classifications, NASA administrators at levels 2 and 1 with authority to make launch decisions testified that they never heard about the reclassification before the explosion (Lewis, 1988, p. 139). More than five weeks after the disaster, the Problem Assessment System at Marshall Space Flight Center still classified the pressure seal as 1-R (redundant). The criticality of this part was never communicated effectively to those who needed to know.

- On January 27, 1986, the evening before the disaster, Morton Thiokol engineers recommended against the next morning's launch because of concern over how the critical O-ring seal would function in the below freezing weather that was predicted. Previous shuttle flights had shown that more gas escapes in cold weather conditions. Levels 1 and 2 NASA officials were not fully informed about the Thiokol engineers' recommendation against launching or about the three-hour teleconference between Thiokol and Marshall representatives in which that recommendation was discussed. The conference ultimately resulted in Thiokol managers reversing their engineers' recommendation. Thiokol managers rejected delay after perceiving comments from Marshall level 3 officials to mean that NASA wanted no further postponement following a series of delays. That a lengthy debate about the *Challenger*'s safety had occurred the evening before launching was never communicated to NASA levels 1 and 2 by formal reports or by rumor. NASA launch director James Thomas told presidential commission member Robert Hotz, "I can assure you that if we had that information [engineering reservations about O-ring seal performance under cold weather conditions], we wouldn't have launched if it hadn't been 53°" (Lewis, 1988, p. 108). Neither were reservations about shuttle safety communicated to the seven astronauts whose lives depended on that safety.

- Further evidence of communication breakdowns surfaced. NASA engineer Ben Powers' reservations about safety problems failed to be carried up the formal chain of command, and no one bypassed that chain to communicate directly to headquarters. Officials from Rockwell Corporation, the primary shuttle contractor, testified to the presidential commission that Rockwell had informed top NASA officials that Rockwell regarded it unsafe to launch in cold, icy conditions. NASA officials testified that they did not perceive Rockwell comments as a warning to postpone launching. This communications breakdown prompted commission chairman William Rogers to say, "If the decision-making process is such that the prime contractor thinks he objected and testified under oath that they took a position it was unsafe to launch, and you [NASA shuttle program director Arnold Aldrich] say that it was not your understanding, that shows us serious deficiencies in the process" (Lewis, 1988, p. 134). Breakdowns were hardly confined to those between the space flight centers and NASA headquarters. They also occurred among NASA centers, causing the commission to recommend measures that would prevent bypassing the national shuttle program managers. Despite changes in NASA structure and procedure, credibility loss and communication problems continued to hamper the space agency, prompting President Bush in July 1990 to initiate another intensive investigation of NASA.

NASA history repeated itself in 1990. NASA launched the $1.5 billion Hubble space telescope despite optical flaws severely limiting its value to space exploration. The report of the official five-month investigation into the causes of this error concluded that the management climate that discouraged engineers from reporting problems to superiors at NASA and to the mirror contractor also contributed to the Hubble failure. A member of the board of investigation said, "The culture has to be encouraged where you don't shoot the messenger. People don't like bad news, but what they like worse is not to be told about the problems. I know it has occurred on many of NASA's projects" (Capers and Lipton, 1990, p. 3A).

Overlooking Romanian Atrocities

During his four years as U.S. ambassador to Romania, David Funderburk tried unsuccessfully to convince superiors in the State Department that "Nicolae Ceausescu was a murderous tyrant undeserving of U.S. favors. . . . 'It was like beating my head against a brick wall.' . . . We reported what was really happening and the whole litany of horrors that Ceausescu was carrying out, but my reports weren't reaching the top people, and they certainly weren't being factored into our relationship.' . . . Now the world knows that Funderburk's descriptions were accurate. Ceausescu ran a police state. His people were virtually starved, while Romanian farm products were sent abroad. Women were penalized if they refused to have babies. Clergymen and opponents were killed" (Feinsilber, 1990, p. 4A).

Why did Funderburk's superiors fail to receive his repeated attempts to communicate true conditions in Romania? Much of the answer can be explained by the communication concepts of *selective attention* and *selective perception,* which are discussed more fully in Chapter Two. Ambassador Funderburk was regarded as a protégé of Senator Jesse Helms, a critic of the State Department. Department superiors therefore discredited Funderburk as an unreliable source and were selectively inattentive to his messages. In addition, the White House and State Department during this period (1981–1985) wanted to encourage independence from Moscow of the kind Ceausescu displayed. Washington superiors might have been inclined to ignore messages that detracted from the favorable prevailing perception. "Funderburk said George Bush, who was then vice president, Alexander Haig, who was secretary of state, and businessmen who wanted to trade with Romania 'trekked over to Bucharest to do homage to Ceausescu.' [Funderburk] said he asked the visitors to press Ceausescu to honor his human rights commitments, but they 'had been told just to ignore Funderburk'" (Feinsilber, 1990, p. 4A). Clearly, this communication gap hindered efforts to uncover atrocities and attempt to prevent additional ones.

Missed Signals Threaten Airline Safety

In January 1990, Avianca Airlines Flight 52 ran out of fuel and crashed, killing seventy-three people. This crash occurred in large measure because of communication failures. The pilot told regional air traffic controllers forty-five minutes before the crash, "We need a priority. We're low on fuel." But the pilot's request was never communicated to the six local controllers responsible for guiding the plane into Kennedy International Airport, according to Lee

Dickinson, a member of the National Transportation Safety Board investigating the crash. One reason for this missed communication appeared to result from differences in terminology. The pilot used the term *priority* instead of the term *emergency*, which would have placed his flight at the head of the landing queue. While requesting priority attention, the pilot told controllers that the plane held inadequate fuel to reach the alternate landing site. New York area controllers told federal investigators they were never told about Flight 52's fuel shortage from the regional traffic control center. Further complicating communications was the fact that the flight crew spoke in Spanish among themselves and in English to the air traffic controllers (Maykuth, 1990, pp. 1A, 4A). The National Transportation Safety Board, on February 21, 1990, cautioned pilots and air traffic controllers to use explicit language and to clarify messages, if necessary. The board blamed the Avianca pilots for failing to use standard terms like *fuel emergency* or *minimum fuel* and blamed the controllers for failing to clarify what the Avianca pilots actually meant by priority, especially when a foreign airline was involved. According to a letter from the board to the Federal Aviation Administration, "the safety board believes that air traffic controllers should question flight crews when there is any indication that flight safety may be compromised. . . . The safety board is aware of similar misunderstandings of communications between flight crews and air traffic controllers, especially in the traffic environment around New York City" (Cushman, 1990, p. B3). The board said that it was investigating several other such cases of faulty communication that jeopardized airline safety.

Miscommunication not only contributed to the Avianca crash itself but also hindered rescue efforts, according to a police report of the disaster. "Communication between the crash site and the hospitals was poor, doctors said, and hospitals did not know how many injured they would receive or when they would arrive" (Schmitt, 1990, p. B3).

In February 1991, a USAir jetliner collided with a Skywest commuter flight, killing thirty-four people. Preliminary investigation of the accident blamed human error by an air traffic controller who allowed the jetliner to land on the same runway previously cleared for use by the commuter flight. Further investigation found that communication problems with an Aeromexico flight probably distracted the controller at a crucial time. Radar communication equipment was also found to give a faulty view of the runway, which was further obstructed by light poles. These accidents, along with 212 runway incursions (near misses) recorded by the Federal Aviation Administration (FAA) in 1989, have emphasized the need for reform of the air traffic control system. Joseph Del Balzo, the FAA's director for systems development, testified in 1990 that "the FAA is developing better runway and taxiway designs, improved lighting and signs, and better training and communication procedures" (Phillips, 1991, p. 35).

Faulty Communication Contributes to Woman Freezing

In December 1989, a fifty-nine-year-old woman froze to death on a city bench despite eight citizen calls to police dispatchers summoning help. After the first call, a veteran police officer said he went to the woman, who was said to be sick, convulsing, and partially disrobed and was lying on a bench at a bus stop. The officer radioed dispatchers to report that the woman was "just a DK," a police term meaning drunken person. Citizens continued to call police dispatchers asking when police would arrive. After several more calls over a two-hour period, a bystander flagged down a passing patrol car. The officer from that car examined the woman and determined that she was dead. This constituted a tragedy not on the order of the *Challenger* and Avianca disasters, but a human tragedy nonetheless. Certainly part of the blame can be attributed to policies that fail to care for society's neediest. The veteran officer was suspended pending investigation for failing to take the woman to a hospital, normal police procedure in such cases. The officer contended that he actually went to the woman and she refused to go to a hospital. Whether that officer acted properly or improperly, part of the blame also must go to the dispatchers, who the police commissioner said assumed the officer had properly checked the callers' reports. Thus when additional calls came to the dispatchers during and after the time the officer was on the scene, they were ignored. These additional calls reporting conditions on the scene never prompted a police follow-up. (Dispatchers paid attention to only one source—

the original officer—and never acted on the subsequent messages.) Faulty assumptions by the officer and dispatchers were all part of a communication breakdown and a personal tragedy.

Communication Snafus Hamper Grenada Invasion

U.S. military forces invaded Grenada in 1983 and succeeded in freeing American students with minimal loss of life and damage to the island. Communication breakdowns hampered the invasion, however. Because landing troops were given little information about their targets, the troops first went to the wrong campus. They were given only tourist maps because detailed maps from the Defense Mapping Agency were not yet ready. As the result of incompatible radio equipment, army officers were unable to call in supporting fire from navy ships. They resorted to ham radios, sent couriers to vessels by helicopter, and in one case, according to a Senate Armed Services Committee report, used an AT&T credit card to place a call on a civilian telephone to Fort Bragg, North Carolina, in the hope of having a request relayed. The Senate report called this communication gap "unacceptable" (Wilson and Weisskopf, 1986, p. A24). Discoveries about lack of preparedness, faulty communication, and overcentralized command structure led to changes instituted in time for Operation Desert Storm in 1991.

Disaster and Rescue on the El

During the morning rush hour on March 7, 1990, a Southeastern Pennsylvania Transportation Authority (SEPTA) elevated train derailed while underground, pinning hundreds of commuters under Philadelphia's center. The crash disabled the communication system on the SEPTA train, preventing the motorman from contacting his dispatcher. A trolley operator finally reported the accident to his supervisor at 8:22. Nine minutes elapsed before the city fire department heard about the accident. And because the first report failed to convey the accident's scope, the fire department underresponded. It sent only a fifteen-member team of fire fighters and paramedics to cope with hundreds of wounded commuters trapped in tons of wreckage. On another front, the director of Philadelphia's Emergency Medical Service summoned surgeons and other emergency physicians from several hospitals to the accident scene. The emergency medical effort involved constant communication among hospital emergency rooms, counseling centers, and city agencies. Medical care received high marks for being fast, effective, and humane. Hundreds of people were treated, 170 were admitted to area hospitals, and the death toll was limited to four by a monumental effort.

A few weeks after the accident, information became public that "SEPTA workers uncovered signs of trouble with the motor support systems . . . before the motor of one car fell, triggering the deadliest accident in the agency's history, but none of the problems was passed up the chain of command. . . . 'If you look at a lot of the glitches we have encountered so far, it isn't people doing things they shouldn't do,' said SEPTA deputy general manager Howard H. Roberts, Jr., 'It is that everybody isn't aware of what everybody else is doing' " (Hollman and Tulsky, 1990, p. 1A). Communication was therefore instrumental in both the cause of this disaster and the successes and shortcomings of the rescue effort.

Communication Affects Government Performance and Citizens' Well-Being

The events just recounted, as well as many others, demonstrate the importance of government communication to international, national, state, and local affairs. Whether a government job is primarily managerial or technical, involves preparing budgets or analyzing educational progress, or is routine or nonroutine, effective communication is crucial to solid performance. Yet communication is not important for its own sake. As with planning, budgeting, program evaluation, and other managerial tools, communication is important because it affects people's quality of life and sometimes whether they continue to live. Communication affects citizens' trust in government and citizens' control over government. It influences employee morale and productivity and permeates all facets of government. Because government decisions and actions often affect more people and with greater consequences, communicating in government tends to be more important and often more difficult than communicating in business.

The next sections focus on other characteristics that make government communication different. Government communicators and those who communicate with governments need to understand these differences.

How Government Communication Is Different

No other communicator matches government for the quantity, variety, and importance of communications. Only government, in this case the federal Defense Communications Agency of the Department of Defense, can control the nation's telephone lines and other communication networks during a national emergency. Corporations or service agencies typically cannot match government for the volume of communications sent and received. A General Services Administration handbook estimated in 1955 that over a billion government letters were sent each year, enough to circle the globe five times if laid end to end. The mind boggles at how many letters, memos, reports, cables, facsimile and radio transmissions, computer and other messages involving virtually every facet of life American governments send and receive today.

Multiplicity and Range of Audiences

Not only do governments communicate more frequently on a greater range of subjects than businesses do, but government communication also typically involves more audiences and more diverse audiences. Businesses today generally communicate more often than they did previously with shareholders, customers, government regulators, consumer advocates, and others. However, the audiences of individuals, groups, and organizations considering themselves shareholders or clients of government services tend to be larger and more diverse than the audiences for business.

Government audiences are often demanding as well as diverse. The legacy of the citizen participation movement that grew out of the 1960s is that government's audiences now expect and demand more of governments as senders and receivers of communication. The diversity and demands of audiences mean that public managers must consistently communicate at intrapersonal, interpersonal, group, organizational, and public communication levels. This diversity of audiences and levels of communicating requires the ability to analyze audiences and flexibility in communicating with them.

Political Realities

Political realities profoundly affect government communication as they do other aspects of public administration. Political appointees and government careerists need to communicate effectively with each other. Yet appointed officials and careerists tend to lack the common experience of moving through the ranks, similar training, or shared perspective that is more common with their business counterparts. Turnover among political appointees (the average tenure of a federal assistant secretary is estimated at eighteen months) compounds the problem of learning how to communicate effectively with superiors. Appointed directors or commissioners of state and local government agencies likewise rarely outstay the careerists in their departments. Public managers often get to know the communication preferences of one boss at about the time a replacement appears. Political appointees are often perceived as dilettantes or hacks by careerists. Likewise, career managers are variously perceived as ineffectual drones or aggressively intransigent bureaucrats by political appointees. Even in local, state, and federal service where appointees possess professional qualifications, such misperceptions often exist. And such distrust is particularly difficult to overcome considering the typical brevity of this relationship. Communication between appointees and careerists is difficult if they fail to perceive that they are on the same management team.

Government agencies are also more likely to experience intervention from political party officials, legislators, public interest groups, and other political actors than are typical business firms. While politics tends to be underrated as a force in business, it can hardly be overrated as the dominant driving force in government agencies.

Amount of Public Scrutiny:
Communicating in a Fishbowl

Because government is seen as the "public's business," citizens as individuals or organized in interest groups justifiably deem it their right to know what government does. News media correspondingly consider it their duty to report on virtually every facet of government judged to be newsworthy because it involves politics, scandal, tax dollars, or simply the public interest. For these reasons, the decisions, thoughts, and even life-styles of public officials and administrators are far more likely to receive public scrutiny than is the case for their business sector counterparts, Donald Trump notwithstanding.

Common policies reinforce this general demand for government openness. The U.S. Freedom of Information Act and counterpart state acts make government "information in the possession of agencies *presumptively public and available* unless it fits specified exemptions" (Cooper, 1989, p. 109). This policy contrasts with the prevailing private sector practice, in which business information is presumed to be private unless required to be public. The Federal Register Act that requires major federal executive branch decisions to be published in the *Federal Register* has counterparts throughout state and local governments. Likewise, widespread open meetings or "government in the sunshine" laws require that high-level policy-making meetings be open to citizens, reporters, and others or require agencies to keep a record if meetings must be closed. This again contrasts with prevailing business practice even though corporate annual meetings and other major forums have tended to become more open in recent years.

Greater scrutiny of government at all levels means that government communication is more likely to be seen outside the agency and therefore must be crafted with multiple and unintended audiences in mind. Any public manager who ignores this principle invites a rude awakening. Governments have also become more active acquirers as well as senders of information. No business collects as much information about citizens as does government. Some of the issues surrounding the tension between the public's right to privacy and the public's right to know (through government, its agent) are addressed in Chapter Seven.

Legal Considerations: The Rules of the Game

As indicated in the previous section, what communication takes place and how tend to be more stringently regulated in government than in business. To be sure, most businesses have policies about what information should be reported, by whom and to whom, when, and how. Indeed, many of these restrictions are imposed by government requirements affecting stock transactions, personnel decisions, truth in advertising, and the like. Since governments tend to be even more stringent in regulating themselves and each other, businesses tend to have relatively greater flexibility overall about how they communicate.

To accomplish its intended purpose, government communication must often reflect legal and procedural factors. Legal guidelines, especially those concerning personnel actions, tend to be more prevalent and extensive in government than in the business sector. Failing to take legal and procedural guidelines into account often produces communication failures. For example, a charge of unprofessional conduct against a Camden County, New Jersey, teacher suspected of sexually assaulting seven sixth-grade girls was dismissed on procedural grounds because of a "fatally flawed" written statement from the superintendent of schools. The district superintendent's statement said: "The school administration has received complaints from several students/parents regarding treatment by [the teacher] which statements have also been given to the Camden County Prosecutor's Office. The statements mentioned leave me to charge [the teacher] with conduct unbecoming a teacher."

According to a representative from the New Jersey Department of Education, this statement was flawed because the superintendent "never mentioned statements made to him directly, nor did he validate the accuracy of or authenticate photocopied statements that he said were given to the prosecutor" (Stilwell, 1990, p. B1). After the school board had voted 9–0 to fire the teacher, the superintendent's defective statement caused charges to be dismissed. If the sixth-grade teacher were guilty of these charges, the dismissal could put a sex offender back in the classroom unless the district board of education refiled charges. Even if the teacher were innocent, this faulty communication delayed ruling on the substance of the charges, placing the teacher under suspicion all the longer. Since the teacher involved will continue to draw his $27,000 salary until there is an official ruling, the flawed statement will also cost taxpayers money.

Multiplicity and diversity of messages and audiences, greater politicization, heightened public scrutiny, and more rigid legal restrictions combine and interact to make government communication more necessary and more difficult. Indeed, a communication paradox exists: the greater the need to communicate, the more difficult it is to communicate (Falcione, 1984). Conditions that make communication so essential—the need to overcome intransigent barriers, existing untrusting climate, political and managerial sensitivity of the situation—make communicating all the more delicate and difficult. The rest of this book provides readers with the framework, knowledge, and guidelines for overcoming such communication difficulties. Chapter Two examines major communication barriers that must be avoided or overcome to communicate successfully in government.

2

Recognizing and Overcoming Barriers to Effective Communication

Blockages in the communication system constitute one of the most serious problems in public administration.
—*Herbert Simon, Donald A. Smithburg, and Victor A. Thompson, 1950, p. 229*

The most immutable barrier in nature is between one man's thoughts and another's.
—*William James*

Chapter One emphasizes the importance of communication to public administrators by highlighting the often disastrous consequences of miscommunication. This chapter more fully and systematically discusses the major barriers to effective government communication, some of which caused problems in the situations recounted in Chapter One. The intent here is to make readers more aware of different obstacles to communicating and to suggest ways of avoiding or overcoming those obstacles. Some of the knowledge and technique for coping with communication barriers is addressed in this chapter. Much of it is addressed in later chapters referred to in this chapter. Specific barriers to be discussed include differences in frame of reference, physical distance, hierarchy, information overload, distractions, language, prejudice, and faulty communication skills. These barriers can impair or block communication at all three major stages: *encoding* (devising a message), *sending,* and *receiving.* While these are not the only barriers to government communication, they are the ones most likely to challenge public administrators at all levels of government.

Differences in Frame of Reference

Probably the most common and troublesome barrier involves differences in frame of reference—between NASA and Morton Thiokol representatives, between Ambassador Funderburk and other State Department officials, and between many others on a daily basis. Why can two reporters covering the same public hearing write totally different stories about what happened? Each brings to the job different physical capabilities (hearing and eyesight), nature and length of professional experience and training, values, social background, and attitudes about government. Each may also bring substantially different editorial positions from his or her newspaper or station. In the 1991 Persian Gulf War, some early reports of the decimation of the Iraqi Republican Guard were later blamed on inexperienced reporters. Reporters with Vietnam experience realized that pilots and other soldiers tend to be overly optimistic when assessing damage. As with reporters, public administrators, other government employees, and citizens outside government bring a frame of reference to any situation. Each tends to perceive messages filtered through this frame of reference. In government communication, different frames of reference can lead to selective attention, selective perception, and selective retention (Schachter, 1983).

Selective Attention

Public administrators, like others, typically devote more attention to messages they perceive as important to them, agree with their frame of reference, or bring them satisfaction. Public managers also tend to ignore or avoid messages they perceive as unimportant, dissonant, or negative. This tendency, *selective attention,* accounts for many unread reports, unattended briefings, and avoided contacts. Former Romanian ambassador David Funderburk discovered

this as did Defense Department analyst Sam Adams, who tried unsuccessfully to convince others that Vietnam War body counts were
being deflated, which likewise was a message an administration did
not want to hear.

Selective attention tends to widen information gaps since
those government employees or citizens predisposed to a particular
topic will seek out information on that topic while others will be
selectively inattentive to such information. Frequently, people with
the greatest need to know are the most selectively inattentive and
therefore the hardest audiences to reach. Examples include potential
AIDS victims or gay bashers, teenage unwed mothers, crack addicts,
and employees who habitually abuse office hours. Selective inattention typically occurs because the message is perceived as irrelevant
or unpleasant, the sender is perceived as untrustworthy or unknowl-
edgeable, or the receiver has too many distractions. The basic problem is how to transform selective inattention into attention by
persuading audiences that a message affects them, can benefit them,
and takes precedence over competing messages or activities.

Public administrators fail to communicate if their message is
not even heard or read by the intended audience. Utilizing or overcoming selective attention therefore deserves considerable thought
and planning, as discussed particularly in Chapters Five and Seven.

Selective Perception

Even if a message is heard or read there is no guarantee that it will
be understood in the way it is intended. NASA officials failed to
perceive Rockwell Corporation officials' comments about icy conditions before the *Challenger* launch as the warning Rockwell officials testified they intended. Misunderstandings or misperceptions
occur frequently in government. U.S. Supreme Court justice Louis
D. Brandeis understood the problem of perception gaps when he
wrote, "Nine-tenths of the serious controversies which arise in life
result from misunderstanding, from one man not knowing the facts
which to the other man seem important, or otherwise failing to
appreciate his point of view."

The basis for these perceptual differences begins before we
remember. In the classic management training film "What You Are

Is What You Were When," Morris Massey claims that our experiences and socialization before we are ten years old establish our lifelong pattern of reactions to all situations. Children growing up in families deeply affected by the Great Depression still scrimp as adults, value economy, and are motivated by fear of job loss. People reared in the more affluent period following the Korean War tend to look for more factors in a job than merely job security. Public administrators must learn about their employees' backgrounds and formative experiences if they want to understand their employees' perceptions more fully.

Selective perception can be shaped by family background, physical and personality characteristics, political and religious affiliation, cultural differences, organizational affiliation and position, professional experience, and other factors. James Q. Wilson (1989) observes that administrators' motivation to protect "turf" or autonomy shapes agency perception on issues. This frame of reference helps explain, for example, why the military generally preferred Melvin Laird to Robert McNamara as secretary of defense. Under Laird the Pentagon lost budget and personnel but was allowed considerable autonomy. Under McNamara, the Pentagon grew considerably but retained less control. Chapter Three discusses factors that influence perception in terms of audience analysis. Chapters Four through Seven stress the importance of understanding the characteristics and frames of reference of key government audiences. Chapter Five in particular addresses the use of multiple sources, bypassing, distortion-resistant messages, and other techniques for avoiding or minimizing misperception.

Because of the tendency of audiences to perceive selectively, administrators need to consider the *loop* in which their message travels. A message asking employees to observe office hours, for example, could be sent to a general loop—all employees. Offenders, nonoffenders, salaried professionals, and hourly employees would get the same message but interpret it selectively according to their circumstances. Some nonoffenders might resent being included in this warning. Some salaried professionals might perceive a move to put everyone on a time card. Another tactic involves tightening the loop—tailoring the message to fit the audience. Other situations require widening the communication loop to involve more audiences. Chapters Three and Seven address audience segmentation tactics.

Selective Retention

Even after a message is received and perceived, it is subject to selective retention. People remember information and meanings selectively rather than uniformly. Retention depends upon the nature of the message, degree of agreement with the message, message position, medium used, frequency, and other factors. In general, retention tends to improve if a message is positive rather than negative, is important to the receiver rather than inconsequential, is repeated in various ways through different media, and comes at the beginning or end of a talk or report rather than buried in the middle. Chapter Three discusses communication tactics involving message, medium, and audience aimed at improving retention. Chapters Four through Seven apply these and other tactics to major audiences of government.

Physical Distance

Physical distance often causes or aggravates government communication problems. Where large distances are involved, adjustments in communicating often become necessary. Distance typically requires greater reliance upon written and telephone communications. Face-to-face communications under such conditions require travel that is expensive and more logistically difficult than calling or writing. Face-to-face communication often must wait for the occasional site visit, inspection, or visit to headquarters.

Even in this era of electronic communications, however, geographical proximity is important for picking up the informal, face-to-face comments and cues that remain so crucial in government. Public administrators in regional offices—or even in annexes to agency headquarters—often find out late, if at all, what is happening at headquarters. That, according to chronicler Theodore White (1975), is why Daniel Moynihan kept his White House basement office instead of moving to more elegant quarters in the annex. Moynihan wanted to be able to talk informally to the chief of staff in the men's room. Aides want offices close to the chief executive or agency head for more reasons than personal status. Proximity usually improves access. Classic research in social psychology reveals that individuals located near stairways, entrances, and other heavily trafficked points have more communication and information (Festinger, 1963). Access cuts both ways, however. Proximity also makes it more difficult to keep a "low profile" when that is desired.

Written messages can be made more uniform for distant audiences, and the literal content is easier to recognize. Yet letters, telegrams, and memos are still subject to interpretation—selective perception. Written messages covering long distances can also be subject to delay. Electronic mail and faxes help reduce the wait typically caused by distance and provide quick feedback on content. But they too omit some of the oral cues—tone of voice, nature of breathing—that the telephone provides. The telephone is useful, therefore, in following up on written messages, in confirming decisions, and in eliminating some distortions. Teleconferencing picks up some of the visual cues that telephoning misses but misses cues (such as the amount of perspiration and micro eye movement) that are available only when sender and receiver are in each other's physical presence. Other chapters discuss overcoming problems of distance when communicating to superiors (Chapter Four), subordinates (Chapter Five), other government agencies (Chapter Six), and segments of the public (Chapter Seven). Uses and abuses of communication technology to overcome distance are addressed in Chapter Ten.

Hierarchy

Bureaucratic hierarchies, whether in government or involving government's audiences, tend to block, reduce, or distort communication. As it travels up a hierarchy, communication is generally screened or filtered in terms of both quantity and quality. Since top officials would be overloaded unless the volume of information received were reduced, subordinates must limit the *quantity* of information as it goes up the chain of command. Downs (1967) demonstrated how screening half of a message per level as it traveled up a hierarchy of four levels would result in a top official's getting only one sixty-fourth of the original message. This reduces the original message quantity by 98.4 per cent. Such hierarchical screening also affects message *quality*, since those officials abstracting a message often use selection rules different from each other's and from their superior's.

"Empty suits" also disrupt communication within hierarchies. "Empty suit" is a new name for the classic "yes-man," who puts his image, appearance, and style before performance; who dresses for success and uses vocabulary power but produces little tangible accomplishment. What the empty suit does best is sell himself to superiors, but this often means avoiding risks and hushing up problems that may occur. "The empty suit may open a gap between his level and the level below him. It's not just that he occasionally sells subordinates out, if that's what it takes to sell himself upward. As psychologist Harry Levinson notes, 'People who handle things expediently are often people who can't sense what's going on beneath them.' Information stops flowing upward. The best people, tired of looking to their empty suit boss for direction that never comes, soon go elsewhere" (Kiechel, 1989, p. 228).

Message quantity and quality are likewise affected when communication is downward in a hierarchy. Tactics for overcoming hierarchical barriers are described in other chapters, particularly Chapter 5, which discusses using multiple sources and channels, removing or bypassing organizational levels, using distortion-resistant messages, applying counterbias, and so on.

Information Overload

Though information loss becomes a barrier to accurate communication, so does information overload—the sheer quantity of information transmitted, received, and stored. Part of this overload results from the rapid expansion of knowledge. Phillip Lewis (1975) observes that it took approximately 1,750 years (from A.D. 1 to A.D. 1750) for human knowledge to double. Developments such as movable type led to the next doubling by 1900, only 150 years later. Another redoubling is estimated to have occurred in 1950. Now, advances in computer technology and other breakthroughs result in a doubling of human knowledge about every eight to ten years. No wonder public administrators have difficulty keeping up!

The volume of knowledge is only one factor that is producing information overload. Speed and ease of communicating also play roles. Computers, teleconferencing, fax machines, and telephones make it quicker and easier for government officials, reporters, citizen groups, and businesses to transmit messages. And because it is now easier to send and store information, people tend to send more messages than they would if it were more difficult or costly. A computer specialist, grade II, in a state finance department can generate volumes of tax records or other information in minutes, even seconds. Dumping an entire data base is usually easier than selecting relevant information or making use of an entire data base. Methods for avoiding overload include tailoring information to audience needs (Chapter Three), reducing unessential reporting (Chapter Five), and specifying decision rules for what information is essential (Chapter Five).

Distractions

At any time, intended audiences may be distracted by other messages, job assignments, agency protocol, personal interests, and the like. In his study of administrative feedback in eight federal bureaus, Herbert Kaufman observed that bureau administrators often had enough information to provide adequate feedback on subordinate behavior (Kaufman and Couzens, 1973). Competing policy priorities, legislative requests, and turf battles sometimes diverted them from sorting and analyzing that information.

Today's government managers must cope with increasing complexity and ambiguity. Managerial work is increasingly "characterized by brevity, variety, and fragmentation" (Mintzberg, 1973, pp. 31–35). Bruce Adams (1979, pp. 546–548) has observed that for top-level federal administrators "there is no time to think very deeply or broadly about anything. The busy work drives out the time for reflection. . . . In Washington, the urgent drives out the important. . . . A system that runs people ragged for 12 to 18 hours a day shortens their perspectives and squeezes out their creativity

and imagination. They reach the point of diminishing returns."
This pattern is repeated in seats of government across the country.

Public administrators can expect to deal with a wide variety
of managerial issues as well as frequent interruptions by staff
members, lobbyists, and citizens. Rarely can government managers
expect to work continuously on one problem until it is resolved.
Like jugglers, they must keep all issues airborne, without letting
them crash. Such fragmentation and interruption hinder communication by distracting the audience's attention from a message. As
communication receivers, public administrators need to recognize
distractions that inhibit their getting and understanding someone
else's message. Techniques for combating distractions include establishing personal and organizational priorities (Chapters Three
and Four); knowing an audience's work load, pressures, and procedures (Chapters Three and Four); avoiding language or communication styles likely to distract an audience (Chapters Three and
Four); and convincing an audience that your message warrants attention despite competing distractions (Chapters Five and Seven).

Language

Language, whether a foreign language or technical or bureaucratic
jargon, can create communications barriers. Diplomats, Peace
Corps volunteers, and others have long accepted the need for bilin-
gualism. "Street-level bureaucrats"—teachers, police officers, social
workers, and others in direct contact with citizens—are finding it
increasingly necessary to speak a second language, such as Spanish
or Chinese (Lipsky, 1971). *Civil Service 2000*, a report on the future
composition of the federal work force, estimates that Hispanics will
comprise nearly 29 percent of new entrants to federal service. This
will make Hispanics the largest growing minority in the federal
work force over the next decade. The report says that, especially in
the Southwest where Hispanics comprise a large percentage of new
entrants into the labor market, "Federal employers may see composition of their staffs shifting quite rapidly to include more Hispanics" (Johnston and others, 1988). The additional federal employees
who speak Spanish as a first language may reduce some language
barriers with Spanish-speaking clients and may complicate com-

munication with some colleagues and clients. Those involved will
need to address such potential language barriers.

Differences between English and other languages are not the
only language barriers. Far more pervasive—and more serious since
they are often more difficult to detect and correct—and those language barriers caused by technical and bureaucratic jargon. Some
of these language differences are relatively new. For example, a
Dallas construction worker was denied a construction job in Chicago when he "failed" clause R-3 because a computer analysis of his
pre-employment physical exam showed that he was "pregnant." He
could have told a human being that he was not pregnant, but he
knew too little computerese to communicate with the computers or
those who operated them. "Eventually he found someone who was
willing to decode the computerese into English [so that he knew on
what basis to challenge his rejection] and the job offer was rein-
stated" (Peterson, 1979, p. 22).

Computerese, bureaucratese, officialese, and legalese are "languages" that government employees use every day. These and other
types of jargon can aid communication if both the communicator
and the audience accurately understand what the jargon means.
Symbols, codes, and the like can even be used to create distortion-
resistant messages, as discussed in Chapter Five. All too often, however, public administrators and employees write or speak jargon
without being certain that their audience will understand it. Consider the following ordinance from a Wisconsin town.

> 132.06 Use of receptacle by other than owner; as to
> junk dealers. The using by any person or persons or
> corporation other than the owner or owners thereof,
> or his, her, its or their agent, of any such can, tub,
> firkin, box, bottle, cask, barrel, keg, carton, tank,
> fountain, vessel or container, for the sale therein of
> any substance, commodity or product, other than that
> originally therein contained, or the buying, selling, or
> trafficking in any such can, tub, firkin, box, bottle,
> cask, barrel, keg, carton, tank, fountain, vessel or con-
> tainer, or the fact that any junk dealer or dealers in
> cans, tubs, firkins, boxes, bottles, casks, barrels, kegs,

cartons, tanks, fountains, vessels, or containers, shall have in his or her possession any such can, tub, firkin, box, bottle, cask, barrel, keg, carton, tank, fountain, vessel or container, or so marked or stamped and a description of which shall have been filed and published as provided in s.132.04, shall be, and it hereby is, declared to be, prima facie evidence that such using, buying, selling, or trafficking in or possession of is unlawful within the meaning of 132.04 to 132.08 [Lutz, 1989, pp. 228–229].

Are junk dealers, at whom this regulation is targeted, likely to understand that if they reuse any of the containers listed they are breaking the law? Misusing legal and bureaucratic jargon in this manner decreases the likelihood of compliance and increases the likelihood of health hazards, fraud, or other problems the ordinance was intended to prevent.

Jargon also creates problems if readers or listeners think they understand it and act on the basis of what is actually a misunderstanding. Sometimes jargon is so unclear that attempts at interpretation fail altogether. A Department of Energy regulation proposed in 1982 stated the following: " 'Nothing in these regulations precludes the secretary or his delegate from designating information not specifically described in this regulation as unclassified controlled nuclear information.' When asked if the proposed regulation meant that the Secretary of Energy or any low-level bureaucrat to whom he hands the power of censorship could suppress any information, including unclassified information long in the public domain, officials were unable to answer since they weren't sure what the regulation meant" (Lutz, 1989, p. 200). Here a lack of clear communication hindered the interpretation and implementation of federal nuclear energy policy. In sending and receiving government communications it pays to be aware of potential barriers caused by actual or pseudolanguages and to take appropriate precautions. Chapters Three, Four, Five, and Seven address this issue.

Prejudice

Prejudice—prejudging an idea, person, group, organization, cause, or the like—is one of the most troublesome communication barriers in government. Such *pre*judging inhibits or prevents careful evaluation of people, ideas, proposals, and so forth on their actual merits. The prejudging that too often occurs between political appointees and careerists is a case in point. Destructive prejudging can occur at all levels of government, even the highest, as the White House and State Department prejudice about the credibility of former ambassador to Romania David Funderburk shows. In a May 1972 memo to Chief of Staff Bob Haldeman, President Richard Nixon wrote: "One department which particularly needs a housecleaning is the CIA. The [first] problem in the CIA is muscle-bound bureaucracy which has completely paralyzed its brain and the other is the fact that its personnel, just like the personnel in State, is primarily Ivy League and the Georgetown set rather than the type of people that we get into the services and the FBI." President Nixon's prejudice against people from Georgetown University and Ivy League schools inhibited a balanced appraisal of CIA employees whom Nixon wanted removed and replaced with "his kind of people." Some experienced, able professionals would be removed because of the president's stereotype.

Dealing with prejudice requires recognizing that it exists and understanding the major reasons underlying it. President Nixon's prejudice against Ivy League and Georgetown graduates resulted partly from his dislike of faculty positions against the Vietnam War taken at these and other universities. In that same memo, Nixon asked Haldeman to stop CIA recruiting at Ivy League and other universities that were taking action against the war. There is evidence that another reason for President Nixon's prejudice may have been envy and the regret that he lacked the credentials and connections that Ivy League graduates possess. Knowing the underlying reasons for stereotyping and prejudging can help public managers convince those who do the prejudging or those who might fall victim to such prejudice that the reasons are illogical or counterproductive. One of the keys for dealing with prejudice is sound audience analysis, as introduced in Chapter Three. Chapter Five discusses prejudging the value of information sources, and Chapter Seven addresses the problem of changing prejudicial attitudes among government's publics.

Faulty Communication Skills

The foregoing barriers to communication are compounded by faulty communication skills, themselves a formidable obstacle. Faulty skills can occur at every stage of the communication process. Weak encoding skills can lead to faulty transmission of a message. A message poorly organized, clumsily worded, and inappropriate in tone and length creates its own barriers. Such messages, like the Wisconsin town ordinance cited above, are unlikely to produce the intended results.

Even after a message is encoded or assembled, the inappropriate choice of a medium can jeopardize it. Henry Mintzberg (1973, p. 38), in his study of business and public sector executives, relates the following: "One manager recounted an interesting story that highlights the difference between face-to-face and documented communication. At head office, a number of people had developed a dislike for a Swiss employee [whose native language was French]. She used the word 'demand' instead of 'ask' in her memos. Only when she visited the head office was the problem resolved. In face-to-face contact, it became clear that she was simply using the word that seemed most appropriate to her. The verb 'to ask' in French is 'demander'!"

In this instance, using a medium that provided less and slower feedback allowed an existing language difference to create communication, administrative, and personal barriers between the employee and headquarters staff. Chapter Three discusses the choice of medium and the characteristic advantages and disadvantages of different media. Examples and applications are presented in other chapters relating to specific kinds of audiences. Faulty communication skills also create pitfalls during message decoding, which involves receiving and interpreting the message. Various distortions in interpretation are addressed earlier in this chapter under perception differences and in all subsequent chapters.

This chapter has discussed the most significant barriers to effective government communication while covering some key communication concepts and terms public administrators need to know. More detailed discussion of communication theory and concepts can be found in Fisher (1978), Littlejohn (1978), Berger and Chafee (1987), and Krone, Jablin, and Putnam (1987). An important tool for identifying and combating potential communication barriers is having a realistic conceptual framework of government communication. Chapter Three develops and applies a model that increases understanding of the key elements in government communication and their interrelationships.

3

Applying a Strategic Model to Government Communication

Nothing is so useless as a general maxim.
—*Thomas Macaulay, 1967, pp. 235-269*

It all depends.
—*Harvey Sherman, 1966*

This chapter provides a conceptual model accompanied by research-based knowledge that can help public administrators avoid or overcome the communication barriers discussed in Chapter Two. In so doing, Chapter Three examines the following topics: a strategic contingency model for government communication, setting objectives for communicating, analyzing audiences, diagnosing the management situation, analyzing message senders, choosing appropriate media, crafting the message, and using the entire strategic contingency model.

A Strategic Contingency Model
for Government Communication

Chapters One and Two stress the difficulty of communicating in government. Government communication frequently involves complex and sensitive messages, multiple senders and audiences, a multistage process, diversity of values and goals, and a need for confidentiality balanced against the public's right to know. The challenge of communicating should not be underestimated because it is a daily management activity. Government communication requires even more forethought, precautions, and effort *because* administrators must communicate on the job every day. Its very pervasiveness makes administrators tend to underestimate the complexity of communicating and to fall into routinized, mechanical behavior, even into counterproductive habits. Using a conceptual framework or model, such as the one described here, can help public managers become more conscious of the key factors and nuances involved in communicating and avoid mechanical or inappropriate practice. I use the term *model* since administrators and scholars understand that term as generally applying to a conceptual framework rather than exclusively to mathematically justified equations. Thinking in terms of this conceptual model will help public managers communicate more systematically, leaving less to chance.

The basic framework is simple to understand, harder to practice. *Effective government communication involves analyzing situations and designing appropriate strategy.* As Figure 3.1 shows, four *situational factors* involving the *objectives for communicating*, the *audience*, the *management situation*, and the *sender* influence two *strategy design factors*—selection of a *medium* and choices made in crafting the *message*. This model captures the government reality that medium and message need to be appropriately designed to fit the purpose, audience, management situation, and sender if communication is to be successful. These six factors are common to all situations of communicating in government. The specific characteristics of these factors will typically vary from situation to situation. For example, in every communication situation in government an audience exists. The audience's position, role, affiliation, size, interests, knowledge, and so on and the amount of impact from the message will vary for different audiences. How government administrators should communicate depends upon the characteristics of their audience and the other situational factors.

The strategic contingency model also captures reality in that the four situational factors affect one another. If an administrator's

Figure 3.1. A Strategic Contingency Model for Government Communication.

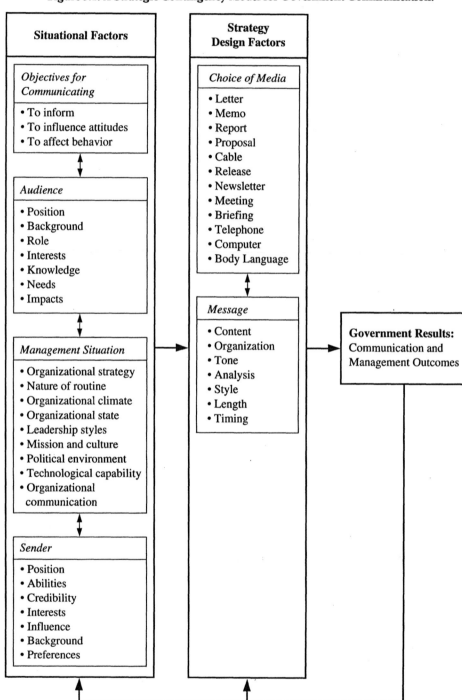

objectives for communicating primarily involve increasing political and financial support for his or her program, that administrator needs to target *audiences* with the ability to provide such support. Likewise, the appropriate choice of *sender* often depends on the *management situation.* Crisis situations, for example, often require top leaders to communicate direction and assurance to those handling the crisis. The four situational factors are shown in their general order of importance. Objectives and audience usually influence communication strategy more than do management situation and sender. In some situations, however, the latter two factors may dominate. The two strategy design factors likewise affect each other. Having to communicate technical content, for example, usually makes written media more appropriate than a telephone conversation. A report can be reread if it is not understood the first time. Complicated material is more difficult to grasp and remember during and after a telephone conversation.

Both situational factors and strategy design factors influence communication and management outcomes—government results. Personal and political factors and careful strategy helped persuade Saudi Arabia to invite U.S. troops into the Persian Gulf in 1990, as related in Chapter One. Sometimes skillful communication can overcome the force of difficult situational factors to produce favorable outcomes—such as peace treaties or agreements that benefit all parties. In other instances, skillful communication may be thwarted by an overwhelmingly unyielding situation, as has occurred too often with negotiations to achieve just peace in the Middle East. The way a message is received and the kind of management outcome produced in turn provide feedback about the appropriateness of the communication strategy. Message content, choice of medium, and other design variables may need to be changed to achieve better results the following time. The outcome of a message may also affect situational factors. A political attack on an agency may produce a more stressful organizational climate and disrupt agency routine, for example.

This framework is a strategic contingency model for government communication because it holds that effective communication strategy is contingent upon a set of factors that need to be assessed and acted upon if communicating is to be done intelligently. This model assumes that there is no one right or best way to communicate in all government situations. The most polished oration is unlikely to succeed if it is conveyed to a group of uneducated, homeless citizens by an obviously affluent bureaucrat who has little affiliation or credibility with that audience. On the other hand, a halting, ungrammatical message might succeed if it "fits" the intended audience and breaks down potential barriers.

Contingency thinking has long held an important place in managerial *leadership* (for example, Fiedler, 1967; Vroom and Yetton, 1973; Hersey and Blanchard, 1982), *decision making* (for example, Lindblom, 1959; Vroom and Yetton, 1973), *motivation* (for example, Vroom, 1964; Porter and Lawler, 1968), and *organizing* (for example, Perrow, 1970; Thompson, 1967; Lawrence and Lorsch, 1967; Levine, Backoff, Cahoon, and Siffin, 1975). A growing body of literature now emphasizes the importance for managers and professionals to plan, market, and implement strategically to improve government performance (for example, Bryson, 1988; Campbell and Garnett, 1989; Rabin, Miller, and Hildreth, 1989; Rainey, 1991). So too must public administrators *communicate strategically* for better results. Even though no general agreement exists about what *strategy* or *strategic* means, several concepts consistently emerge. A strategic approach involves systematically integrating information across fields, departments, and organizations; considering more than the technical aspects of managing; thinking situationally—taking relevant political, economic, administrative, social, legal, and personal factors into account; and devising strategy appropriate to organizational strengths, weaknesses, and competition.

Communicating strategically also involves the following:

- Systematically integrating knowledge of human behavior, communication technology, managerial and organizational politics, communication skills, and the social and behavioral sciences, along with knowledge of public management and the technical subjects communicated
- Recognizing that communicating in government is more than a technical process of following the mechanics of grammar, style, and so on and therefore requires considering administrative, political, legal, economic, and personal factors

- Analyzing the objectives for communicating, the audience, the sender, and the management situation, as well as one's own skills and preferences as a communicator
- Devising strategy appropriate to the total communication situation rather than communicating the same way in every situation or following some ideal, "proper" way to communicate.

In light of the foregoing, government communication in reality has more in common with contingency and open-systems theory—with their emphasis on environmental influences and multiple ways to accomplish objectives—than with classical management's emphasis on a "one best way" of doing things. The model presented here draws heavily from the thinking of strategic planning and management and organization design and of management contingency theory.

This book follows a strategic approach throughout, emphasizing that effective communication results more from careful planning and deliberate choices about audience, sender, medium, content, format, style, length, tone, and the like than from happenstance or innate skill. Good communicators, like good physicians and good managers, are skillful diagnosticians, sizing up key factors in a situation and acting accordingly. Each component of the model is discussed below to help readers become more fully aware of the different situational and strategy design factors. Working through the process and the factors should also help readers begin to internalize the logic involved.

Setting Objectives for Communicating

The communication process usually starts when one identifies objectives for communicating, although consideration of audiences, senders, and management situation usually influences choice of purposes. Principal purposes of communicating are to inform or gain information, to influence attitudes, or to affect behavior. Government managers or professionals are often engaged in two or even all three of these purposes.

In trying to inform the public about how AIDS is transmitted, the surgeon general and other public health officials are also trying to change attitudes and behaviors. Informing is rarely an end in itself but the means toward behavioral change. Public health officials aim to prevent the spread of AIDS by persuading individuals to avoid risky sex and potentially contaminated needles, blood, or other body fluids. At the same time, public health officials aim for more enlightened behavior toward AIDS victims such as children who want to attend school with their friends. Changes in behavior—whether concerning people's health, spending, investing, choice of homesite or transportation—are typically the bottom line of public policies or actions.

Since behavioral science research has repeatedly shown that attitudinal change is often a prerequisite to behavioral change, public education efforts target attitudes as well. For example, desired changes in attitude include greater public sensitivity to the real causes of AIDS and less irrational fear of casual contact with AIDS victims in workplaces, schools, swimming pools, and other public places.

In government management, *objectives* are typically regarded as more specific and more operational subsets of *goals*. This book uses the term *objectives for communicating* to emphasize the importance of identifying specific and, if possible, operational and measurable purposes for communicating. Here are two examples of specific communication objectives: "to persuade the State Board of Higher Education to approve a new degree program in public administration by December 31, 1992" and "to inform agency employees about procedures for a coming reduction in force and their rights and protections during that process."

Counterproductive memos, department meetings, and the like often result because the staffer who wrote the memo or the official who called the meeting had a vague objective or too many objectives to be accomplished. The chapters in Part Two, Communicating with Key Audiences to Achieve Public Management Results, emphasize primary objectives in communicating with superiors and elected officials, subordinates, colleagues, actors in other government agencies, and government's publics. With all of these audiences, public managers will need to inform, to change attitudes, and to motivate changes in behavior. Clarifying direction, reporting progress, responding to requests for information, making recommendations, delegating assignments, and motivating action are all objectives for communicating and all are the stock-in-trade of public managers.

Analyzing Audiences

Writing, speaking, and other sending skills usually receive the first and greatest attention in training sessions and how-to books. Yet much evidence exists that the audience *receiving* role is the most important to communication success (Frandsen and Clement, 1984; Gortner, Mahler, and Nicholson, 1987). Public administrators typically spend more work time as receivers than as senders. Also, knowledge about intended and unintended audiences is prerequisite to crafting and sending a message intelligently.

The more that public managers know about their audiences, the more accurately they can tailor their message to avoid communication traps. Too often, audience analysis is forgotten in the rush to deliver the message. Such an omission is tantamount to delivering an adult reading readiness program without first conducting a needs assessment or social marketing study to discover whether anyone needs or wants that program.

While all communications involve three elements—the *sender* (writer or speaker), the *message,* and the *audience*—many communicators underestimate the audience's importance and make several false assumptions, among them the following (Mathes and Stevenson, 1991):

1. The person addressed is the primary audience.
2. The audience is a group of specialists in our field.
3. The message has a finite period of use.
4. The author and the audience will both remain available for reference.
5. The audience is familiar with the assignment.
6. The audience has been involved in daily discussions of the material.
7. The audience awaits the message.
8. The audience has time to read or listen to the entire message.

To which I would add two additional false assumptions:

9. Only the intended target audiences will get the message.
10. One style of writing or speaking is appropriate for all situations.

Though J. C. Mathes and Dwight W. Stevenson drew up their list (comprising the first eight points) for engineers, public managers and staff professionals make these same assumptions daily. And the larger the government agency involved, the more disastrous such assumptions can be. Public managers know from experience the risk of making any of these assumptions. A memo to a colleague airing frustrations over administrative red tape may end up on the desk of the bureau chief or appear in the *Washington Post*. A budget-request briefing may assume more technical knowledge than a legislative committee possesses, thereby producing more questions and less funding.

A safer course than making these assumptions and "letting fly with a message" involves *audience analysis*, a process that requires three steps:

1. *Mapping audiences* to learn who the intended and potential audiences are, what functions they serve, and their priority
2. *Constructing or consulting profiles of target audiences*, particularly important and recurring audiences, to learn their background, characteristics, preferences, and how the message will affect them
3. *Designing communications strategy* (choice of medium or media, message content, tone, length, format, and so on) appropriate to objectives, audience, and the management situation.

Mapping Audiences

Figure 3.2 presents an *audience map* for identifying intended and unintended audiences. Audiences fall into these three categories: *primary audiences*—who make decisions or act on the basis of the information a message contains; *secondary audiences*—who are affected by these decisions and actions; and *immediate audiences*—

Figure 3.2. Audience Map.

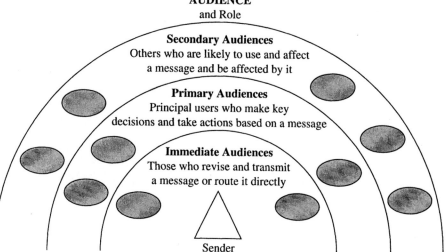

AUDIENCE
and Role

Secondary Audiences
Others who are likely to use and affect
a message and be affected by it

Primary Audiences
Principal users who make key
decisions and take actions based on a message

Immediate Audiences
Those who revise and transmit
a message or route it directly

Sender

Source: Adapted from Mathes and Stevenson, 1991, p. 15.

who route the message directly or transmit the information it contains.

Primary Audience. The primary audience consists of those persons who will make the most important use of a message. The message must first meet the needs of these users. Primary audiences can be organizational superiors, subordinates, or equals; but they are the top-priority users. The message is primarily intended for them. Primary audiences often include the head of an operating unit and the chief executive of an agency or department. In the communication of public information, the general public or segments of the public are primary audiences. For example, smokers and potential smokers are the primary target audience in the surgeon general's public education campaign against smoking.

Typical primary audiences are the decision makers but their actual decisions are often determined by the evaluations or recommendations of staff members. An audience analysis should indicate which of the decision makers' personal concerns are likely to override organizational concerns. An analysis should also consider known personnel who make evaluations or recommendations to the decision makers. In time, both the line and staff personnel will change. Roles, rather than individuals, provide continuity. An entire audience can change between the first reference to a specific project and the last report on that project. For this reason, references to past messages and details of background need repeating, even when the intended primary audience knows some of these details.

Secondary Audience. The secondary audience consists of those who are affected by decisions that the primary audience makes on the basis of the message. Secondary audiences are likely to use and affect a message and be affected by it, even though they are not the principal users. Secondary audiences often include staff specialists in the same unit, managers and staff specialists in related units, clients, and reporters. Recognizing secondary audiences can be more important than it might appear. While these people cannot affect decisions directly, they often can influence primary users or undermine decisions through faulty implementation. When a secondary audience is responsible for implementing decisions based on a message, you may need to use clearer language or include additional information that is necessary for secondary audiences to act appropriately. For example, financial journalists for the *Wall Street Journal, Barron's, New York Times,* and "Wall Street Week" are an important secondary audience for information coming from the Securities and Exchange Commission, Federal Reserve Board, Treasury Department, and related agencies. Such journalists are not bankers, investment brokers, insurance and other corporate executives, managers of government funds, or other principal users of this information. Nevertheless, by further disseminating government policies and actions in channels and formats that primary audiences can use, financial journalists play a key role in implementing government financial policies. In this instance they also help the public information offices of these agencies perform the role of immediate audience, a conduit to primary users.

Immediate Audience. The immediate audience is the individual or group to whom a message is addressed. In large organizations, many people act as channels for routing information. Sometimes these people are also part of the primary audience—for example, an immediate superior who requests a memo for his or her use only. Often people are part of the secondary as well as the immediate audience. The financial journalists discussed above are examples. Subordinates who have little direct decision-making power but who must implement decisions resulting from the information they route to decision makers fit this category. It is easy to mistake the immediate audience for the primary audience and thereby to design the message inappropriately.

Multiple Roles of Some Audiences. As illustrated above, some audiences play more than one role, complicating analysis. In many small local government agencies, for example, the immediate audience is often the primary user as well. In large departments, many people act as channels for routing information. Sometimes these people are also part of the primary audience. Often they are part of the secondary audience as well as the immediate audience. For example, supervisors may have no direct decision-making power but must implement decisions resulting from information they route to decision makers.

   Analyzing the role or roles an audience plays is crucial to knowing what it needs from the message, how much background and detail to include, what medium or media to use, and so on. The success of public health information campaigns has been improved, for example, through effective use of evaluations before and during such a campaign to determine a target group's literacy level, health needs, life-style, communication preferences, and other relevant information (Rogers and Storey, 1987).

   As receivers of information, public managers should inform those who communicate to them what their audience role is so that those senders can tailor the message and medium accordingly. For example, this may involve signaling, "Write a memo to me, but tailor it to my boss, the primary audience."

   Once public managers have *mapped* their audiences, recognized what basic functions (conduit, decision maker, implementer, and so forth) they serve, and established audience priority, important audiences need to be *profiled* according to the audience profile shown in Exhibit 3.1.

Profiling Audiences

In the audience profile, information on the audience's background and preferences usually remains relatively stable, changing only gradually over time. Affiliations, experience, communication preferences, and credibility with audience are therefore less likely to be situation specific than are the audience's knowledge and interest in a particular topic, what the audience and others need to get from a message, and the impacts of that message. This profile information will change as the topic and management situation change.

Consider now each element of the audience profile. *Name* and *title* must be complete and correct to address the audience properly. Users may want to note permissible nicknames or required titles for addressing this audience. A full, correct title helps identify an individual's role and relative position in the organization. Be careful to avoid the assumption that a title correctly defines a role. For example, elementary school secretaries often play administrative roles as assistant to the principal or interim principal and need to be treated as such. Knowing the *organizational role* of an audience is crucial because roles are often more important than individual positions or personalities. Research shows that people interpret messages and react to them in different ways according to their positions and roles in an organization (Dearborn and Simon, 1958; Tompkins, 1984). What each person perceives as the issue or facts of a case depends largely on his or her position and role in the organization. Miles' Law, attributed to Rufus Miles, Jr., has great relevance for government communication. According to Miles' Law, "Where you stand depends on where you sit." Organizational role forces agency directors, for example, to take a broader perspective than program directors concerned primarily with their single program or project. Cost-conscious Office of Management and Budget analysts are predictably perceiving plans for a new AIDS research laboratory differently than are research administrators from the Federal Food and Drug Administration and the Department of

Exhibit 3.1. Audience Profile.

NAME:

TITLE:

BACKGROUND

Organizational Role: (for example, manager, staff adviser, analyst, watchdog)

Routine: (daily tasks, daily problems)

Age: Gender:

Educational Level and Fields:

Professional Experience: (positions, organizations, duties)

Geographic Identification: (for example, nationality, regional preference, cosmopolitan or local orientation)

Group Affiliations: (political, social, and so on)

PREFERENCES

Communication Preferences: (preferred medium, style, length, tone, likes/dislikes jargon or gimmicks)

Credibility: (sender's credibility with this audience, credibility of others with audience)

Characteristics Specific to Topic and Situation

TOPIC   Knowledge of Topic or Assignment that Message Is About:

Interest in Topic or Assignment that Message Is About: (intrinsic interest, practical need-to-know, and the like)

NEEDS   What Audience Needs from Message: (for example, data, critique, progress report, recommendations)

Other Uses Message Will Serve: (for example, background for others, reply to others, justification for policy)

IMPACTS   Impact of Message on Audience and on Others: (for example, creates extra work, brings good/bad news, involves others)

Source: Adapted from Mathes and Stevenson, 1991, p. 41.

Health and Human Services. When receiving or sending messages, public managers need to be aware of their own organizational role in order to avoid letting that role unduly affect interpretation.

Knowing an audience's *routine* can reveal when that audience is usually too busy with correspondence to take phone calls, when the most promising lulls occur for asking questions, and what kinds of activity are likely to engender resentment (more reports to read) or bring welcome relief.

Knowing the *age* of an audience may be less important and in some instances may cause awkwardness. On the other hand, knowing a person's approximate age often tells something about that person's values and preferences for formality or informality, for example. Assuming values or positions on the basis of a person's *gender* is even riskier. Avoid it. Note gender if a mistake is possible in addressing the audience, as with the first names Leslie, Dana, and so on. Homework on each particular audience helps avoid stereotyping.

Educational level and fields are indicators of an audience's general knowledge base. For example, Frank Macchiarola, former chancellor of the New York City Public School System, surprised some attorneys and witnesses with his ability to question witnesses testifying before the New York State Study Commission for New York City in 1973–74. A thorough profile of Frank Macchiarola would have told New York City officials that he held a law degree in addition to a Ph.D. and therefore his knowledge of questioning and hearing procedure was to be expected. Dr. Macchiarola modestly and shrewdly did not flaunt his legal training and experience beforehand, but he made them count when the hearings were held.

Professional experience is probably a better indicator of job-related knowledge than is education. If Dr. Macchiarola had only taken courses in cross-examination technique and procedure, he could be expected to question witnesses, but with less proficiency than his experience also equipped him. Knowing that a superior, for example, has served lengthy stints in budget and personnel offices indicates that she has probably developed considerable savvy about budget and personnel matters.

Geographic affiliation can often be revealing. Westerners, for example, frequently value water and wildlife issues highly. Urbanites often take different positions on city-suburban issues than do suburbanites. As before, check carefully to avoid misleading assumptions. Some staunch urban advocates live in the suburbs to please their families.

Much of the background information discussed above can be obtained from official biographical sketches found in government organization manuals that the U.S. government, states, and major counties and cities publish. Legislative directories, sometimes published separately and often known as bluebooks or redbooks, are another source. Sometimes additional biographical information can be obtained directly from the audience or the audience's agency.

Knowing *communication preferences* is a must. Some government audiences prefer brief memos, as did a former boss, Governor Nelson Rockefeller. Others prefer an informal conversation in the hall. Some of your government colleagues may revel in legal or technical jargon while others loathe jargon. Knowing some of an audience's major preferences or peeves helps one avoid alienating that audience because of communication style, format, tone, wording, and so forth.

Recognizing their *credibility* with an audience can also make public managers more effective communicators. Budget analysts who have less credibility than others with their budget director, for example, usually need to convey more technical detail in their briefings for the director until the director recognizes that they "know their stuff." If I know that someone else has greater credibility with an audience I wish to reach than I do, I often ask that person to convey my message for me. Often it is even more effective to disassociate myself and my name from the message that now is carried by another standard-bearer. My ego can stand seeing someone else be the conduit, especially if he or she succeeds with audiences that I might not.

An audience's *knowledge of topic or assignment that the message is about* is even more crucial to a sender's communicating success than is that audience's general knowledge. An audience's general knowledge of university administration may not translate into specific knowledge about retrenching universities intelligently, for example. It pays to assess an audience's specific knowledge of that subject by asking that audience beforehand, asking others who know that audience well, or reading that audience's writings on the subject. The audience's *interest in topic or assignment* is as important as its knowledge. Public servants, lobbyists, and others who are interested in a topic can become knowledgeable with sufficient educating on a subject. On the other hand, experts in a subject may no longer be interested, thereby requiring facts, arguments, consequences, or something else in a message to increase its salience for them.

Knowing *what an audience needs from a message* is also crucial to communicating successfully. Does the audience need background information? A report on progress? Decision options? A critique of another plan? The specific needs the message is to serve should influence message content, format, length, and other features.

Likewise, it pays to find out about any *other uses a message will serve.* Suppose a budget examiner discovers, for example, that her boss requests a memo critiquing the report of her colleague *and* that her critique will go to that colleague for his guidance in making revisions. She will still need to convey her honest assessment. She owes that to her employer, her profession, and her colleague. But her memo may need to show greater tact if she values a positive working relationship with her colleague. Having been "burned" before by seeing a report circulated far more widely than I imagined and to people my report mentioned, I am now more careful to find out other uses, both intended and unintended. If these other uses are not specified when a report, memo, letter, or the like is assigned to you, ask about them.

Of all the characteristics listed in the audience profile, *impact of message on audience and others* is the most likely to be neglected, in my experience. Yet, if the profile shows that recommendations will create extra work for an audience, the message should take that into account by showing how the extra work can be handled, why benefits will outweigh costs, and so on. Precautions such as these often make the difference between accomplishing objectives and failing to communicate.

It is, of course, unnecessary to complete a formal profile for every communication task. Many communications are so brief, straightforward, or inconsequential that profiling all audiences (in such situations) would be wasted effort. Some audiences, however, particularly deserve careful analysis: those communicated with regularly, those on whose behalf messages are sent, and those who can make or break important messages. An agency public information office, a correspondence control unit, or an administrator's immediate staff can prepare and maintain audience profiles to ease the administrator's task. Keeping these profiles in a paper or computer file for further reference enables public managers to refresh their memory about the kinds of detail and nuances needed to get their message across. Such profiles can be attached to requests for replies or other assignments. This kind of audience analysis is effective regardless of whether a message is written or spoken. Profiles can be tailored to particular audiences. From time to time it may be necessary to drop some characteristics and add others to make such profiles more useful. The importance of considering audience when developing and executing communication strategies is emphasized throughout this book. Indeed, this book is primarily organized around communicating with government's important audiences. Chapter Seven, especially, discusses audience segmentation strategies. Further discussion of audience analysis can be found in Gibson and Hanna (1976).

Diagnosing the Management Situation

Most government communicators probably consider their audiences before sending messages. Greater use of audience mapping and profiling will make their acquisition of knowledge of audiences more systematic. Effective communicators, however, must also assess the *management situation,* which affects the ways messages are sent, received, and interpreted. When sending or receiving messages, being aware of such factors as those shown in the management situation profile presented in Exhibit 3.2 will help public managers and staff professionals communicate more effectively.

An agency's, a company's, or an association's *organizational strategy* profoundly shapes communicating. Much of the crucial communicating in any organization involves identifying its overall strategy, communicating that strategy to employees and others, and communicating internally and externally to get the strategy implemented. Knowing, for example, that an agency is pursuing a strat-

Exhibit 3.2. Management Situation Profile.

Organizational Strategy: (for example, empire building, turf protection, diversification, or coalition building)

Nature of Management Routine: (for example, strong attention to routine or aversion to routine, routine or variety the norm, personnel familiar or unfamiliar with routine)

Work Load: (for example, unit overworked or underworked, work load concentrated or shared, work load requires specialization or generalization)

Organizational Climate: (for example, open or secretive, tolerant or unforgiving, supportive or competitive, calm or stressful)

Organizational State: (for example, prospering or declining, secure or threatened, experiencing normalcy or crisis)

Primary Leadership Styles: (for example, autocratic or democratic, risk taking or risk averse)

Primary Motivators: (for example, rewards or sanctions, praise or blame, economic or psychological)

Political Environment: (for example, politicized or apolitical, dominated by office politics or party politics, Democratic or Republican oriented)

Organizational Mission and Culture: (for example, military, paramilitary, philanthropic, research, service, or regulatory)

Technological Capability: (for example, has adequate computer capability, fax capability, and satellite uplink and/or downlink)

Organizational Communication: (for example, written or oral media emphasized; formal or informal communications predominate; communications primarily upward, downward, or lateral; routing structured or unstructured)

---

egy of coalition building rather than turf protection to help it weather budget cuts probably indicates greater willingness to send and receive requests involving other agencies.

It also helps to know the *nature of management routine* when sending messages to an agency or receiving messages from it. Does the management routine of the target agency, unit, or individual primarily involve managing caseloads? Administering grants or contracts? Developing policy? Evaluating programs? Administering budgets? Managing support services? Does the intended message fit into or run counter to the management routine? Audiences are less likely to know how to handle messages that do not fit readily into their management routines. On the other hand, messages that are not routine can provide diversity and get special treatment if crafted appropriately.

Knowing the type and amount of an audience's *work load* helps in several ways. Work load often gives clues as to the kind of attention your message will receive. A report sent to an already overworked unit will probably be at least temporarily delayed or ignored. This knowledge suggests some strategies: submitting the report earlier or later to avoid peak load, channeling the report to processors not overworked, or attempting to convince someone that the report deserves special attention. Underworked units looking for action to justify their existence may be ripe targets for a proposal, report, or other message. Public managers who want to bury a message can do that better during peak work loads. Public managers on the receiving end need to be particularly alert to detect important messages that might get lost because of overload. Air traffic controllers face this problem constantly.

Knowing something about *organizational climate* provides clues about receptiveness for sending or receiving messages. For example, managers and professionals within the U.S. State Department need to consider their department's substantial need for secrecy and multiple reviews of all messages. They should expect longer lag times before their messages are cleared and will need to design each message to satisfy more reviewers.

Research generally shows that people who feel threatened or stressed are more likely to misinterpret messages. If you are sending a message into a situation where workers are unduly stressed for some reason, build more precautions into the message to anticipate the greater likelihood of error or misinterpretation.

Organizational state is also a particularly important variable, a lesson I learned the hard way. As a program assistant to Governor Rockefeller of New York in 1971, I saw the Attica Prison riot's devastating effects on those at the prison and also on those trying to cope with this crisis. The resulting forty-three dead prisoners and hostages and breakdowns in trust and communication were all serious consequences. In an effort to add some levity to what was a rather grim scene in the governor's office, a junior staff member inserted a routine reply about the governor's being unable to attend a speaking engagement. My friend and colleague, who would normally have reviewed and edited this letter, would undoubtedly have enjoyed and appreciated a little humor in light of all that had happened. The staff member, however, should have realized that during crisis, normal routines are set aside. Indeed, normal routing had changed so that the staff member was assigned a routine reply that was usually handled by the correspondence control unit. The draft reply went directly to the assistant director of state operations, who reviewed the governor's correspondence. He failed to see the humor and rightfully admonished the staff member for taking liberties with this assignment. In light of the Attica tragedy, this attempt at humor, however well intended, was in poor taste. And because of organizational crisis, the chances of that reply going out unchanged, thereby embarrassing the governor and getting the writer into trouble, were heightened.

Receiving and interpreting messages effectively is particularly crucial during times of administrative, political, or other crisis—exactly when an organization's capacity to receive and interpret messages promptly and accurately is most likely to be impaired. For these reasons, it helps to establish and practice special communication procedures and systems for crisis situations, a topic addressed more fully in Chapter Eight.

Knowing that a *primary leadership style* used in a bureau is, for example, autocratic, with information and decision making centralized in the chief and several deputies, should indicate that these officials are the primary audience no matter to whom the message is addressed. Choice of medium, content, style, tone, and so on should reflect this knowledge. I have given briefings when I was convinced my primary audience consisted of one comptroller and one assistant comptroller in an audience of sixty people. My basic message was therefore geared to those two people. Knowing something about *primary motivators* also provides some useful cues. Discovering, for example, that most employees in a unit are motivated by salary, benefit, and security rather than the intrinsic nature of their work suggests greater effort in explaining why a message deserves their attention.

The *political environment* affects communication in obvious ways. When individuals are sending or receiving messages in highly politicized situations, for example, they must pay particular attention to political nuances in wording and tone. Politics also affects choice of sender. Democrats in New York City, Chicago, and Camden (New Jersey) have often utilized Republicans to convey their requests to state governments when those governments were Republican dominated.

Learning about a target unit's *organizational mission and culture* usually provides useful insights into its communication practices. For example, paramilitary agencies, such as police forces and fire departments, typically have a command structure and discipline similar to military organizations. Communication in such organizations, especially in police departments, tends to be more formalized, emphasizing written reports, manuals, logs, and the like. Thus communicating with a police department would normally be more structured and formal than communicating with a department of cultural affairs and recreation. Departments of cultural affairs and recreation typically have a different mission and organizational culture. In fact, such agencies really have two missions: promoting cultural activities and providing recreational opportunities. Conflicts in priorities, employee orientation, and operating procedures can be anticipated in such agencies, thereby requiring adjustments in communication.

An agency's *technological capability* will influence the choice of medium. If a unit lacks a fax machine, documents may need to be sent via express mail, transcribed by telephone, or downloaded via computer. A training director in a federal agency who wants to conduct televised training at all field office sites simultaneously will need to learn whether these sites have adequate satellite downlink or cable hookup capability. If the field offices lack this capability, other receiving sites, such as public schools or motel conference centers, could be found.

Organizational communication is clearly another key factor in the management situation. Learning an organization's preferred medium (or media) and degree of formality, for example, can help in one's choice of media, style, and tone. If routine routing patterns are followed, this helps the sender know who the likely audiences of a message are and the message can then be tailored for them. If no regular routing is followed, a message may have to be crafted for multipurpose, general audiences and be less tailored.

Factors in the management situation are more subtle, more difficult, and more likely to be overlooked than are factors in the audience or sender. The management situation profile can help identify key situational factors, but it should also be regarded as a tool to use and adapt as necessary. Other variables also deserve attention in various situations. The profile, however, emphasizes variables particularly relevant to communicating. Analyzing the management situation would be a burden for administrators if such analysis were used only for communicating. The kinds of information included in the management situation profile are critical to functioning effectively in an administrator's own agency and to dealing with other organizations. Effective administrators gain much of this knowledge in the course of their work and only need to organize such knowledge mentally for communicating. Chapters Four, Five, and Six provide pointers for assessing an agency's internal management situation. Chapter Six also offers guidelines for assessing another agency's management situation. Additional useful insights into diagnosing management and organizational situations can be found in Kotter (1978) and Gortner, Mahler, and Nicholson (1987). Computer software such as the *Situation Analyst*© is also available to help managers and planners diagnose management situations.

Analyzing Message Senders

Factors regarding the *sender* or *senders* of a message can be diagnostic factors since knowledge about senders influences choices of medium and message. But factors concerning message preparers and senders are also part of the strategy design process. Message senders need to analyze, for example, their own characteristics to discover whether they are automatically or subconsciously favoring their own communication preferences over those of their audiences. Many government analysts, for example, so prefer the relative safety of written reports to the trauma of public speaking that they continue to write reports even when their bosses prefer greater brevity and the give-and-take of oral briefings. Assessing themselves as senders and their bosses as receivers would tell them that their personal preferences were inappropriate to the audience and management situation. Self-knowledge of preferences, credibility with the audience, and level of expertise on the topic also help public administrators decide when someone else should serve as the message sender. Research has shown that communicators judged trustworthy (expert, experienced, unbiased, and so on) can produce several times the opinion-change that communicators with little credibility can produce. Choosing a sender that has greater credibility with the audience increases the likelihood of success. For both sending and receiving communication, introspection leading to greater self-awareness of strengths and shortcomings generally leads to improved performance.

Message receivers need to assess the sender to gauge the sender's role and perspective, knowledge and experience, and professional credibility; potential impacts on the sender; and other characteristics. This helps receivers (1) judge the message's accuracy and significance and (2) know how to reply if a reply is required.

Choosing Appropriate Media

Another important communication strategy decision concerns the choice of medium or channel. The range of media available to government communicators has been expanded by modern technologies. Standard communications media include the report, memo, letter, press release, magazine or newspaper article or editorial, newsletter, meeting, briefing, speech, hearing, rumor, personal visit, radio, and network television. These have been supplemented to include cable and satellite television, computer networking, electronic mail, automatic message systems, videotaped messages, and the like. Some media are used primarily for internal government communication (memo, staff meeting). Other media are utilized more when one is communicating with external audiences (press release, radio, television). Almost all media can be used appropriately internally and externally, however, depending on the message, audience, skills of the sender, and objectives for communicating. Some research findings follow; these findings can help public administrators choose media intelligently.

Different Communication Media Are More Effective with Different Audiences and in Different Situations

Research summarized by Tompkins (1984, p. 688) shows that oral communication, allowing feedback from subordinates, is the "preferred single medium of downward communication" in organizations. Writing is more effective when combined with oral messages to allow feedback. Studies show that "management is ill advised to depend on the written medium alone, particularly in one-message campaigns" (Tompkins, 1984, p. 688). In addition, some audiences prefer certain media. Mintzberg (1973) has documented the preference of busy chief executives for oral communication, even rumor, to formal, written messages. The preference of video-age young people for short, visually oriented messages—what futurist John Naisbitt (1984) calls "blips"—has prompted some governments to emulate political campaigners in making their messages short and visual.

The choice of an appropriate medium depends on content as well as audience. On the one hand, financial information, for instance, is difficult to convey solely by briefing, even when an audience prefers oral messages to written ones. Financial and other technical data are often conveyed more precisely by written documents, often with oral explanation available. On the other hand, written messages are often risky when political, administrative, legal, or personal sensitivities are involved. Written messages do not allow the sender to gauge the audience as the message is being sent and to adjust the message on the basis of the perceived audience response. Even more important, written messages often have a life of their own—ending up in the hands of unintended audiences and showing up years after they were written. Written messages are also more likely to be interpreted as official and thus harder to recant or alter later. Administrators would do well to ask themselves whether writing is worth the risk in the situation at hand.

Nonverbal media (expressions, gestures, and body language)

convey messages that accompany a spoken message such as a public speech or communicate something by themselves, as with a shrug or a frown. Administrators must be careful to avoid saying one thing with words and contradicting that message with body language. For instance, President Nixon's facial expressions, eye movement, and other body language sometimes gave the impression that his words were insincere. The mannerisms, voice, and eye contact of President Reagan, on the other hand, tended to increase the perception that his words were sincere. Evidence generally shows that nonverbal signals convey more accurate messages than do spoken words (Falcione, 1984). Some useful resources on body language include Ruesch and Kees (1956), Harper (1982), and Breasure (1982).

The creative use of modern technologies enables governments to reach audience segments better than ever before. Word processing and computer data banks can produce letters of instruction to voters, for example, which not only appear to be personalized, individually typed letters but can reflect information about residence, past voting regularity, education level, and the like. Cable television provides the means for segmenting communication to groups with different interests, languages, and geographic locations. The Monrovia, California, High School routinely calls parents after work to inform them about their child's attendance, academic progress, or an upcoming school event. The "caller" is an automated calling system, a computer that delivers preprogrammed messages. The Federal Aviation Administration uses voice recognition technology to provide a weather advisory system with a vocabulary of more than 2,000 words to 800,000 licensed general-aviation pilots. Modern technologies such as these can help segment audiences more effectively but also require accurate knowledge of audiences to avoid the "garbage in–garbage out" problem. Also, the logistical advantages of high-tech channels may be offset by the anxiety many groups and individuals experience from technology that they do not understand. For these people and others who prefer social contact, the coffee klatch may be the appropriate channel to use.

Objectives for communicating also affect the choice of medium. For example, Rogers and Storey (1987, p. 837) note that "while the mass media may be effective in disseminating information, interpersonal channels are more influential in motivating people to act on that information." People are more likely to act on information when social and environmental support is present. Utilizing people as role models or opinion leaders helps provide support, as does building in on-site interpersonal channels for reinforcing appropriate behavior. For these reasons, neighborhood meetings and householder interaction are important to the success of the Neighborhood Watch crime prevention program (Rogers and Storey, 1987). In summary, different media have different strengths and weaknesses with different audiences and goals for communicating. There is no substitute for knowing which media work best for a particular audience or objective. While the acceptability of a medium usually depends on the specific sender, audience, objectives, and situation, some general characteristics are useful to recognize. Table 3.1 presents a comparison of the advantages and disadvantages of the media most commonly used in government.

Using Multiple Media Increases Communication

Some research indicates that conveying a message via multiple channels or media interferes with message retention, but the bulk of research supports the value of redundancy, especially when the message is within the audience's ability to process the information (see Frandsen and Clement, 1984; Tompkins, 1984). A typical finding reported that within three days people forget about 80 percent of what they read (Maude, 1974). If they both read and hear the message, they forget only about 35 percent of it. The importance of backing up oral messages with briefing papers, memos, or other documents is also supported by administrative experience as is supplementing written messages with oral explanation. Using different media can help audiences with different physiological barriers. Many senior citizens, for example, need written *and* spoken information to piece together messages their diminished eyesight or hearing alone would miss.

In a report entitled *Leadership for America: Rebuilding the Public Service,* the National Commission on the Public Service emphasizes the need for using multiple media: "To describe and celebrate public careers, government should open new channels of

Table 3.1. Major Government Communication Media.

Medium	Advantages	Disadvantages
Telephone	Speed Two-way Convenient	No record of conversation No visual cues
Face-to-face	Personal contact Allows visual cues Two-way	Timing may be inconvenient Requires spontaneous thinking May be difficult to end Status differences may be obvious or exaggerated Expressions and other nonverbal cues can con- tradict oral message
Meeting	Allows interaction of dif- ferent minds Allows members to see who is on the team Combines visual and audio	Can be time-consuming Can be unproductive if improperly planned and conducted
Memorandum	Brief or extensive Message can be planned Provides record Read at receiver's convenience	One-way Limited control over who sees the memo
Formal Report	Comprehensive Sender can control organi- zation and wording Read at receiver's convenience Provides record	May take much time to read Content and language may be difficult to understand Often expensive One-way
Computer	Instantaneous Can be sent to multiple audiences Can allow quick feedback Can be coded Typically distortion- resistant since generally sent intact	Ease of sending may lead to unnecessary messages or to too many audi- ences getting a message Equipment or user fail- ures can thwart use Still basically one-way un- less interactive at the same time

Source: Adapted from Uris, 1970, pp. 27–28 and Lewis, 1987, p. 8.

communication with America's college students—at job fairs, and through electronic bulletin boards, computer software, and/or video cassettes" (National Commission on the Public Service, 1989, p. 28). The commission made this recommendation after finding that relatively few federal agencies use the medium of campus visits to educate and recruit the best and the brightest. The commission also found that other channels are underutilized.

Multiple media or channels are just as important when administrators *receive* messages. Providing multiple media for citizens to communicate with government enables people who are inarticulate in one medium to voice their opinions or needs via another. In many localities, citizens who are reluctant to write or to appear at a public hearing, for example, utilize radio call-in programs to communicate with public officials. The City of Tucson is just one government that is sponsoring television call-in programs with city officials and telephone access twenty-four hours a day. Multiple media help too in gaining feedback from government subordinates and field offices, as discussed in Chapter Five.

Crafting the Message

Knowledge about the audience, objectives for communicating, and the management situation helps senders tailor a message whether that message is official or unofficial and whether it is aimed at an internal or an external audience. Key variables to consider when crafting a message include wording, content, length, style, organization, tone, analysis, and body language (when it applies).

Appropriate *wording* often depends on the audience's preferences. Some words trigger audience reactions that are counterproductive. For example, Mayor Fiorello LaGuardia's former personal secretary hated the word *input* when used for example in "Your input is needed on this." Using this word invariably irritated her, usually weakening the effect of the entire message. In an administrative writing workshop for a state department of education's professional staff, I asked participants to name the words that irritated them most, words they wanted staffers and colleagues to avoid. This turned out to be one of the most productive exercises in the workshop. Even the management situation affects wording. Those tempted to transform certain legal documents into readable prose should consider the fact that many stuffy phrases have specific judicial interpretations. Trying to simplify wording in such cases might obscure rather than clarify legal meaning.

Message *content* should be shaped primarily by the objectives for communicating and the audience's knowledge and needs. Too often, however, content is shaped by limitations in the sender's knowledge. This problem can be avoided somewhat by giving senders more time and information to become knowledgeable instead of insisting on quick turnaround in every instance. Occasions arise, as discussed in later chapters, when a quick response is essential. Many of these situations can be anticipated, however, and the content for reports, replies, speeches, and the like prepared in advance.

Length is another message design factor. Often managers will be told how long their report or briefing should be. In other cases they will need to consult audience profiles to remind themselves of preferred length. Presidents and governors tend to prefer memos of two pages or less. Other audiences may prefer longer, more detailed messages. Whatever the length, it is important not to confuse brevity with conciseness. For example, some memos are brief but unnecessarily wordy. What was said in two pages was worth only one page. On the other hand, some presidential briefing memos require more than eighty pages to cover broad, complicated topics; yet they are concise. No unessential content or wordiness has been added. Some communication experts and many government communicators prefer brevity in most cases. Government managers would do well, however, to let their diagnoses of needs, knowledge, and so on dictate the length of their messages. They should then keep those messages concise unless strategy dictates otherwise.

The crafting of writing or speaking *style* should be guided by the audience's preferences, by organizational norms, and by the content of the message. As a rule of thumb, the more complex the content of a message, the simpler, more direct the style should be. Conveying a complex subject in a complex style places a double burden on audiences. Deliberately complicating style to confuse receivers is the kind of ethical issue addressed in Chapter Nine. Senders must also take their own skill levels into account. Some public managers could not speak or write elegantly even if the audience and management situation required that style.

Another strategic communication choice involves message *organization*. If a report is for a busy official unlikely to read more than a few pages, put key findings and recommendations up front in an executive summary or digest. If certain information needs to be absorbed before a reader can understand your recommendations, follow findings with recommendations. Alan K. Campbell, former director of the Office of Personnel Management prefers an inductive organizational pattern that provides him with the information and allows him to draw his own conclusions. The most useful patterns for organizing your message are described in Chapter Four.

Tone is how your message "sounds" to your audience. The tone of a written or oral message can be businesslike, aggressive, servile, warm, hostile, and so forth. As discussed in Chapter Four, tone is created by choice of wording, content, format, and other design factors, as well as how particular audiences perceive the message. In my experience, more government communicators get into trouble because of inappropriate tone than because of the wrong or inaccurate content. Take special precautions, therefore, to craft appropriate tone.

The *analysis* of a message focuses on its logical soundness. Does your report, for example, attribute cause when the conditions for causation are missing? Does your briefing present only one or two options when other reasonable options exist? Analysis is another key strategy design factor addressed in Chapter Four.

The *timing* of a message is a factor not built into the message itself but nevertheless extremely important. *When* a message is sent or received is often the key to its success. Reports of changing crisis conditions need to be sent immediately, whereas many press releases may need to be delayed until after the event publicized. Another major decision involves sequencing—which audiences should get the message first, which next, and which last. In some situations primary audiences, such as key legislators, should get a message first so that they do not become insulted. In other instances a message must go first to an intermediate audience who will be needed to influence the primary audience. These message variables will be addressed more fully in subsequent chapters.

Using the Entire Strategic Contingency Model

We have now worked through the situational and strategy design factors in the strategic contingency model for government communication. Exhibit 3.3 systematizes this process of diagnosis in the form of a communication strategy worksheet. This worksheet is my attempt to systematize and operationalize the conceptual process of diagnosing relevant factors and devising appropriate communication strategy. This heuristic, along with the audience map, audience profile, and management situation profile, is referred to throughout the rest of this book as an aid both to my explanations and to the reader's systematizing and internalizing the conceptual process, which probably is used often but perhaps subconsciously. The

Exhibit 3.3. Communication Strategy Worksheet.

Objectives for Communicating	Audience(s)		Management Situation
(Be precise—for example, "Getting the project committee to fund my proposal." Number each objective, then rank by priority.)	Intended:	Key characteristics	Management climate:
	Primary:		Likely impact of message:
	Secondary:		
	Immediate:		
	Unintended but potential:		Political implications:

Consider the above factors when designing strategy for

Medium (Media)		Sender	Message
Oral	Written	Appropriate preparer(s) of message:	Basic thrust/content:
Face-to-face	Letter		Tone:
Interview	Memo		
Phone	Report		Style:
Meeting	Proposal		
Teleconference	Cable		Length:
Briefing/speech	Brief	Appropriate sender(s) of message:	Organization:
	Release		
Other	Other		Timing:
Combination	Combination		

value in making this conceptual process conscious and systematic is to sharpen the reader's diagnostic and strategy skills further. My aim and the reader's is to make this strategizing process so ingrained that the reader later has to rely less on the worksheet and accompanying heuristics. There may well be situations, however, that are so important or so frequent that the reader may want to analyze them formally and devise strategy in order to avoid barriers or errors.

The model's six sets of factors are incorporated in the communication strategy worksheet in abbreviated form so that readers can get in one glimpse an overview of the entire strategy process we have just worked through—from setting objectives for communicating to crafting the message. Readers can consult the more detailed maps and profiles for further information as needed.

An example may serve to show how the communication strategy process works. Dorcas Hardy, when head of the Social Security Administration (SSA), initiated a strategic planning process that resulted in a set of strategic objectives for that agency. Some months later, however, a survey of SSA managers found that many managers were unaware of all the agency goals issued. The survey also showed that a majority of the managers felt that their subordinates were unaware of or uncommitted to agency goals and that many subordinates felt poorly informed about strategic and long-range planning efforts in the SSA. The survey further showed responses indicating low morale among managers and employees. Commissioner Hardy was thus faced with evidence that many managers and employees lacked an understanding of her strategic planning process and lacked motivation and morale. She needed a communication strategy.

The *objectives* of that strategy included informing managers and employees throughout the agency of the new strategic plan, motivating them to support the plan's goals, and convincing them that she was committed to alleviating conditions that hurt morale. The intended primary *audience* would be agency managers and employees who would have to achieve the objectives and outside officials whose political support would be needed. The important secondary audience would include other agencies whose cooperation would be necessary, news organizations, and key client groups. A reading of the *management situation* would indicate that employees might need to be convinced that a new direction was worth their effort and that a new politically appointed administrator was to be trusted. Examining characteristics of the *sender* would indicate that given the importance of the messages (agency strategy and commitment to improving morale) and the need to convince employees of her commitment, the commissioner herself should communicate to those audiences. Assistants would be less effective substitutes. Because of the need for persuasion and the need to allow for questions and discussion and because previous memos and newsletters and other *media* had obviously failed to get her message across, Hardy, in the spring of 1988, held regional management conferences with SSA employees around the country. The key *sender* used this more personal, two-way medium to convey her *message* about the need for change within the SSA and also to receive suggestions from participants about how to better manage and motivate employees. Commissioner Hardy appointed a team to review more than a thousand suggestions obtained from the management forums, to select priorities, and to propose action. This strategy supplemented efforts to communicate via the *Commissioner's Bulletin* and other SSA publications and helped to improve communication and motivation within the Social Security Administration.

Part Two of this book provides guidance for applying the strategic contingency model and communication knowledge to governments' key audiences.

PART TWO

Communicating with Key Audiences to Achieve Public Management Results

4

Relating to
Administrative Superiors
and Elected Officials

Be selective. Be concise. Don't tell someone what you
know; tell them what they need to know, what it
means and why it matters.
— *General David C. Jones, U.S. Air Force Chief
of Staff, as quoted in* Air Force Guide, *1963*

Good counselors lack no clients.
— *William Shakespeare,* Measure for Measure,
Act 1, scene 2

One of the many complexities that make government management
highly challenging is having many "bosses." For division directors,
bureau chiefs, principals, or the equivalent, bosses are the agency
commissioner, secretary, or superintendent, their assistants, and
perhaps managers in another administrative layer if the agency is
large. At times, chieftains of other agencies, the chief executive and
staff, legislators and staff, and members of various publics make
demands of public administrators. This chapter focuses on the
special nature of communicating to administrative superiors and
elected officials, those inside and outside an agency to whom administrators typically report or are responsible. Topics covered include knowing the audience, understanding the management situation, building professional rapport and credibility with superiors

71

and elected officials, clarifying administrative direction, responding to requests for information, building support for agency, program, or project, making policy or administrative recommendations, and requesting financial, political or other resources.

Knowing the Audience

To communicate strategically with superiors and officials, administrators should first be aware of audience profiles, the management situation, and objectives for communicating. Administrative superiors and elected officials share certain similarities. Both sets of audiences have busy schedules, must maintain a broader perspective than that of a single program or project, expect some deference from subordinates, and must be sensitive to political issues, media attention, and public opinion.

On the other hand, there are some important differences between these two groups, differences that require different communication strategies. For example, elected officials usually have less certain tenure than administrative superiors. They are also typically more directly sensitive to voters who control their tenure and to media coverage that shapes voters' opinions. In addition, barring special circumstances, administrators will have less frequent contact with elected officials than with administrative superiors. Indeed, one of the difficulties of communicating with elected officials stems from this infrequent contact. One writer put it this way: "Imagine a marriage in which the partners could meet face-to-face only once a week—and then see every word they exchanged subjected to public scrutiny the next day in the newspaper! These are precisely the conditions under which elected and appointed officials labor in . . . government" (Kellar, 1983, p. 46). To combat such infrequent contact, administrators need to maintain regular channels. Instead of waiting for a crisis or an urgent request, administrators should maintain regular contact through the following media:

- Periodic progress reports that discuss issues and problems rather than ignore or sugarcoat them
- Agency or unit newsletters and reports that keep elected officials (and staff) informed

- Briefing papers that highlight particular, relevant issues, problems, and policies—counterparts of the British white and green papers for briefing key governmental actors
- Issue agendas that list and discuss central issues to be addressed at a particular meeting or during a longer period
- Periodic telephone calls to bring elected officials or staff up-to-date and to keep the administrator's agenda part of their agenda
- Periodic meetings or study sessions with officials or staff to keep them informed and involved
- Reports, both written and oral, of how citizen complaints have been handled that officials have referred to the agency (If administrators can report solutions to problems that have not yet reached the officials' attention, so much the better!)

Knowing and using the kind of information provided by the audience profile for both administrative superiors and elected officials will improve an administrator's "communicating average." As a rule, administrators should use the medium, style, format, tone, and length their audience prefers rather than those that they themselves prefer. If an administrator discovers, for example, that his agency's chief executive prefers oral to written communication, as do many executives (Mintzberg, 1973), he had better find ways to deliver his messages orally instead of in writing. If on the other hand, profiling that executive indicates two-page memos are the order of the day, the administrator had better learn to convey messages that way. Richard Thornburgh, attorney general in the Bush administration, "cut out virtually all daily and weekly meetings with top department officials. Instead, he receives frequent memos from division and agency heads that he reads and returns with red pen marks. . . . 'I like some precision in what I have to decide and oftentimes the discipline of putting something down on a one- or two-page memo will accomplish that,' Thornburgh said" (Purdy, 1989, p. 10A). Not only do Justice Department managers need to adjust their communicating style to include more memos, but they also must be prepared for the unannounced visits the attorney general likes to make.

Lawrence Lynn emphasizes how public executives think and act differently and the importance of knowing those differences.

Joe Califano was very different in the way he could be reached than an Elliot Richardson, or even Caspar Weinberger. Califano is a political animal and has a relatively short attention span—highly intelligent, but an action-oriented person. And one of the problems his analysts had is that they attempted to educate him in the classical, rational way without reference to any political priorities, or without attempting to couch issues and alternatives in terms that would appeal to a political, action-oriented individual. . . . I think that it is not that difficult to discover how a Jerry Brown or a Joe Califano or a George Bush or a Teddy Kennedy thinks, how he reacts. All you have to do is talk to people who deal with them continuously, or read what they say and write. And you discover the kinds of things that preoccupy them, the kinds of ways they approach problems [Kirst, 1980, pp. 86–87].

In addition to Lynn's sound advice for assessing superiors and elected officials: consult them directly, if appropriate; seek information from their aides or secretaries; check official directories and manuals for biographical sketches; obtain résumés; or consult clipping or correspondence files. A useful tactic is to request sample memos, reports, letters, speeches, and so on that the superior or political official judges to be excellent or ask to attend briefings conducted by people the superior regards highly. These examples provide some tangible models to follow.

Administrative superiors and elected officials are often so busy that a brief message is all they have time to digest. When I worked for the governor of New York, there were weeks when I would not see the governor personally and days when I had no personal contact with my boss, the chief of staff. I sent brief messages via quick notes that asked for direction on an issue. Often to guard my superior's time, these notes required only yes or no responses, and the superior could check the appropriate box without having to write a detailed message. Such brief messages can also be posed via electronic or voice mail, with the response via the same medium.

Other ways to communicate briefly with busy officials include accompanying them to the elevator, to their next appointment, or to their car. In these situations administrators need to be
especially prepared since time is short, the superior may be moving
quickly, and distractions will occur. Because of the greater likelihood of misperceptions and crossed signals while trying to talk on
the move, this tactic should usually be used only when less distracting opportunities cannot be arranged. Even then, communicating
on the run requires greater care to verify what each of you meant.
It helps for each of you to summarize what you regard to be the key
points and decisions made. Some officials and superiors welcome
talk at such times. Others dislike surprises and insist their secretary
be informed in advance that someone wishes to accompany them.

Establishing positive working relationships with the secretaries of superiors pays dividends in other ways. Many government
officials are difficult to reach but communicate regularly with their
secretaries. Department heads and White House staffers during the
Eisenhower presidency knew that the key to reaching the president
was often via his personal secretary, Ann Whitman. If administrators
or staffers are on good terms with the secretaries of superiors and the
secretaries know the administrators have credibility with their
bosses, these secretaries can be good conduits. For many details, communicating with the secretary may work better if the secretary is the
one who will actually act on the message—for example, mail agendas for an upcoming meeting—of if the secretary is likely to keep
questioning the superior until he or she gives a response. In this
manner, administrators can have their message repeated without being present and without appearing to be overly persistent.

Administrators need to be cordial and cooperative to stay on
good terms with the boss's secretary. If secretaries think they are
being manipulated or sense lack of cooperation, administrators may
lose a valuable ally. The same guidelines apply to communicating
through press secretaries, staff advisers, or other people who serve
as immediate audiences linking administrators to superiors or officials. Getting to know such people and treating them with respect
may often be as important as relationships with their bosses. In my
experience, public administrators who treat legislators and execu-

tives deferentially but who treat the staffs of these officials shabbily usually get their messages undermined at least once.

Understanding the Management Situation

Another cardinal rule, in addition to knowing the audience's communication preferences and preserving superiors' time, is to compare assessments of each management situation to be addressed. Comparing notes on information such as that in the management situation profile (Exhibit 3.2) is vital because different actors usually have different insights based on their managerial perspective, types of contacts, and background. Middle and first-line managers usually possess detailed knowledge of public programs and management operations. Agency executives usually have a broader perspective of how a program or project fits into the agency's overall operation and of the broader administrative and political implications for that agency. Elected officials can supply an interorganizational perspective because they or their staffs are in touch with many agencies as well as interest groups and voters. Officials can therefore serve as barometers of how policies or actions are perceived by other agencies, interest groups, and individual voters. Sharing information builds a richer understanding of an agency's management situation and helps avoid communication barriers created by different frames of reference.

Administrators can obtain knowledge of the management situation by consulting the other key actors, reading administrative files and news clippings, reviewing government and consultants' reports, and tapping agency and interagency grapevines. It is important to avoid becoming paralyzed by exhaustive (and exhausting) situational analyses that unduly delay action, however. Consult enough informed sources to supply the key perspectives. Consulting superiors and officials to gain their understanding of the management situation helps administrators communicate more intelligently with these audiences and others.

Purposes for Communicating
with Superiors and Elected Officials

A number of objectives exist for communicating with administrative superiors and elected officials. Communication with superiors and officials builds credibility, clarifies agency direction, provides information for decision making and for citizens, builds essential support for agency policies and programs, conveys policy and administrative recommendations, and acquires necessary resources. Even though public administrators may not communicate as frequently with superiors and elected officials as with colleagues and subordinates, communication with superiors and officials often influences their effectiveness most directly and significantly. The rest of this section—and this chapter—focuses on specific purposes for communicating with these key actors.

Building Professional Rapport and Credibility with Superiors and Officials

In pointing out that one important objective for communicating is to build rapport and credibility with superiors and officials who influence an administrator's work and career, I am *not* suggesting administrators talk or write to these audiences primarily to build an image. Make no mistake about this, for that tactic often backfires. A former colleague in the New York governor's office was known for constantly sending memos to the governor and chief of staff. This ploy to keep his name in front of superiors was recognized and often resented since the memo barrage wasted his superiors' time. He would have been better off avoiding unnecessary communication and making the most of those essential opportunities. In the long run the best route to credibility with superiors is proving one's integrity, competence, and reliability. These are qualities displayed in all communications and managerial tasks. There is no shortcut to credibility! Credibility is built over time and through many large (and small) efforts. Managers should recognize that every time they speak, write, or listen to a superior or official this communication affects their professional credibility.

Listening Effectively. Poor listeners damage their administrative credibility by missing assignments, misunderstanding the boss's intent, or making other errors. Listening is the management skill administrators use the most but are prepared for the least. To begin with, listening is more than hearing. Hearing is a physical process

of changing acoustic energy in the form of sound waves into mechanical and electrochemical energy the brain can understand.
Listening is the mental, psychological process of attaching meaning to what we hear. Hearing is necessary for listening to occur but
in no way guarantees it. In his classic piece "Listening Is a 10 Part
Skill" Ralph Nichols identifies ten bad habits that hinder listening
(1957, pp. 56–60): (1) thinking the subject is dull and automatically
tuning out, (2) mentally criticizing the speaker's delivery instead of
listening to what she says, (3) overreacting to something the speaker
says and dwelling on that instead of listening, (4) listening only for
facts instead of listening for larger meanings and expressed feelings
as well, (5) taking notes or outlining everything instead of listening
for overall meanings, (6) faking attention while concentrating on
something else, (7) tolerating or creating distractions, (8) avoiding
difficult material—mentally bailing out when technical or complicated ideas are presented, (9) letting emotionally laden "trigger"
words upset concentration and rapport, and (10) wasting thought
power. While most people speak at about 100 words a minute, an
audience can mentally process about 400–500 words per minute
when listening. Poor listeners let their attention wander while waiting for the speaker to catch up instead of analyzing what the speaker
has said.

Effective listening involves avoiding these ten pitfalls and
taking the following steps. (1) Get *physically* ready to listen—facing
and looking at the speaker, getting close enough to hear, maintaining an alert posture, removing distractions such as other work,
noise from televisions or radios, or competing attention from other
people. Unless one takes these physical actions, listening is already
jeopardized. (2) Get *mentally* ready to listen. Concentrate on what
the speaker is saying rather than on talking or preparing to talk.
Administrators cannot listen effectively when they are talking or
thinking about the next point they will make. By doing this they
may miss something that makes their contemplated next point irrelevant or counterproductive. Such inattention irritates superiors
and any other listeners for that matter. (3) Practice *active listening*
by using the gap between speaking rate and listening rate to good
advantage. Get mentally involved in the subject (even if dull) by
thinking of ways the message affects personal or agency perfor-

mance or how it relates to subjects of interest. Use the slack time constructively to make mental summaries and analyses of what the speaker says. How do the ideas hang together? How do they fit with the ideas of others? (4) Listen for more than content. Listen for tone of voice, and observe expressions, body language, and other nonverbal signals to ascertain additional meaning. Listen also for emotional content. Government and business administrators too often become preoccupied with information and shy away from receiving (or sending) feelings. Because administrators and other professionals often are reluctant to express feelings openly, listeners must be more alert to interpreting feelings conveyed indirectly or partially. Yet feelings that underlie a policy position or reaction to an administrative action are crucial to personal and organizational success. Expressed feelings indicate support or resistance, enthusiasm or burnout, or other important cues.

Effective listening also involves verifying what listeners think they understand. The following techniques help listeners test their understanding (Verderber, 1981). *Paraphrasing* involves restating the content or intent of a message to show what the receiver understood from that message. Example: "As I understand it, you want me to conduct a system analysis of the capital budgeting process." *Questioning* requests further information about content or intent. Example: "What do you mean by 'playing this one close to the vest'?" *Interpreting* points out alternative meanings or a special significance. Example: "What I hear you saying is that you are worried about the outcome of our departmental reorganization." Interpreting a statement is often an effective way to prompt a clarification. If the interpretation is too dogmatic or reads too much into the sender's remarks, however, it may offend him. *Supporting* reinforces the sender, helping her feel better about self, behavior, or message. Example: "Your assessment of training needs makes a great deal of sense to me." *Giving personal feedback* directs feedback not at the message but at what the sender has done or what the sender is like. Example: "Do you realize that you appear to be badly overworked?" In my experience, administrators generally concentrate more on sending messages, but they would be more effective, credible communicators if they gave appropriate attention to these listening/receiving skills.

Crafting an Appropriate Tone. Another way to build rapport and credibility with superiors and officials is to use an appropriate tone when speaking or writing. Tone, as defined in Chapter Three, is how a message "sounds" to an audience. In the strategic contingency model, what constitutes appropriate tone, like other factors, is contingent upon the objectives for communicating, management situation, relationship between sender and audience, and even choice of medium and message content. A formal reprimand to a chronically tardy employee needs an evenhanded, businesslike tone. A speech to motivate subordinates needs emotion to accompany information. While crafting appropriate tone is necessary when communicating with all key audiences, tone for superiors and officials requires special attention. For this reason, tone is addressed in this chapter with the intent that readers apply the principles outlined here to other audiences as well.

Administrative superiors and elected officials typically expect some signs of deference in messages from subordinates. They look (or listen) to see whether subordinates understand and acknowledge the official relationship between them. Sounding presumptuous and aggressive can annoy some superiors, thereby damaging rapport and credibility. On the other hand, superiors who value themselves and their subordinates often react adversely to a servile tone. Effective public managers do not want subordinates who grovel. They want subordinates who show initiative and confidence. In most cases, administrators need to strike a balance between these extremes, as shown in Table 4.1.

Again, following a contingency perspective, administrators need to recognize the many exceptions to the guidelines in Table 4.1. Some bosses and staff professionals are so sensitive about their status and authority that what others consider obsequious tone is what they expect. Other superiors may demand an aggressive tone. A sound audience profile should supply information about the type of tone a superior wants.

As already noted, administrators can help create appropriate tone through their choices regarding message content and medium; they can also do this through their selection of wording, style, and format. It is difficult to convey a positive, optimistic tone if content says, "Someone else got the assignment you wanted." Yet using

Table 4.1. Achieving Appropriate Tone in Messages to a Superior.

Aggressive/ presumptuous tone	Appropriate tone	Obsequious tone
Writer/speaker fails to recognize the status and authority of superior and is therefore too presumptuous about telling superior what he or she should do. Writer/speaker is cocky about his or her own efforts and fails to recognize prerogatives of superior to accept, reject, change, or ignore the writer's/speaker's ideas.	Writer/speaker presents ideas or recommendations forcefully and without apology but also recognizes the prerogatives of the superior.	Writer/speaker is too extreme in describing how good or important the superior is and how inadequate and unimportant the writer/speaker is. Writer/speaker is apologetic and timid in expressing his or her own views.

Examples

"Here are the recommendations from my study of necessary budget cutbacks in the Education Department. Our financial situation is urgent. You must adopt these cutbacks without delay in order to straighten out our mess."	"Here are the recommendations from my study of budget cutbacks in the Education Department. As you know, our financial situation is urgent. The cutbacks I propose are intended to help us cope with revenue shortages."	"I would appreciate it if you would kindly consider these recommendations for cutbacks in the Department of Education. You may well need to refine these recommendations. If you need me, I'm willing to do what I can."

Degree of deference

Not enough	Proper amount	Too much

more positive wording, conveying the same message in a more personal medium (in person or by letter rather than the more impersonal memo), and supplementing that content with some encouraging content ("You're in line for the next good assignment") can soften the blow. Recognize, however, that your audience's perception of tone is what really counts. For example, a letter of commendation may contain positive content and wording conveyed in an impressive format. But if the relationship between sender and receiver is basically distrustful, the letter may be perceived as sarcasm or a manipulative ploy. That is why assessing the audience and management situation is so crucial.

Using Sound Analysis. Another design factor critical to establishing and maintaining credibility with superiors and elected officials is analysis. Analysis involves using sound logic in developing and conveying a message. Readers may have seen, as have I, a solid briefing come apart and the presenter's credibility tarnished because computations on a visual aid were incorrect. Credibility can also be lost because many high-level public executives and elected officials resent being presented with a "stacked" argument or getting recommendations that exclude viable options. Elected officials dislike getting reports that omit essential evidence or reasoning, reports that leave loose ends. An administrator's standing is therefore on the line every time she briefs superiors, prepares a report for elected officials, or communicates in other ways with these audiences. Following are a few guidelines to help administrators check the soundness of an analysis.

- Double-check the accuracy of information you convey in writing or speaking. Since people often see or hear what they know to be correct data rather than what they have actually written or said, have someone else also check the accuracy of information you plan to convey.
- Be sure to include evidence and reasoning essential to your analysis. Review the analysis for unanswered questions, missing logical bridges, faulty transitions, missing or weak data, inappropriate examples, and other problems that could give the audience difficulty. As above, enlist the help of a test audience to catch errors in the analysis.
- Avoid stacking the evidence of argument, using misleading quotations, or engaging in other practices considered to be unethical or inappropriate. Most superiors are smart enough to detect such ploys and will resent being manipulated.
- Anticipate potential counterarguments superiors might make and be prepared to refute them (tactfully). Public executives and elected officials typically value people who can assess different

positions. In addition, because they often have to respond quickly they generally value people who can "think on their feet." Preparing for counterarguments makes it look like administrators are "quick on their feet" even if that is not their strength. Administrators or staffers fail to serve their superiors well, however, if they constantly supply the quick answer instead of researching an issue and thinking it through.

- If a report claims that one condition "causes" another, all four conditions of causation must be met. That one condition or event (1) *always occurs after another* and (2) *the two are correlated* does not establish causation. An educational study in the United States several decades ago found a high correlation between foot size and level of reading achievement. Children with big feet tended to be better readers. But there must also be (3) *no other plausible cause or explanation between the two conditions or events* and (4) some *conceptual justification between the two events or conditions.* There is another plausible explanation for the high correlation between foot size and reading achievement. The older children get, the larger their feet grow and the more reading instruction and practice they have had. Age of child affects both foot size and reading level. This explanation is also more conceptually satisfying. People can understand some relationship between age and reading level. Using the terms *cause* and *causation* carefully will help administrators avoid embarrassment.

- Articulate the assumptions, methods, constraints, and limitations superiors and officials must know to interpret an analysis accurately. Without this information, an audience may be handicapped. Avoid overdoing such explanation, however. Busy administrators and officials rarely have time or inclination to dwell on such methodological issues that are often best handled in an appendix or explanatory endnote.

Listening more effectively and paying attention to tone and analysis will hardly guarantee credibility and rapport with administrative superiors and elected officials. Competence in these matters is just part of the necessary overall competence. Mistakes in listening, tone, and analysis, however, can quickly undermine hard-earned rapport and credibility. This objective is addressed first because it relates to all other objectives for communicating.

Clarifying Administrative Direction

Another important objective for communicating with superiors and officials is to clarify administrative direction. This involves clarifying *macro* overall direction and *micro* direction on specific jobs or assignments. At the macro level administrative direction involves *mission,* those primary goals or end states toward which an agency or program is directed, and *strategy,* the basic game plan for accomplishing mission (Campbell and Garnett, 1989). Government agencies that communicate a strong, shared sense of overall direction or mission have a powerful advantage in motivating their own employees, dealing with clients, and responding to legislators and elected executives. Peters and Waterman (1982) and Peters and Austin (1985) found that sense of mission is one characteristic common to excellent firms and agencies. Much of the success of public agencies like the Strategic Air Command, National Forest Service, Federal Bureau of Investigation, and National Aeronautics and Space Administration and programs like the Peace Corps results from the strong sense of mission imparted to their employees, elected officials, and citizens. These and other agencies experience loss of performance, status, and morale when that strong sense of direction is lost. NASA after *Challenger* and the scandal-plagued Department of Housing and Urban Development are good examples of this. What administrators can do to communicate a sense of direction to subordinates is addressed in Chapter Five.

Gaining a Sense of Overall Direction from Superiors and Officials. Administrators must first receive direction from others, typically administrative superiors and elected officials, before they can act in concert or convey a sense of direction to subordinates. Otherwise, they will never understand their organization's direction and where they fit in, and they will never communicate that sense to others. This is one of many situations where being a passive audience waiting to be informed is disastrous. By actively seeking a sense of direction from those in a position to know, administrators show commitment to their agency and program and help sensitize superiors to the importance of sharing this message. If superiors balk at sharing their sense of agency direction, several possibilities exist. One, they may themselves fail to understand agency direction and may now be stimulated to find out. Two, superiors may be deliberately vague about mission and goals to delay opposition over specific goals. Three, superiors may distrust subordinates or their reasons for knowing agency mission. Or four, superiors may be trying to maximize their power by hoarding such knowledge. These last two cases require efforts to educate superiors about how instilling a sense of direction in others usually improves performance and morale, makes superiors look good, and ultimately increases their power (Bennis and Nanus, 1985; Kouzes and Posner, 1987).

Sense of direction is rarely conveyed in one message but more realistically imparted over time in many ways. Several methods exist for finding out a sense of direction.

- Encourage leaders to issue a "charge to the troops" at a staff meeting or a retreat. Allow enough time for questions and discussion. Retreats are particularly conducive to addressing mission and strategy since they remove daily distractions like phones and in-baskets and place employees together for an extended period of time. Communication is often more open and productive than at agency quarters, where the trappings of unequal rank and status exist.
- Encourage leaders and the training department to schedule seminars or workshops addressing overall agency or program direction. Knowledgeable insiders can be utilized as instructors and facilitators, or outside consultants can be used. Methods such as nominal group technique (Delbeca, Van De Ven, and Gustavson, 1975) are useful for identifying employee sense about existing direction and for developing new goals and strategies.
- Request that leaders communicate a sense of direction via agency or program newsletters, briefing papers, videotaped interviews, sharing of press releases with staff, or via other media.
- Consult documents that convey statements of mission, legislative intent for agencies or programs, and related information. These include legislative histories of acts such as those in the

U.S. Code, Annotated, and in similar state and local codes, government and agency manuals, and agency rules and regulations. Also useful for gaining a sense of direction are executive orders and executive and legislative bill memorandums, press releases on key issues such as an agency or program's creation, budget documents, agency or program plans and annual reports, and agency or program reviews or audits.

To increase the odds of perceiving administrative direction correctly, make sure to read a range of documents and consult people at different levels and positions both inside and outside the organization. If most of these sources communicate the same basic sense of mission and strategy, public managers can feel fairly confident that they have gained an accurate perception. If they get widely divergent readings, their organization is doing a faulty job of conveying a sense of mission and strategy. Checking sources again, consulting additional sources, and advocating direction-sharing actions such as those listed above ought to help. If the problem is more fundamental—an organization or program lacks a firm sense of direction—then discussions, retreats, and workshops can help develop a better sense of mission and strategy.

Gaining a Sense of Direction on Specific Assignments. Clarifying administrative direction at the micro level means being certain that specific assignments are understood. Here, too, administrative superiors and elected officials should make efforts to convey assignments fully and accurately. This often fails to happen, however. I have charged out of my boss's office ready to tackle a new assignment only to realize I was missing information crucial to succeeding. My research on administrative delegation in government reveals that this occurs all too often. In such instances, administrators need to exercise good receiving skills to glean what they need to know from superiors. When being delegated an assignment, whether short- or long-term, some of the more salient questions to ask are these:

- What actual results are expected at the completion of this assignment? What specific products (reports written, cases closed, and so on) are expected?

- Do I have the necessary information to complete this assignment effectively—information about deadlines, resource constraints (budget, personnel, equipment), policy restrictions, information sources?
- How does this assignment fit with other assignments now handled by others both inside and outside my agency? With whom should I collaborate? Which people or units should I avoid? For what reasons?
- How does this assignment resemble or differ from previous assignments? What can I repeat successfully and what should I change?
- What is the superior's sense of the management situation in which the assignment will take place?
- What are the potential pitfalls or problems I should particularly try to avoid?
- Are there any alternative plans if difficulties arise?
- How, when, and by whom will my progress be checked?

If the person or committee delegating an assignment fails to cover the above points, be sure to ask questions. Also take the opportunity to *restate the assignment* so the delegator can check your understanding. If questions or restatement points up differences in perception, address these differences immediately rather than wait for problems later. Intelligent questions demonstrate interest and competence. One of the quickest ways to tell whether someone understands a subject is by the quality of questions he or she asks. Excessive or trivial questions and requests for detailed guidance on an assignment show a lack of independent judgment. Most good bosses want subordinates who are self-starters rather than those who need constant hand-holding, so avoid overquestioning. The reverse of this process—how to communicate an assignment to subordinates—is addressed in Chapter Five.

Responding to Requests for Information

All public managers spend part of their time responding to superiors' requests for information. How well they respond affects their credibility with superiors and elected officials. Managers should observe the following guidelines:

Respond Quickly and Accurately. Requests by superiors and elected officials for information are often urgent and disrupt important work. Michael Cohen's *The Effective Public Manager* (1988) offers sound advice on handling requests for information: supply the necessary information promptly, then get back to other work. Complaining about the request or postponing it rarely helps. Unless administrators can educate the right people on whether the information is really essential, they should respond to the request accurately and quickly. It will not go away. Of course, if they learn that the request is really perfunctory and no adverse consequences will result from ignoring it or providing a cursory reply, they should give the request the attention it deserves.

Respond with an Appropriate Medium. Often a request specifies the reply medium: "Send us a report." "Call me back with the answer." If no medium is specified, choose medium or media tactically. Consider general expectations. A rule of thumb in government is to respond with like medium. Answer a letter with a letter, a phone call with a phone call. A call by a legislative staffer requesting information on agency staffing levels for tomorrow's hearings should not be answered by letter or report unless it can be received in time via messenger or fax. Consider other factors besides custom, however. As noted in Chapter Three, choice of medium is affected by message content. Technical analyses are difficult to convey by telephone. A useful strategy involves using multiple media. Follow up a written analysis with a phone call to see whether questions arise, or follow up a preliminary explanation with detailed documents.

Obtain Feedback on the Adequacy of Response. Following through to learn whether an information response satisfied the audience is the step administrators often omit. Yet calling, writing, or stopping by to ask if a response did the job and how it might be improved accomplishes several important objectives. One, follow-through diplomatically allows senders to find out whether the response was received. If not, they can supply another without waiting for a second (and more irate) request. Two, follow-through provides valuable feedback that senders can apply toward the next response. Were assumptions about the intended audience and uses for the information correct? Was the information supplied inadequate, appropriate, or excessive? Was the information clear to all audiences? Did any repercussions arise? Three, follow-through shows that the administrator who supplied the response is conscientious and thorough, someone to be relied upon. This enhances an administrator's credibility and that of his or her organization. Four, follow-through provides a legitimate reason to contact the administrative superior, elected official, or staff member from whom the request was received. This follow-up contact often provides additional insights about the management situation involved and helps build rapport and credibility with those important audiences.

Building Support for Agency, Program, Policy, or Project

Some administrative communications, such as annual reports, budget presentations, legislative packages, or grant proposals, have the central objective of building support for an agency, program, policy, or project. Yet other communications to administrative superiors and elected officials may influence the credibility of an agency, program, or project as well as an administrator's own professional reputation. Over time, shoddy or missing responses to information requests create an image of a careless or incompetent unit, thereby undermining support. A history of well-researched and cogently written reports enhanced the Advisory Commission on Intergovernmental Relations' reputation and influence. Building credibility and support should therefore be one of the objectives for each communication to administrative superiors, elected officials, other government agencies, news organizations, and relevant publics. Discussion of these last three audiences is provided in Chapters Seven and Eight.

Concentrate on Actual Performance. Acquiring support is difficult or transitory if a program or unit has inadequate performance to support. Obtaining internal and external support to clean up an administrative mess does happen, as the 1989 efforts to reform HUD show. Rescue appeals lose their persuasiveness if made too often or too long, however. Indeed, a strong case can be made that HUD has traditionally received less political and financial support because performance problems damaged its credibility. To help address a problem of agency image, I was once asked to be a keynote speaker on the topic "Marketing and Promoting the Department of Employment Security." My advice to that agency audience, and to readers: concentrate on mission and performance—and communicate the results of that performance to key target audiences. Worrying first about external image will likely fail. In government and politics image is sometimes perceived as being more important than reality. But image without substance is difficult to maintain. Most professional public information officers I know recognize the folly of promoting image without performance. Putting image first also runs contrary to a public administrator's sense of ethics and professionalism. Performance to benefit relevant publics—to improve people's lives—is our mission in government. If mission and performance are taken seriously, credibility, image, and resources generally follow. In my government experience, grants, budget, positions, administrative authority, and other support tend to go, in the long run, to agencies and programs that demonstrate competence to use that support effectively.

Communicate Successes and Problems. Establishing a competent level of performance supplies administrators with ammunition to communicate. And communicate it they must. Administrators should never assume that organizational (or individual) performance will automatically be recognized and rewarded. They should assess results to see what is worth sharing. Likely prospects for communicating to superiors and officials include project or program starts, completions, and milestones; innovations or promising pilot projects; instances of serving program clientele; cooperation with other agencies or groups; turnarounds or improvements in measured performance; instances of cost reduction; and effective uses of new technologies. Administrators would do well to recognize that many public executives and elected officials react well to personal accounts involving individual clients, citizens, or employees. Such accounts often give decision makers a tangible feel of situations or issues that aggregate data cannot. Too much reliance on anecdotal information can mislead superiors and elected officials if the accounts are selected for being particularly favorable or unfavorable, sensational, or interesting rather than for being representative. A balance of aggregate information and flesh-and-blood personal accounts goes further in building rapport and credibility.

If done carefully, it also pays for several reasons to communicate problems and shortcomings honestly. One, communicating problems honestly gives an administrator greater credibility with key audiences than reporting only successes. Research on persuasion generally shows that more balanced information or arguments are more credible (Berelson and Steiner, 1969; Miller, 1987). Knowledgeable elected officials and public executives know some problems must exist and become wary if only good news reaches them. Two, reporting problems openly and accurately typically brings less criticism than situations in which a reporter, external agency, or whistle-blower finds the problem and makes it known. Not only do superiors and officials hate to be surprised by problems; if they find out from another source, it might appear that the program or agency was attempting a cover-up. Four, by honestly informing key audiences of problems and needs, they will be in a better position to provide support. Savvy government administrators know which legislators they can call on to help their cause. If administrators have to convey problems or deficiencies up the line, they can soften the blow by also reporting some successes, when possible, and including proposals for addressing the problem, showing that they are not just dumping problems on superiors.

Making Policy or Administrative Recommendations

Assessing audiences and management situations will tell which situations require making recommendations to superiors or elected officials. Some may only want the information summarized; some may even want to see the raw data and draw their own conclusions. Frequently, however, superiors and officials want an administrator's best advice in the form of policy or administrative recommendations.

Drafting Recommendations. When drafting recommendations, keep the following points in mind:

- Highlight recommendations by numbering them, listing them rather than burying them in the narrative, using a different typeface, and labeling the recommendations with a heading. Many solid recommendations get lost because they are not set apart and clearly identified.
- Use the form and style that the primary audience prefers or at least is familiar with. Often agency manuals such as the General Accounting Office's *Project Manual* specify the form that recommendations must take. If an agency has no such form or the form leaves much to be desired, I recommend the following. Recommendations that can be operationalized typically have three elements, actors, actions, and constraints. In the following example, these elements are labeled.

Actors
The State Department of Education and Board of Higher Education

Actions
should establish a Joint Commission to Improve Teacher Training

Constraints
by January 1, 1993, at a cost of no more than $250,000.

Actors can be single or multiple. Actions should be clearly specified with action verbs (establish, report, audit, provide, and the like). And constraints typically specify time, budget, information, or human resource constraints. In most cases the elements of recommendations shown here should be present unless more ambiguous recommendations are needed for tactical reasons.

Tactics for Sequencing Recommendations. Sequencing is as important in getting recommendations accepted as is form. Merely presenting recommendations in the order in which they are formulated misses using communications strategy. Instead, consider using one or more of several different possible *sequences* or organizational patterns. Frequently, a sequence based on descending order of *importance* makes the most sense. Research and practice both show that public executives and elected officials are too busy to wade through reports or memos or endure long briefings waiting for key recommendations. Starting with the most important recommendation and progressing to less important ones increases the chances of an audience seeing or hearing key proposals and recognizing them as significant. In addition, if only a limited number of recommendations can be accepted, presenting them in order of importance makes it easier to drop those below the cutoff point. Never assume, though, that others agree which recommendations are important or that an audience recognizes when recommendations are listed by importance. It helps to specify that recommendations are presented in descending order of importance and whose priorities this ranking represents. The writer's alone? The entire staff's or committee's? The agency's? These clues give an audience additional guidance in interpreting the recommendations.

Policy recommendations, budget requests, equipment "wish lists," and other proposals can, by contrast, be presented in order of *perceived receptivity*. This involves placing first those recommendations the proposer perceives the audience will most likely accept, in the hope of establishing rapport and credibility. If an audience approves of initial recommendations, it is more inclined to think the proposals that follow also have merit. This "pump priming" tactic can work, but administrators should be careful not to put their own favored proposals so far down the list that the audience has used up its receptivity by the time it gets to theirs. Moreover, public administrators would be avoiding professional responsibility if they catered to the predilections of their audience without reflecting their own priorities.

Another way to present recommendations is in order of administrative *feasibility,* placing those that are easier to accomplish first. This also can have a "pump priming" effect and can be useful if easier actions are logical steps to more ambitious actions. This borrows from the logic of mixed scanning, beginning with those steps that are easier to accomplish and reversing course if problems arise. It follows even closer the logic of incrementalism, proceeding cautiously in small steps. A trap in this tactic is putting so much emphasis on administrative feasibility that more difficult, but more important, actions or decisions get relegated to the bottom. Often in government it is more crucial to accomplish a few major actions than to accomplish many minor and more feasible ones.

Time sequence, ordering recommendations in the sequence in which they need to be decided or implemented, facilitates planning and scheduling. This pattern could be applied to proposals addressed in a meeting or stages in a project. As with receptivity, chronological order may run counter to importance. The most urgent decisions or actions are not necessarily the most crucial ones; they just need attention sooner.

A pattern that stresses *geographic location* presents recommendations grouped by federal region, agency field office, municipal service area, or some other geographic unit. This emphasizes to an audience that each geographic area gets attention in the recommendations, a point often politically sensitive. If some geographic units are not the subject of recommendations or the proposals must treat units unequally, another pattern, such as order of importance, probably makes more sense.

Sequencing by *neutral order* can often be politically prudent to avoid the appearance of favoring some administrative units, geographic areas, or programs according to their sequence. Presenting recommendations by number of region, for example, signals an audience that Region V is no less valued than Region I, but just has a higher number. Presenting proposals in alphabetical order (by name of program, project, department, or employee) likewise can help avoid ruffling the political feathers of those who fear they are lower in the pecking order. If administrators or analysts use some form of neutral ordering, they should explain what their sequencing scheme is—for example, in strict numerical or alphabetical order—and never deviate from that pattern. If a superior or official fails to perceive the logic behind a sequence or detects unequal treatment in a sequence, the attempt to appear neutral may backfire.

An *inductive* pattern reasons from the specific to the general, providing pieces of information and requiring the audience to generalize (induce) recommendations from the information given. Listing recent, specific employee tangles with ethical issues, for example, letting a superior draw the generalization that an overall agency ethics policy is needed is an example of inductive sequencing. As mentioned in Chapter Three, some public executives and officials like to draw their own conclusions and prefer inductive reasoning. Most busy officials, however, want staff to offer recommendations that officials can accept or reject. Another potential problem occurs when the audience, perhaps less familiar with the subject than is the one preparing the recommendations, induces generalizations that are not really warranted by the data. More common when presenting proposals is to organize a report or briefing *deductively*, beginning with a generalization or major point (ethical concerns are widespread in this agency) and allowing the audience to deduce specific facts or examples from that generalization (ethical issues must exist in code enforcement if they have already been found in purchasing and personnel). Communication research generally shows that when an audience may not already agree with you, presenting data and analysis first is necessary to persuade that audience before it can accept your recommendations. If an audience is already likely to agree with you, recommendations can precede analysis.

Managers need to decide whether one sequence is most appropriate or whether using a combination of sequences is required. For example, a list of military base closings and realignments may sequence recommendations by geographic area within an overall priority order. These sequence patterns are not confined to recommendations, but are versatile tools public managers can use for organizing many kinds of written or spoken messages to different audiences.

Requesting Financial, Political, or Other Resources

Resource requests are important forms of recommendation. The skill with which administrators request and obtain resources significantly determines managerial and organizational effectiveness. Several pointers can help.

Assess Resource Needs First. Without knowing what budget, equipment, positions, buildings, expertise, political clout, or other resources a program or agency actually needs, making intelligent requests is impossible. Some public managers are constantly on the lookout for desks, grants, computers, or other resources without knowing whether an actual need exists. Such opportunism may pay off if a constructive use can be found or if one arises later. This tactic has particular value when financial retrenchment hits. The resources already stockpiled help to weather lean times. The risk in such tactics is twofold. (1) Resources that are not really needed often stimulate wasteful use on the grounds that "now that we've got it, we might as well use it for something." Care to guess, for example, how many government computers are used merely as expensive "toys"? (2) Being allocated marginally useful resources now, even if offered for the taking, may jeopardize ability to acquire more badly needed resources later. Office space, equipment, personnel positions, political favors, and other resources typically are in short supply these days. Agencies, programs, and projects often have to take turns for "their share." If a program or agency gets its share now, it may be put at the end of the queue. Knowing what resources are really needed, now and for the foreseeable future, prepares an administrator for seizing opportunities that arise.

Know What Resources Are Available. In addition to knowing needs, it also helps to learn what organizational resources are available, in what supply, and at what monetary or political cost. Reviewing budget bills, executive budget documents, an agency's internal budget, prior budgets, personnel ceilings and staffing plans, equipment inventories, office space utilization plans, and the like provides insights into who may have slack or disposable resources that could be acquired. Seeing plans that a department is getting new office space often means the existing space can be acquired. Administrators are advised to supplement official sources with their own contacts and the ever-present grapevine. Establishing cordial relations with people in the general services or other administrative service agencies sometimes helps in getting notified of available office space, cars, or equipment. Likewise, establish good ties with the personnel or civil service agency and budget office. More information on communicating with other government agencies appears in Chapter Six.

Seek or Create Opportunities for Pooling Resources with Other Units. Pooling resources with other governments, agencies, divisions, or staffs makes sense in several ways. First, most governmental units need to conserve existing resources by supplementing them with those of other organizations. Sharing underutilized buildings, purchasing or payroll systems, technical expertise, and even employees generally demonstrates economical management. Second, collaborating even in minor ways builds relationships for future actions. Administrators may never know when external support will be necessary. Third, legislators, elected executives, and voters usually like to see cooperation among governmental units. In their eyes, cooperation generally means teamwork, administrative effectiveness, and fiscal prudence. And the greater the fiscal stringency in a jurisdiction, the more resource pooling is generally encouraged or required. Collaboration, provided it is real, can ease pressure on a budget and enhance agency credibility. Making official or unofficial contacts in different agencies helps identify such opportunities. Local colleges near the capital of West Virginia acquired space in the capitol complex for classes and training. The West Virginia Civil Service agency needed space for its own training and meetings. Having no extra funds to acquire space, the agency provided expertise and personnel to help plan and staff the training center in exchange for access to meeting and training rooms. Neither the colleges nor the agency alone would have been powerful enough to claim so much prime space. By collaborating, all participants benefited.

Understand an Audience's Negotiating Style. Before managers frame resource requests, it helps to know whether the audience expects to haggle or expects an already pared, no-nonsense request. Many administrative superiors and elected officials expect subordinates to make a maximum request, listing what they ideally would want, with the understanding that this will get negotiated down to a more realistic level. This constitutes practice typically advocated by authorities on negotiation (Brooks and Ordiorne, 1990; Susskind, 1987; Cohen, 1983). Such "wish lists," however, should not be too unrealistic since research on communication and persuasion generally finds that extreme claims or positions are likely to hinder persuasion (Miller, 1987; Weiss, 1969).

    Other public managers expect subordinates to do their own

5

Strengthening Exchanges with Subordinates

Communication is at the very heart of the leader-
follower or leader-constituent relationship.
—*John Gardner, 1990, p. 85*

The first executive function is to develop and maintain a system of communication.
—*Chester Barnard, 1938, p. 226*

Whenever public administrators must communicate with superiors
and elected officials, as discussed in Chapter Four, they probably
postpone other duties and give this task priority attention. To do
otherwise invites unnecessary problems. Yet communication with
subordinates also deserves public managers' best effort even though
subordinates typically lack the rank to reprimand them for inattentive listening or lackluster reports. Communicating with subordinates deserves special attention for several reasons. (1) Public managers spend most of their time relating to subordinates (Corson and
Paul, 1966; Mintzberg, 1973). (2) The most capable public managers
are limited by time, experience, and physical energy. They therefore
rely on others, primarily subordinates, to accomplish most of their
results. (3) An administrator's rapport with and results through

subordinates influence the administrator's reputation with superiors. Credible subordinates are often consulted before their boss is
promoted. (4) Public managers, through daily communication with
subordinates, shape and sharpen their communication skills, skills
used with other audiences as well. This chapter addresses a number
of topics that apply to communicating with all major audiences,
especially with subordinates: building rapport and trust with subordinates, avoiding the typical imbalance of downward communication, facilitating upward communication from subordinates, and
organizing an effective communication system.

Building Rapport and Trust with Subordinates

Central to communicating effectively with subordinates is developing a sense of trust and rapport. When ordered, subordinates may
communicate to superiors when trust is lacking, but such communication tends to be perfunctory, incomplete, and inaccurate. Communicating is often difficult when trust exists; it is almost impossible without trust. Trust is essential to effective communication of
all kinds between superiors and subordinates. It is essential to establishing trust and sharing with subordinates to avoid treating them
as "inferiors" and to treat them as equals who contribute to the
agency team. I use the terms *superior* and *subordinate* not because
I support the concept of hierarchical relationships but because those
relationships are embedded in government reality and the terms are
ones public managers understand and use. The terms *superior* and
subordinate are typically associated with vertical relationships. This
chapter and the rest of the book, however, advocate emphasizing
lateral rather than *vertical* relationships and concepts. Lateral communication in government is generally more open and accurate than
vertical communication. Public managers can significantly improve
vertical communication by making it more like lateral communication—removing or bypassing hierarchical levels, emphasizing subformal, informal, and personal communication rather than official
communication, and creating a climate in which subordinates feel
and act like equals in the process of serving the public. The pages
that follow provide guidance for building greater trust and rapport

with subordinates—the foundation for sound communication and productivity.

Acknowledge Strengths and Limitations

A logical start involves self-awareness. If, for example, a public manager realizes he lacks the kind of charismatic personality subordinates would follow without question, he should then work on building trust through the many daily opportunities that arise with subordinates. If large groups do not bring out a manager's best, he should de-emphasize speeches to the entire staff in favor of conversations with smaller groups and individuals whenever appropriate to the purpose.

Trying to be someone else rarely instills trust. Leveling with subordinates can also be effective in enhancing trust if a minimal trust level already exists so that a manager knows her leveling will not be held against her. For example, a manager's confiding that she functions better in smaller groups may show subordinates that she is willing to trust them by sharing a shortcoming. This may also foster empathy since many subordinates may share a discomfort with large-group settings. Subordinates are likely to recognize the paucity of large-group meetings anyway. Leveling with them lets them know the manager is not indifferent to subordinates' need for information but is using other forums to communicate. Subordinates, in my experience, are far more likely to trust a competent but human boss than one who never admits failings. Bennis and Nanus (1985) note that excellent leaders recognize their limits and utilize subordinates to fill those gaps. I have seen subordinates make enormous efforts to compensate for the shortcomings of a boss they trusted and liked.

Know Subordinates

Knowing subordinates occurs at several levels. On a personal level, subordinates tend to appreciate superiors taking enough interest to know something about subordinates' families, hobbies, birthdays, anniversaries, and so forth. Such personal interest goes a long way in developing rapport with subordinates and can be motivating for many subordinates.

On a professional level, knowing about subordinates' work interests, preferences, and abilities enhances rapport and trust. For example, *knowing* that a subordinate has trouble hearing with his left ear, prefers to be given assignments in writing, and tends to wilt under criticism from superiors and *acting* on this knowledge will help avoid mistakes that undermine that subordinate's trust. Developing an audience profile for subordinates, or at least key subordinates, would be a useful start.

Be Aware of the Management Situation

The management situation in an agency influences confidence between superiors and subordinates. This holds whether the management situation is in the present, past, or future. Present legislative attacks for performance failures, memories of a previous administration's devious tactics, or anticipation of future employee layoffs can all strain relations. Encouraging subordinates to air a particular concern can help alleviate it. A management consultant, hired to discover why a factory suffered from substandard quality and productivity and hostile labor relations, was repeatedly told about how Sam, the plant manager, intimidated and humiliated employees. When summoned to the manager's office, one employee actually threw up on the way. Another employee burned Sam's car to retaliate for indignities. The consultant went to see the plant manager, who turned out to be a mild-mannered man name Paul. The consultant discovered that Sam had been dead for nine years, but his memory still debilitated morale and productivity. Having the plant manager, supervisors, and teams of employees discuss the organization's history, including Sam's reign of terror, helped clear the air. The plant later won a company award for quality (Dumaine, 1990). Sensitivity to present and past management situations also makes sense in government. After striking air traffic controllers were fired by President Reagan, Federal Aviation Administration managers examined prestrike practices and learned new managerial styles to adjust to the new work force (Ulrich, Quinn, and Cameron, 1989).

Because almost every public managerial activity involves

communication with subordinates, the next section addresses some of the central purposes of downward communication: conveying mission and goals, motivating and evaluating employees, assigning tasks, and conveying task information.

Avoiding the Typical Imbalance
of Downward Communication

Downward communication usually involves issuing specific task directives, conveying information related to task and to organizational practices and procedures, providing feedback on job performance, and fostering a sense of mission and team (Katz and Kahn, 1966). There is a tendency in government bureaucracies for task directives and job instructions to dominate downward channels, leaving communication on agency mission and performance feedback underutilized (Gortner, Mahler, and Nicholson, 1987). If this imbalance occurs, public employees can become desensitized to task-related messages and starved for communication about their performance and about agency direction.

Imbalance in downward communication often causes other organizational dysfunctions, such as depressed morale, preoccupation with routine tasks, and indifference to overall agency performance. Avoiding or correcting this typical imbalance involves (1) being aware of whether a current imbalance exists and (2) deliberately increasing messages about overall direction, overall performance, and employee performance while keeping task-related communication to a necessary minimum. Keeping a message log that identifies *date* and *type of message* helps identify and correct imbalances. The types can be *task* (directives, instructions, task information), *agency direction and feedback* (goals, strategy, agency successes and failures, problems and opportunities), and *employee performance* (group or individual praise or criticism, performance appraisal, feedback on consequences of employee efforts). Public administrators can also create other categories that make sense to them. With this typical imbalance in mind, this chapter addresses the underemphasized types of downward communication first.

Conveying a Vision—A Sense of Mission and Culture

Before conveying an agency's or unit's mission, public managers
must first understand it themselves. Chapter Four encourages managers to actively seek out that vision if superiors fail to provide it.
A sense of vision or direction takes time to acquire—and to impart.
Once managers have a basic understanding, they can begin to convey direction to others in the following ways.

*Avoid Overestimating Subordinates' Information and Underesti-
mating Their Intelligence.* Managers should never assume that subordinates possess all necessary information to do their jobs
effectively. Subordinates typically report that they are starved for
information or are at least underinformed about how their role fits
into the total agency mission. Rarely do subordinates think they
have too much information about organizational direction (Kaufman and Couzens, 1973). To combat this condition, public administrators should give as full a picture as possible rather than
providing only necessary information. In my experience, "need to
know" is interpreted too strictly in most situations. In my government experience, more damage has been done because lack of information handicapped subordinates in fulfilling their duties than
because agency plans or confidences were inappropriately divulged.

Consistent with this book's strategic contingency approach
to communicating, withholding specifics about mission or goals
may make sense for tactical reasons. Clearly communicated policies
and goals often trigger opposition since groups or individuals then
see specific points to rally opposition against. A time-honored tactic
involves keeping potential opposition guessing until it is too late
to defeat a plan. President Reagan observed this tactic when push-
ing through omnibus budget cuts in 1981. This tactic may succeed
in minimizing opposition initially but intensifying it later, even
during implementation.

Quinn (1980) provides guidance on whether to provide
general or specific direction. He suggests using general goals to
promote cohesion or to create a sense of identity and mission. Specific goals are more effective for creating a challenge and precipi-
tating action and to signal major departures from previous

direction. Whether general or specific goals are used depends on one's purpose as well as the audience and management situation. If opposition comes from within your agency or you suspect an employee will leak your overall game plan to outside opposition, withholding some specifics may be warranted. In such situations, though, I have found that taking employees into one's confidence usually works better than keeping employees in the dark. A lesson basic to success in creating a new sense of mission and organizational culture is this: employees have been traditionally underestimated and they then live down to expectations. Instead, administrators need to act as though people at all levels want to contribute to agency success (Dumaine, 1990).

Tailor Content and Media to Your Audience. Use terms subordinates can understand. They may lack your perspective or experience with agency strategy, but they are smart enough to realize if you talk down to them. When choosing media, use those most likely to reach your audience. As discussed in Chapter Four, retreats and discussion sessions with both the full staff and smaller groups often work well for addressing overall mission or direction. Video or audio recordings of employee conversations with top officials and stories or columns in agency publications are other vehicles. If some employees are more likely to pay attention to editorials that appear in their electronic mail than to read an agency newsletter, communicate accordingly.

Communicate Agency Vision Through Actions. In addition to the usual media for conveying a sense of mission—meetings, retreats, agency publications—actions command attention. Public administrators need to recognize that actions communicate louder than words. If, for example, managers are trying to communicate a change in agency culture of greater tolerance toward risk taking, they better not crucify the first subordinate who shows initiative but makes a mistake. Which message do you think would guide subordinates? If you intend to convey a need for closer teamwork on your staff, show your willingness to tackle the unpleasant jobs right along with subordinates. Chris Argyris and Donald Schön (1974) emphasize that actual behavior, what they call *theory-in-use*, generally supersedes one's *espoused theory*—formal pronouncements. Therefore, managers should strive to make actions consistent with verbal statements of direction or they will be giving subordinates mixed signals. Smart subordinates will take their cue from actions rather than directives.

Communicate Through Other Behavior Models. Using the behaviors of others as models reinforces and supplements a manager's own example. Locating what management scholar Michael Beer calls "universities" within an agency allows employees and public managers to learn from each other more naturally and effectively than does imposing a model from above (Dumaine, 1990). Making different programs or units the model for different behaviors minimizes the competitive aspect and creates a win-win rather than zero-sum mentality. For example, one program within your agency might be used as a "university" on adjusting to change. Another might be the model for handling paper flow.

Seeking out what is done well and using that as an example for others accomplishes several things. First, it gets managers better in tune with what is happening. Second, subordinates learn that managers are interested in what they do well and not just in finding their mistakes. Third, once a unit gets acknowledged for excellence in one aspect of performance, it often wants to excel in other ways. Fourth, multiple "universities" increase the different kinds of learning that take place in an organization. Articles can be written about such centers of excellence for the agency publication. Videotapes can be made for others to see. On-site observations or learning tours can be arranged. Such site visits are usually motivating for the observers as well as those serving as models.

Communicating to Motivate Subordinates

Communicating to motivate is central to public management whether the purpose is to change agency culture and direction or to improve individual performance. Our communication, whether oral, written, or nonverbal, motivates or demotivates subordinates intentionally or unintentionally. It therefore pays to know how to motivate through communication. Essentials of that process follow.

Learn What Motivates Subordinates. Communicating to motivate involves as much receiving as sending. The traditional conception that one motivates subordinates primarily by giving them inspirational pep talks is overrated. Constructive listening and observing to discover employees' interests, ambitions, and satisfactions are vastly underrated and underutilized as motivational techniques. Theories such as Maslow's needs hierarchy theory, Herzberg's motivator-hygiene theory, and McGregor's Theory Y, which claim that people are motivated by the same general factors or processes, have typically not been supported by research and have typically proved to be ineffective for motivating specific people on specific jobs (Steers and Porter, 1987; Lawler, 1981). Research and experience have typically shown that some people are motivated strongly by money—others by status, security, affection, sense of fairness, desire for leisure, or other factors. Since what motivates people is so individualistic, an essential management task is to learn what motivates subordinates. This typically involves receiving skills—asking, listening, and observing. Specific methods for doing this include the following. Initiate informal contact to get to know the subordinate better as an individual. Discuss over lunch or at an informal meeting what the subordinate would like to get out of this job and what he finds rewarding or annoying about the current job. It often motivates subordinates for managers to listen to their successes and problems. Public administrators can ask other trusted managers about a particular subordinate's behavior, performance, and potential and examine relevant employee records to learn more about his background, interests, and abilities. Administrators can also observe the subordinate's nonverbal behavior. Does he say he's motivated but put in the minimum time? Do his general expression and body language indicate overall satisfaction or frustration? Do the quality and quantity of his work indicate a high degree of motivation?

If managers cannot get accurate feedback about the nature, quality, and quantity of a subordinate's performance, then motivating that employee becomes uncertain since they cannot tell whether they are rewarding sound behavior or criticizing it. Sound receiving, then, is crucial to motivating a subordinate effectively. When what managers learn from the subordinate's verbal communication and what they learn from that subordinate's nonverbal communication agree, they can feel confident that their assessment of the subordinate's level and type of motivation is valid. When verbal and nonverbal signals conflict, the nonverbal cues probably are more accurate.

The same communication skills of questioning, listening, reading, and observing also apply for learning what motivates and demotivates a staff as a working team. We know now that a different dynamic exists in motivating team effort. Individual motivators do not automatically aggregate to team motivation. In fact, overemphasis on individual motivation can undermine efforts to motivate team cooperation.

Send Motivational Signals. Once managers have discovered what motivates and demotivates their staff members, both individually and collectively, they are in a sounder position to send motivational signals of their own. Motivational cues can be sent in various ways. The agency's *official reward system* communicates volumes to employees. If, for example, no rewards for team performance (for instance, merit bonuses for reaching unit goals) exist, employees may quickly conclude that individual performance takes priority. Communication also occurs through *written and oral statements*. A periodic "charge to the troops" can be motivating, for example, as long as it is not used too often or does not become too mechanical. Reinforcing the kind of performance or behavior managers value is one of the best practices. A letter of commendation, an informal note, a certificate, recognition in a staff meeting or in front of superiors are all ways to reinforce valued performance or behavior. Some government administrators give a "most valuable employee" award each month. The award can be a plaque or even a special symbol that rotates among employees who earn that recognition. Several cautions exist with any such attempt to recognize superior performance, however. One, recognition must actually be for individual or group *performance* rather than because of favoritism or some desire to give everyone a chance to "shine." Two, as with other forms of reinforcement, the recognition should be timely rather than delayed and be tied to specific performance (grants acquired, efficiencies instituted, money saved, employees effectively relocated, and so on) rather than some abstract sense of being deserving.

As with communicating a sense of mission and culture, managers can communicate motivationally through *performance and behavior models.* Here, too, managers should be sure the model actually sends the intended signal. If, for example, administrators want to motivate employees to be involved more in local community affairs, they must be involved themselves. If a manager's words say that she or he values airing views openly, the manager's expressions and actions should convey the same message. Some researchers conclude that up to 90 percent of a message's meaning is attributed to a sender's nonverbal communication (Falcione, 1984), so communicate accordingly.

Providing Feedback on Subordinates' Performance

As with clarifying direction and motivating, providing feedback on subordinates' performance is an underutilized form of downward communication. Communication pervades both major aspects of performance appraisal: clarifying performance standards and conveying informal and formal feedback on performance.

Communicate Performance Standards. Many public managers inhibit subordinates from performing as they intend because they have never effectively conveyed performance standards to their subordinates. Subordinates then must predict the boss's priorities or attempt to do everything to cover all bases. Both superior and subordinate suffer under these conditions. Instead, public administrators need to communicate performance standards using the following guidelines. *Standards should stretch the potential of subordinates yet be realistic.* Unreasonably low standards fail to challenge subordinates and to produce the results expected. Unrealistically high standards frustrate or demoralize employees and often produce the same results as low standards. Research on persuasion generally shows that unrealistic claims are less effective than credible claims in changing attitude and behavior. Involving subordinates in the standard-setting process, as should be done with management by objectives or behaviorally anchored rating scales, provides subordinates with a perspective on what they can realistically accomplish. Previous performance standards and standards in comparable government units serve as other benchmarks. *Convey standards by means of multiple media—documents, presentations, personal conferences—and by example.* Once again, take advantage of communication research showing that repetition with different media is more likely to increase retention and behavior change.

Provide Informal Performance Feedback. Feedback on performance is generally most effective when it is timely rather than delayed, consistent rather than sporadic, and appropriate to the subordinate and management situation. For these reasons, informal feedback often proves more useful for subordinates and superiors than the regularly scheduled six-month or yearly performance appraisal interview. Appraisal interviews in government have been criticized for among other things not being held at all, tending to be rituals without being tied directly to personnel decisions, or resulting in more misunderstanding than existed without them (Rich, 1989). Another problem with the formal appraisal process results from instilling the mind-set that feedback should be given on scheduled dates instead of on a continuous basis.

Since informal feedback is not part of the official record, it is less threatening to subordinates and more likely to be accepted. Managers can also provide informal feedback when it has the greatest learning impact on the subordinate—as the job is being done, when a question or problem arises, or when results of the subordinate's performance become known. Such timely feedback allows subordinates to incorporate suggestions immediately instead of waiting six months to hear about mistakes or to receive reinforcement for good performance. Informal (and formal) appraisals should be contingent upon the subordinate, purpose, and management situation. If criticism to a subordinate who is nearing retirement is unlikely to improve performance and may jeopardize working relations, feedback should be withheld. If a skilled computer analyst has trouble briefing superiors about system operations, patient instruction and encouragement over time will likely prove more effective than a dressing-down during a briefing.

Informal feedback can occur in the hall, at lunch, while working together on a task, or via comments on a subordinate's draft. Praise for individual or group performance may merit an announcement at department meetings or a ceremony, scheduled or impromptu, to celebrate a success. Criticism of group performance is usually better conveyed to the assembled group than to individual members. When criticism is conveyed to the group, reflection and an active search for improvement are more likely to occur. If criticism is conveyed to members individually, they are more likely to feel singled out for blame. Criticism of individual performance is almost always better handled privately with the individual. Criticizing subordinates in front of others usually makes the criticism more threatening and harder to accept. It also makes the bystanders anxious about receiving similar treatment.

Informal feedback involves listening as well as telling. For example, asking an employee to assess his own performance allows that employee to give his perceptions of strengths and weaknesses. The administrator can then compare her perceptions with the employee's, and begin addressing ways to improve performance. This give-and-take process is likely to be more open and constructive than a formal appraisal interview. Likewise, administrators need to be alert to subordinate-initiated messages about both good and bad performance. If, for example, an assistant dean admits having difficulty arranging a university conference, heavy criticism will likely deter him from raising problems in the future. Working with that assistant, coaching him to find ways to get the conference back on track, will likely accomplish several things. One, it will be more constructive in accomplishing the task at hand. Two, coaching will give the assistant more guidance on how to correct such problems in the future. Three, coaching rather than condemning will encourage that assistant, and other subordinates he tells about this, to bring problems to the superior's attention before they become disasters. In such situations administrators must take care to coach subordinates on how to solve their own problems rather than to solve subordinates' problems for them. Otherwise, subordinates will not learn from a situation, and the superior will be victimized by reverse delegation.

Make Performance Appraisal Interviews Constructive. If formal appraisals are to be done at all, considerable effort is required to make them constructive supplements to the informal feedback process. Communicating in an appraisal or evaluation interview has two primary purposes: to assess subordinates' performance so they know where they stand and to counsel employees to help them improve their performance. These two fundamental aims sometimes conflict and are often handled unevenly. Conducting a performance appraisal requires a superior to be both judge and coach, a difficult balancing act. The formal appraisal's assessment provides data for salary, promotion, dismissal, and other personnel decisions. Fulfilling the requirements of the formal evaluation system typically takes agency priority. Communicating assessment results for use in personnel decisions tends to get more attention than does counseling, an often unmet aim of appraisals. The following guidelines are aimed at helping administrators fulfill both purposes of appraisal interviews.

Make appraisal interview strategy contingent upon purpose, audience, and management situation. The two primary purposes of formal appraisal interviews assume that employees want to know where they stand and that if told how their performance measures up, they will do better. According to Strauss and Sayles (1972), neither assumption is universally valid. Some employees have no desire to know where they stand and may become totally demoralized if given a frank assessment. Learning one's faults as perceived by the boss will have little effect on performance if the motivational factors discussed above are missing. In such situations a formal interview may be inappropriate or at least should be handled more diplomatically. If an agency's appraisal system has little influence on salary, promotion, or other rewards, interviews should concentrate less on formal ratings and more on coaching and counseling. Situational factors should influence whether the basic approach to the interview will be on *selling*, convincing the employee of the accuracy of the ratings; *listening* to the subordinate's self-assessment and program for improvement; or *problem solving*, mutually assessing performance and means for improvement. Appraisal interviews usually follow this basic format (Strauss and Sayles, 1972): (1) Superior states purpose and ground rules for appraisal interview. (Including this opening almost always makes sense.) (2) Superior presents evaluation—first strengths, then weaknesses. (3) Superior asks subordinate for reaction to the evaluation. This gives an employee a chance to present his or her perspective, which may be accurate, and to blow off steam. Superior should refrain from trying to refute every point subordinate makes. (4) Superior encourages subordinate to assess his or her own progress and the difficulties he or she is facing and to make suggestions for overcoming difficulties. (5) Interview ends with mutual discussion of what subordinate can do to improve and how superior can help. Unless agency regulations require interviewers to follow a prescribed format, it makes sense to utilize only those parts of an appraisal interview appropriate to the situation at hand.

Create an appropriate climate for the interview. In most cases this means a supportive climate. An audience analysis would predict that subordinates might understandably act defensively in this situation, denying or attempting to justify any performance failures. Creating a supportive climate alleviates some of these problems. There are several ways to establish a supportive climate. Holding the interview on pleasant, neutral ground helps minimize some of the status barriers conjured up by being called to the boss's office. Conference rooms or private lounges often suit this purpose. Sound communication strategy typically involves discussing the subordinate's strengths and successes first to establish a positive tone. Every employee has some strengths and successes to affirm. Interviewers need to be sure, however, that successes are genuine rather than contrived. Subordinates will see through disingenuousness. Presenting a balance of favorable information along with, and preferably before, criticism makes that criticism easier to take. The subordinate realizes this is to be a balanced assessment rather than a one-sided attack. In some circumstances, however, a subordinate feels overconfident rather than threatened. The superior's task then becomes one of piercing that overconfidence by showing a more realistic picture of the subordinate's performance. Even though the tactics may be stronger, the climate still needs to be supportive to enable such criticism.

Assigning Tasks and Conveying Task-Related Information

Since directives and task information tend to clog downward channels, managers should avoid overloading subordinates with orders and job details. When assigning tasks, make the most of the situation by taking the following steps.

1. Explain why this task is necessary and how it fits into the context of other jobs and with overall agency direction. Providing this context helps motivate subordinates, saves floundering time, and lowers the odds that subordinates will be working at cross-purposes.

2. State the actual results expected at job completion. What is expected? A completed analysis? A draft? Working notes? An outline? Without specific targets, subordinates are less likely to fulfill expectations. If the actual results are unclear, ask for clarification from others. Or make known to subordinates that this is an instance where targets are unclear, requiring them to feel their way in the assignment.

3. Describe how this assignment resembles or differs from previous tasks. If subordinates understand that a new assignment is essentially the same as one completed last year, they have a head start on completing it. Likewise, it helps subordinates to know that the product, quality, and quantity supplied for the last assignment would be inappropriate now. Otherwise, subordinates tend to supply what worked before.

4. Provide the information essential to completing this task:

Why is this task important?

Who is this task for? Who is involved? Who should be avoided?

When is the assignment due? Any interim deadlines?

What is to be done?

Where is it to be done?

How is it to be done? (Explain this only if the subordinate is unable to or not allowed to arrive at the best way himself.) Are there any time, cost, legal, policy, political, or other restrictions? Are there any contingency plans if difficulties arise?

5. Check subordinates' understanding of the crucial aspects of this task. Unless a manager has particular confidence in her subordinates, she should avoid asking whether they have questions

about an assignment. Subordinates tend to say they understand. Superiors should ask instead for subordinates to paraphrase instructions and ask subordinates questions that probe their understanding of the assignment (Falcione, 1984).

6. Encourage subordinates to rely on their resourcefulness first but to seek further information or guidance if needed. Recognize that much task-related information cannot be fully anticipated until the subordinates are further into an assignment. When the need arises, information is more likely to be meaningful to subordinates.

Facilitating Upward Communication from Subordinates

Upward communication is vital to public agencies. Management depends on upward messages about how work is progressing, what problems and opportunities subordinates see, what ideas subordinates have for improving performance, what intelligence subordinates gather about what clients and other organizations are doing, and what subordinates feel about the agency, their superiors, and their jobs. Yet ensuring healthy upward communication is usually more difficult and more crucial than communicating downward. Chapter Two describes the tendency of subordinates to filter information at each hierarchical level. The audience profile and sender characteristics of each of these subordinates in a hierarchy will likely differ in terms of department rank and administrative perspective, personal perceptions, background, outside organizational affiliations, and policy agenda. These and other characteristics influence how each subordinate is likely to condense, embellish, or shape messages a public administrator will receive. The powerful tendency for upward government communication to be distorted by minimizing bad news and accentuating self-serving or self-interested messages is well documented (Tullock, 1965; Downs, 1967; Kaufman and Couzens, 1973; Garnett, 1989). Several methods exist for minimizing the distortion effects of communication from subordinates. Some of these methods relate closely to one another but are presented separately here to emphasize different concepts or tactics.

Clarify the Selection Rules Subordinates Are to Apply

One way to help ensure that communication from subordinates provides essential information quantity and quality is to make selection rules more explicit to subordinates.

1. What information is required for decision making? In what format?
2. What information should be excluded?
3. What information is useful but should be condensed or coded?

Before administrators articulate their requirements to others, they should take precautions to avoid building distortion into the foregoing selection rules. Sharing selection rules can be done in several ways:

- Identify for subordinates examples of reports, memos, briefing papers, oral presentations, and the like that have the form, content, coverage, tone, style, and analytical rigor that meet standards. Encourage subordinates to follow these models without doing so slavishly or mechanically. Also share examples of bad practices you want them to avoid. Many agencies have forms or formats for reporting information. If they are well designed, such formats can guide subordinates on what to exclude and what to include and how. Many faulty forms or formats incorporate the wrong selection criteria, however, and therefore build in distortion. These forms or formats deserve to be redesigned, replaced, or ignored.
- Give subordinates constructive feedback on their communications. Return a memo revised the way it should be written. Tell a subordinate what essential arguments and data were missing from his oral briefing.
- Share what you want with subordinates who write correspondence for your signature. From my experience in working with government agencies to improve administrative writing, I conclude that most public managers fail to provide enough guidance to subordinates who write *to* them or *for* them. Adminis-

trators should give subordinates a general idea of the intended content, tone, and strategy whenever delegating a writing assignment. This includes briefing the writer on the purpose for writing, the audience—intended and unintended—and the management situation. If administrators find it helpful, they can use a communicating strategy worksheet to convey this information to the subordinate or staff writer. Administrators can save time by trusting the writer to produce final copy for routine writing tasks. For example, administrators can quickly review final versions of routine correspondence to make sure that what goes out with their name does the intended job. More thorough scrutiny can be reserved for the most sensitive and strategic writing tasks. Administrators need to revise and edit drafts of controversial or key letters, memos, reports, proposals, and the like for content, tone, organization, and accuracy of analysis. Unless style is important for a particular audience, superiors should refrain from revising wording merely because they prefer their own style. Time, effort, and morale are lost when superiors throughout the chain of command feel compelled to interject their own wording for its own sake.

Utilize Subformal and Personal Communication to Overcome Hierarchical Barriers

According to Downs (1967), three types of communication networks typically exist in government hierarchies: formal, subformal, and personal. *Formal* communication networks are typically vertical, follow the formal authority structure, and transmit "official" messages. Formal methods of communicating include official reports, orders, and correspondence; audits and investigations; and grievances.

Subformal networks convey messages that flow through formal channels but not as formal communication and messages that flow along strictly informal channels. (Examples of subformal messages include off-the-record comments by officials and informal conversation among peers about agency business.) Since both types of subformal communication are unofficial, "they can be withdrawn, altered, adjusted, magnified, or canceled without any official record being made. As a result, almost all new ideas are first proposed and tested as subformal communications" (Downs, 1967, p. 113). Subformal communication tends to be *quicker* than formal communication because it does not have to be verified as often or move through as many formal channels. Subformal communication also tends to be more flexible than formal communication for the reasons Downs gives. Moreover, subformal communication is generally more accurate because its greater informality reduces barriers of status and rank, allowing officials to communicate more openly as equals. Administrators will probably get a quicker, more accurate response from subordinates through subformal conversations in the hall or on the phone than through formal written or oral reports. To use subformal communication effectively, administrators must learn and observe the informal, unwritten rules and procedures about what to communicate, to which audiences, and with what media. There is no substitute for knowing the rules and nuances of the subformal communication system. Observing and asking experienced, effective agency administrators will help you learn these unwritten rules and procedures about subformal communication.

Personal communication networks convey unofficial messages transmitted by people outside their capacity as officeholders. Personal messages differ from subformal messages, which are transmitted by officeholders in their official capacity but not for the official record. Rumors and gossip are major forms of personal communication in government. Personal communication tends to be quicker than formal or subformal communication since verification mechanisms are minimal or nonexistent. Some evidence indicates that personal communications such as rumors can be highly accurate (Caplow, 1960). Chapter Eight provides detailed guidance for coping with grapevines and rumors.

Use Redundant, Multiple Channels for Verifying Information

Supplementing normal channels allows administrators to compare information communicated to them, weigh the quality of that information, and investigate the accuracy of some or all messages. Some of these redundant channels should be inside the agency and some should be outside it. *Internal channels* can include any of the following:

- Subordinates working on the same program or project who can supply different but comparable reports
- Organizational peers responsible for different programs or functions who can provide different perspectives on the total bureau or division
- Trusted subordinates even if they are farther down the chain of command
- Subordinates who make good "sounding boards" because of their good contacts, experience, or savvy
- Subordinates who, because of their position, cognitive style, or natural optimism or pessimism, "balance" other sources

Employees themselves, whether individually via suggestion box or collectively via joint management-employee meeting or organized task force, can supply valuable organizational intelligence, particularly on relations with clients or internal operations. Those closest to clients and service operations are worth consulting about such matters. A Florida public utility, for example, was experiencing injuries, absenteeism, and service delays because of dogs biting meter readers. When meter readers wanted to form a team to study the problem, management encouraged this employee involvement. The employee team surveyed households, discovered which had dangerous dogs, and programmed hand-held computers to beep before meter readers went to a dangerous address. "Dog bites (and absenteeism) are down, and morale (and service) is up" (Dumaine, 1990, p. 128). In this situation and many others, employees had the direct motivation and hands-on knowledge to solve the problem.

External sources useful for verifying internal communication or providing new information can include any of the following:

- Members of an agency's clientele who can provide a useful "customer" perspective on the agency's performance
- Personal or professional contacts in other departments who have knowledge about the agency
- Political officials or members of their staffs

- Newspapers, television and radio news reports, reporters, and editors
- · Official reports from other departments or even other levels of government
- Acquaintances from an administrator's neighborhood, church, civic organization, or professional society

Guidelines for using these redundant channels include the following:

- Use multiple overlapping internal and external channels to supplement and compensate for the strengths and weaknesses of other channels.
- Let subordinates know the reasons for using multiple sources and the importance of verifying messages they send. It is important for superiors to stress that they use redundant channels to get different perspectives and insights, thereby enriching the information pool. Superiors should likewise emphasize that redundancy is not used primarily to test the honesty of subordinates. Subordinates will quickly learn from the actions of superiors their reasons for using redundancy.
- "Reduce the penalty for conflicting reports by encouraging a variety of viewpoints and minimizing the threat of investigation" (Downs, 1967, p. 120).
- Eliminate automatic yes-men by avoiding them in personnel selection, getting them transferred, or conditioning them to change their behavior.

To prevent subordinates from colluding beforehand on what information to communicate upward, Downs (1967, p. 120) has counseled superiors to "structure the interests of the subordinates involved so they are in direct conflict." President Franklin Roosevelt made extensive use of this tactic, structuring assignments and access so that staff members often competed against each other in trying to inform and persuade the president. This tactic may work for an FDR, but the resulting competitiveness among staff members may jeopardize staff unity, trust, and teamwork if allowed to get out of hand. If trust—the lifeblood of communication—becomes undermined, vital communication upward will dry up despite multiple sources. Sources may become preoccupied vying for the superior's attention and undercutting each other to get that attention. The adversarial tactic involves enormous risk and is perhaps more appropriate for situations where no alternative upward channels of communication exist, as in "some covert operations or specialized fields of research" (Downs, 1967, p. 120).

Structuring redundant communication channels does lead to wasted effort in sending and receiving overlapping information and, in the extreme, may lead to information overload. Redundancy remains, however, a valuable check on the quantity and quality of the communication received from subordinates.

The Single-Access, Gatekeeper Model

Contrary to the multiple-access approach recommended above is the single-access or gatekeeper model. This model relies on a gatekeeper—a chief of staff or other aide—who controls information flow to the superior by monitoring appointments and correspondence. Communication factors that most influence the use of this model are message volume and the superior's managerial style. When communication flows are too heavy for a superior to handle personally, some of the load must be delegated to aides. If that superior emphasizes coordination and uniformity, he or she may opt for a gatekeeper who monitors incoming and outgoing correspondence and screens appointments and access to the superior. The ultimate gatekeeper was President Nixon's chief of staff, Robert Haldeman, who almost totally controlled access to the president. The disastrous consequences in this situation of a president relying on one person who blocked and filtered communication going both ways has failed to deter other officials from using the gatekeeper model. President Bush's secretary of state, James A. Baker, relies on aide Robert Zoellick. "Every piece of paper that is sent to Mr. Baker must first pass through his desk, where Mr. Zoellick . . . 'institutes some quality control.' He is also the first to see the replies. . . . Over the past year veteran State Department officials have learned that the only way to Mr. Baker is through Mr. Zoellick. 'We've adapted,' one senior State Department official said of Mr. Zoellick. 'We no longer view him as a rival. We view him as the person who can make things happen'" (Sciolino, 1990, p. A12).

If this model is to function effectively rather than hinder communication, several guidelines make sense.

1. Administrators need to choose a gatekeeper with whom they have good rapport and who understands their priorities, values, strengths, and shortcomings.

2. It is important to choose a gatekeeper with enough professionalism to avoid playing ego games manipulating and controlling staff members. Otherwise, access can be given or withheld at the gatekeeper's whim. Out-of-favor aides or other agency officials can be screened with unfortunate consequences. Gatekeepers should actively seek other views or information if their instincts tell them the superior needs different perspectives or information.

3. If administrators rely on a gatekeeper, they must be particularly sensitive to the inherent problems of filtering or blocking information. As the adage states: "the communications bottleneck is usually at the top of the bottle." If administrators suspect that other views exist, they should contact their subformal internal and external sources personally as discussed above.

4. Administrators need to establish some fail-safe procedure for overriding the gatekeeper if other aides, outside officials, or citizens believe that their message must reach the administrator directly. Criteria for overriding the gatekeeper should be established in advance. Once these guidelines are established and discussed, however, subordinates should be allowed discretion in invoking their right to override; otherwise their messages will still be screened. Subordinates who misuse the override policy should be counseled by the gatekeeper and their superior.

Minimize Layers Through Which
Upward Messages Must Travel

Reducing the number of layers through which a message must be transmitted can also improve upward communication. Flatter hierarchies enable employees collecting the original data or providing the actual service to communicate directly, or at least more directly, with superiors. This helps eliminate distortion introduced by extra conduits, as discussed in Chapter Two. Eliminating orga- nizational layers can have other benefits as well. Reducing layers typically increases the managerial span of control. Public managers with wide spans of control must spend less time monitoring each subordinate, allowing subordinates more administrative discretion. When authority is decentralized like this, more communication oc- curs at lower levels, involving superiors in fewer communications. If in this way administrators reduce their overall message flow while retaining access to important messages, distortion and overload will be reduced. As in the business sector, flatter hierarchies appear to be particularly feasible where government performance can be re- ported through objective measures. Managerial control can be maintained despite wide spans of control because performance can be monitored readily and performance gaps more easily identified (Downs, 1967).

The trend in government to reduce layers of middle manage- ment as a response to budget cuts can leave departments populated primarily by top public managers and operating-level supervisors and employees (Carroll, Fritschler, and Smith, 1985). Some good can be made to come out of this condition if more direct commu- nication channels are established between top managers and oper- ating-level subordinates. Without channels linking top administra- tion and operating levels, agency communication flow may become truncated, however. Directives will continue to flow downward, but fewer messages except the most perfunctory ones will travel upward. Administrators will need to establish direct channels with those at the agency's operating level or install some trusted links between the operating level and top management.

Bypass the Chain of Command

Even if too many levels exist in an agency and no efforts to "de- layer" are imminent, administrators can avoid unnecessary layers and distortion in specific situations by bypassing the formal chain of command. Downs (1967) has identified several types of bypassing.

Straight scoop bypasses involve contacting sources two or more levels below you to get the original message or convey orders to those directly responsible for carrying them out. The following examples show effective use of the straight scoop bypass. University of Wisconsin Chancellor Donna Shalala regularly calls or lunches with faculty members to get faculty views firsthand. President Bush conferred with relatively junior rank officers to hear their reactions about the attack to capture Panama's Manuel Noriega. Countless public executives have been practicing management by wandering around (MBWA) with their scheduled and unannounced inspections of agency work sites long before Tom Peters and Bob Waterman (1982) made MBWA a management slogan. At Strategic Air Command headquarters, information from remote radar tracking systems is reported directly and automatically on display panels seen by top officials.

Checkout bypasses (sometimes called trial balloons) can be used to test reaction of other agencies, legislators, and interest groups to a new policy, program, or other idea before going on the record through official communications. Subordinates may use end-run bypasses to get around their superiors to communicate to someone higher. Generally, bypassing undermines the efforts of immediate superiors to stay informed unless the bypasser or the receiver of the bypass informs this superior later. Even if the supervisor is informed later, indiscriminate, frequent end runs damage a supervisor's status and effectiveness with subordinates and clients. Use speed-up bypasses to get information more quickly than is possible through slower, formal channels. Use co-optation bypasses such as briefings or brainstorming sessions to give subordinates at lower levels the feeling that their counsel is personally valued by higher agency officials (Downs, 1967). This kind of bypass makes sense only when officials actually value subordinates' counsel. Subordinates usually recognize and resent insincere efforts at participation.

Bypassing is typically more necessary in government agencies that face frequent crises. During crisis, getting fast, accurate information directly to those in charge becomes essential. Police, fire, military, health, and emergency relief agencies often rely on bypassing in crisis situations as will the executive office of a president, governor, county administrator, or mayor. In addition, administrators who need highly specialized, technical information often need to consult operating-level experts directly rather than the experts' immediate superiors, who lack the specialized knowledge sought. Bypassing can add flexibility, speed, directness, and accuracy to circumvent shortcomings in the formal communication system, but it must be used judiciously to avoid creating other communication, morale, and political problems.

Use Distortion-Resistant Messages

Downs (1967, pp. 127–128) defines *distortion-proof* messages as messages transmitted from the source to the final destination without alteration, expansion, or condensation. Since the intended target audience can introduce distortion while interpreting an unaltered message, the term *distortion resistant* is more accurate. To make a message more distortion resistant, administrators need to (1) transmit the message without revision through mechanical means, such as computer, teletype, or video or audio recording, or via unaltered document; (2) develop prearranged definitions or meanings for interpreting the message—if senders and receivers use standard terms, phrases, or symbols and interpret according to predesignated meanings, ambiguity and distortion can be reduced; and (3) develop prearranged codes and ciphers or interpretations of those codes. Such codes can be brief (for example, "Condition Alert"), conveyed quickly without alteration, and then interpreted according to predetermined meanings.

Distortion-resistant messages tend to be more useful when accuracy and speed of transmission are at a premium, when a high volume of messages exists, when messages are more precisely quantifiable, and when a large organizational distance (many layers) or physical distance exists. Diplomatic, military, and paramilitary (police, fire, emergency health) agencies find distortion-resistant messages useful, particularly in crisis situations. (See Chapter Eight.) Distortion-resistant messages can be used in other kinds of agencies if the above conditions are basically met. When using this method, administrators need to recognize its limitations. A high volume of uncondensed messages might overload the system, making it necessary to use this method only for vital messages. In addition, if coding is used to abbreviate messages, some of the most crucial qualitative data may be lost or distorted because they are more difficult to code precisely than are quantitative data. Even these obstacles, however, can usually be overcome with experience and fine-tuning.

Adjust for Bias by Applying Counterbias

When subformal channels, redundant sources, the elimination or bypassing of levels, or distortion-resistant messages are unavailable or ineffectual, administrators may need to apply their own counter-bias to minimize upward distortion. Savvy administrators know that subordinates and other communicators deliberately or unintentionally interject bias into a message as it travels upward. It therefore becomes necessary to counter that bias, either consciously or perhaps subconsciously, when the message arrives. If administrators accurately assess the kind, direction, and amount of bias, they can correct for distortion. If not, they will introduce further bias. From earlier experience in the ranks, administrators may know firsthand the kind, direction, and amount of bias interjected in upward messages. University administrators from faculty ranks, for example, understand that faculty members and peer committees commonly embellish the records of their colleagues who are applying for promotion or tenure. As deans or provosts, these administrators therefore tend to deflate systematically department or committee claims about a candidate and to inflate any negative information. Members of military inspection teams recall the extensive preparation they probably once took to create a favorable impression on other military or civilian inspection teams. Knowing this, these teams often expect perfection, prefer unannounced inspections, or since they also know the small probability of a really surprise inspection, seek other forms of performance feedback. (See Kaufman and Couzens, 1973.)

Bias is typically of two types. *Information* bias is bias introduced unknowingly from inaccurate or incomplete information. *Tactical* bias is bias deliberately interjected to influence decision making or otherwise gain tactical advantage. Deliberately deflating enemy troop strength as in Vietnam and intentionally skewing case-load numbers to make the pitch for more caseworkers are examples of tactical bias. If administrators suspect unintentional information bias, they should seek additional information or discount the information in the probably biased message. If they suspect deliberate, tactical bias, they can apply counterbias away from the perceived purpose. If administrators have no direct knowledge about the kind, direction, and amount of bias, it helps to recognize that subordinates tend to interject bias that favors their personal self-interest and the self-interest of their unit, program, or policy; to embellish claims for needing greater resources; to deny or deflect responsibility for performance failures; and to follow routine procedures in collecting information that emphasizes official sources.

It also helps to understand that in applying counterbias superiors tend to exercise counterbias in favor of their personal self-interest and the self-interest of their unit or strategy; to discount information about the future in favor of information about the present or past; to apply counterbias in favor of quantitative, measurable factors and away from qualitative factors; and to apply counterbias in favor of quantitative factors that can be verified readily and away from factors harder to verify (Downs, 1967, p. 122).

Predictably, when evaluating cases for promotion or tenure, many university administrators emphasize scholarly productivity (number of publications) rather than quality of scholarship, which is more difficult to verify. Likewise, recent or present performance tends to be weighed more heavily than future plans, which may not materialize. In exercising counterbias, it helps to consider the general biases of subordinates as well as the typical counterbiases of superiors.

Sometimes distortion takes the form of lies, deliberate misrepresentations for tactical ends. Unless administrators know the subordinate or other communicator well, detecting lies usually proves difficult. Behavioral research has found some ways, however, to detect lies when they are conveyed in face-to-face communication. Exhibit 5.1 covers some of those ways to detect lies. Other research on lying is reported in Ekman (1985). When applying research knowledge, it is important to remember that even behavioral scientists and other experts make errors in observation. Moreover, people under stress or with particular mannerisms may appear to be lying when they are telling the truth. The knowledge presented here should therefore be used with caution. These symptoms are more

Exhibit 5.1. Cues for Detecting Lying.

According to research conducted by Michael J. Cody, School of Communication, University of Southern California at Los Angeles, when people lie, their body language often gives them away.
People who tell lies they have rehearsed in advance tend to:

- Give extremely short answers.
- Answer immediately on hearing the question.
- Nod after telling a lie.
- Rub their hands or other parts of their bodies.
- Display voice tremors. (Subtle tremors can be detected only by a machine.)
- Sound mechanical and expressionless, as though they have said the same thing many times.

People who invent a lie on the spur of the moment tend to:

- Give short answers, not being able to think fast enough what to say.
- Make false starts: start a statement one way, then start again to correct it ("I decided . . ."; then *They* decided to ignore procedures").
- Hesitate more often than usual, with either silent or vocalized pauses (um, ah, and the like).
- Use broad generalizations: *all, never, always,* and so on ("All the clients I helped today were impossible") or load their explanations with empty phrases ("you know," "or whatever").
- Dwell on vague generalities.
- Display excessive movement (scratching, or rubbing hands) or remain inordinately still.

Source: Based on Buchert, 1989, p. 11A.

appropriately used as indicators than as conclusive evidence of lying. If many of these symptoms are present, instead of immediately making accusations it would be more prudent to probe this source further, check other sources, and perhaps discount the uncertain information from this source.

In considering how to apply counterbias, administrators must recognize that cumulative distortion may occur as a message travels upward. Even when immediate superiors recognize bias in upward communication, they may pass along or even enhance that bias if it serves their ends. If, for example, state economic development departments are evaluated on the basis of how much additional business they attract, claims of successful "catches" will tend to be exaggerated. Economic development recruiters and department officials sometimes take exaggerated credit for their role in luring businesses to their state. Economic development directors and even governors have an incentive to "look good" by showing successes and so are more likely to enhance claims than to deflate them. Thus, while counterbias can resist distortion in upward messages, cumulative distortion may still prevail. Downs (1967) counsels that cumulative distortion is particularly hard to overcome in agencies that lack a clientele competent to evaluate agency performance and in agencies where a source of highly technical knowledge exists with no other sources to counter distortion.

Avoid Compartmentalizing Subordinates
as Sources of Information

A strong tendency in government is to compartmentalize expertise and activity. Inquiries about school dropouts are sent to the Department of Education for reply. Officials seeking information about hazardous waste sites turn to the Environmental Protection Agency. Such pigeonholing aids administrative order, but it can also produce dysfunction. It may lead to a closed loop that excludes independent information. John B. Martin (1988, p. 24) shows this in his vivid account of events leading to a mine explosion that killed 111 Illinois miners.

> One of the most remarkable aspects of the whole affair was this: an aggrieved party (the miners) accused a second party (the Illinois Department of Mines and Minerals) of acting wrongfully, and the higher authority to which it addressed its grievance [the governor's office], in effect, asked the accused if he were guilty and, when he replied that he was not, dropped the matter. . . . The logic . . . of the administrative mind has a pigeonhole for everything. Matters which relate to law go to the Attorney General, matters which relate to mines go to the Department of Mines and Minerals, and that is that—but it is scarcely a useful logic when one of the agencies is itself accused of malfunction. Apparently it did not occur to [the

governor's aide] to consult the [mine] inspector directly or to make any other independent investigation.

Through artificial compartmentalizing, useful sources of information are excluded. The aftermath of the aborted invasion of
Cuba demonstrates this problem.

> Shortly after the Bay of Pigs disaster, a number of
> members of the Kennedy circle became increasingly
> uneasy with the decision-making processes of the ad-
> ministration. Arthur Goldberg, the new secretary of
> labor, finally asked the president why he had not con-
> sulted more widely, why he had taken such a narrow
> spectrum of advice, much of it so predictable. Kennedy
> said that he meant no offense, that even though Gold-
> berg was a good man, he *was* in labor, not in foreign
> policy. "You're wrong," Goldberg replied, "you're
> making the mistake of compartmentalizing your cab-
> inet." The secretary went on to point out—much to
> the president's surprise—that the two men in the cab-
> inet who should have been consulted were Orville
> Freeman, the secretary of agriculture and himself.
> Freeman had been a marine, made amphibious land-
> ings, and knew how tough such landings can be; and
> Goldberg had been in OSS during World War II and
> had run guerilla operations [Halberstam, 1969, p. 90].

Maintain Communication Reciprocity
with Subordinates

If superiors keep their subordinates accurately and fully informed,
subordinates are more likely to reciprocate with information. Sociologist George Homans found this human tendency toward reci-
procity to exist when he articulated the concept of *exchange relations*. He found that human exchanges reinforce the way people
behave with each other. Positive behavior tends to elicit positive
behavior in return. Likewise lack of cooperation engenders lack
of cooperation in return. Skillful attention to the preceding eight

methods for improving upward communication will fail if subordinates withhold or distort messages because superiors leave them underinformed and are unwilling to share what they know.

*Reinforce Constructive Upward Communication
and Discourage the Counterproductive*

Probably more important to achieving healthy, accurate upward communication flow than any of the more technical, foregoing guidelines is the feedback subordinates get from superiors. If subordinates get penalized for relaying information about agency problems that source of intelligence will be extinguished. If superiors reward yes-men, agreement with the boss will flourish. Nelson Rockefeller's penchant for yes-men was recognized even by his staunch supporters (Donovan, 1988). The lack of critical, independent information hindered Governor Rockefeller's decisions about the Attica prison uprising and other matters.

On the other hand, if administrators reward subordinates for alerting them to problems or to potential threats, administrators will likely continue to reap such organizational intelligence. Generally, the more unwelcome the message, the more important it is for administrators to receive that message. They can likewise eliminate unnecessary reports and discourage inconsequential memos that create overload and consume subordinates' time to prepare. Official and informal incentives to motivate subordinate feedback are more crucial to improving upward communication than is mandating more reports. Incentives are also important to motivate subordinate managers to encourage constructive upward communication from their subordinates. Unless incentives for effective upward (and downward) communication exist, rational managers will divert attention to the many policy, turf, and other issues that compete for their time. The next section summarizes the chapter by showing how the various elements fit together into a communication system.

Organizing an Effective Communication System

Downward and upward communication need to be organized into a coherent system, as do lateral and external communication, which will be discussed in the following chapters. This section examines the elements necessary to develop an effective agency communication system. Essential elements include communication goals and objectives, an overall climate conducive to communicating, assessment of communication performance, diverse and appropriate communication structures and media, communication policies and procedures, and roles and responsibilities for agency communication.

Establish Overall Communications Policy

Agencies need a broad policy that shapes direction for their internal and external communication. This policy should be more than a written statement; it should also be a philosophy embodied in the attitudes and actions of management and the work force. Because all levels of management and the work force are integrally affected by their agency's policy and practice and will have to implement them, all should be involved in appropriate stages of developing that policy. The specific content of an agency's policy is contingent upon its own mission, personnel, technology, structure, and other factors. Here are some policy statements that make sense for most agencies.

- Management and the work force should recognize communication as a vital agency function and give communication priority attention comparable to that given budgeting and service delivery. Communication is recognized as involving public information and media relations functions but is much broader, encompassing an agency's formal and informal, internal and external flows of ideas, information, and feelings.
- The agency will provide timely and appropriate information on plans and operations to employees so that they can do their jobs effectively and to citizens on matters that affect them.
- Whenever possible, employees will first learn of important matters that affect them and their jobs through internal agency channels rather than the news media or other external channels (Nowak, 1990).
- Internal agency communication should emphasize and reward upward and lateral flows as well as downward flow. The agency

strives for a healthy, balanced communication system able to send and receive a broad range of messages that relate to providing agency direction, motivating employees, giving feedback on performance, and informing citizens, as well as providing essential task-related information.

- People inside and outside the agency are the agency's most valuable resource. The agency should take steps to utilize people's ideas and opinions by providing them with information to enable their participation and with opportunities to participate through a variety of media.
- Agency management will communicate agency and individual accomplishments through appropriate internal and external media and through recognition programs.
- The agency head and public information officer are responsible for the overall direction of agency communication policy, but all managers and employees share responsibility for implementing it. Successful agency communication requires the close involvement and expertise of the public information or communications office but should not be restricted to that department. Effective communication demands the direction and example of top management and cannot be totally delegated.
- The agency's communication performance shall be evaluated regularly and thoroughly by appropriate means. The effectiveness of individual and unit communication will be a key criterion for individual and group rewards.

These policy statements illustrate the broadest level of communications policy. Other, more detailed statements are needed to address bypassing, gatekeeping, disclosure, communications training, use of technology, public information (see Chapter Seven), ethical concerns in communicating (see Chapter Nine), and other germane issues.

Establish an Overall Climate Conducive to Communicating

A strong, appropriate communications policy is a good start. It cannot be relegated to paper alone but needs to be communicated periodically to employees, clients, citizens, news media, and other appropriate audiences by a variety of media. As important to creating a conducive climate is the degree to which communication is a continuous administrative priority. From top administration downward, administration needs to show through the reward system and through example that communication is vital to agency success. Another key to establishing a climate conducive to communicating is the way people are treated when they communicate or fail to communicate. Messages relating to problems and bad news are valued rather than punished. Rosy messages are not unduly rewarded so that attempts are made to make information appear more favorable than it is. A conducive climate, spirit, or philosophy is as integral to a communication system as any of the other, more tangible elements.

Assess Communication Needs

Before organizing or reorganizing communication structures and channels, it makes sense to assess communication needs. Agencies can do this by relying on the public information office to make a needs assessment, utilizing consultants to do this, or involving agency specialists, consultants, administrators, and employees in a joint process. My sense of the matter is that the first two options— using specialists who do some consulting with employees—tend to be used if a needs assessment is done at all. The third approach usually takes more time and effort but can produce a better feel for agency communication needs. Whoever conducts the needs assessment should explore such issues as these: What kinds of information are needed to make key agency decisions? What kinds of information are needed to supply key agency audiences—clients, legislative and executive officials, regulators, and so on? What formats and what media would be most appropriate for conveying this information? What communication occurs now that has no constructive use? Determining the communication needs and preferences of management and the work force is only part of the picture. Agencies should also ask their external audiences what kinds of service and information they expect and how they prefer to be communicated with in terms of both sending and receiving information. Any assessment should address the need for the communication of feelings and emotional support as well as task-oriented information.

A tool useful for assessing communication needs and performance is the *communication audit*. Communication audits assess the status and health of an organization's communication system much like financial audits evaluate financial status and practices. Such audits tend to be detailed, comprehensive assessments. The communication audit developed by the International Communication Association uses multiple methods. *Surveys* assess the amount of information employees receive on selected topics, the amount needed, the quality of communication relationships, satisfaction with communication results, and similar issues. *Interviews* probe in depth issues that surface via other audit methods. *Network analyses* explore communication flows and the roles employees perform (liaison, isolate, and so forth). Sharing of *communication experience* elicits employee descriptions of particularly successful and unsuccessful communication experiences. *Communication diaries* log employee communications over time in terms of subject communicated, with whom, and with what medium. Goldhaber (1986) and Downs (1988) provide detailed explanations of communication auditing.

Establish Communication Structures and Channels

With a firmer grasp of what kinds of messages need to be communicated, an agency can proceed to establish or reorganize appropriate structures and channels. Agencies typically need one or more organizational units to direct and conduct communication activities. These units are usually called public information offices, communication departments, or community affairs departments. Too often, such units have primarily functioned to get information to news media and to the public without being involved with internal communication issues. Increasingly, however, communication or public information units are addressing communication issues more comprehensively. Whether handled by the same organizational unit or different ones, public information, legislative affairs, internal communication management, and communication strategy setting need to be integrated and coordinated, either by a single superior responsible for all, by a coordinating committee, or by some other means. The communicators need to communicate effectively with each other!

Some form of communication command center for handling vital and crisis communication is essential for many public agencies. Another unit that might be useful is an intra-agency communication committee to provide different agency perspectives and advice to the communication officer and staff. Some agencies also contain a communications review committee responsible for assessing and improving agency communications. (Such committees typically review the content and format of agency publications periodically, but they also need to assess the adequacy of other agency communications.) No one structure best serves every agency. Agencies need to establish, test, and refine structures that are appropriate to their overall mission and strategy as well as to their communication objectives, audiences, messages, and management situation. Whatever structures are devised, they should enhance rather than complicate or burden communication.

After conducting a communication assessment, agencies may also need to establish or revise upward, downward, and lateral internal communication flows as well as external flows. This involves official reporting channels that typically follow the chain of command, but it should also consider subformal and personal channels. Bad news is rarely carried by formal, primarily written channels because of the risk of getting spread and misinterpreted. It is essential, therefore, to open and maintain subformal and personal channels to keep this kind of intelligence flowing. In establishing an effective communication system, each agency should develop a capacity for using media that can reach its important internal and external audiences with the different kinds of messages that agency needs to convey.

Several factors determine which media an agency should use, including *diversity* (employing a range of media to reach different audiences), *balance* (of oral, written, high-tech, low-tech information), and *cost* (Is the medium affordable? Will benefits of using this medium outweigh costs?). The advantages and disadvantages of different media are discussed particularly in Chapters Three and Seven.

In addition to establishing communication structures, channels, and media, agencies should develop mechanisms and procedures for identifying and correcting communication breakdowns, gaps, distortions, and other problems. The communications department or intra-agency communication team could function as troubleshooters or facilitators, for example. Richard Stillman (1987, p. 201) has identified some factors that are important in designing a communication system that provides adequate feedback. These factors include the use of understandable and shared *language,* a commonly understood *perception* of issues, close geographic and status *distance,* an adequate capacity to handle communication *volume, freedom to communicate* (climate), and *adequate time and work load* to "receive, digest and comprehend communications."

Establish Communication Roles and Responsibilities

To function effectively, agencies must answer a number of questions. Who has responsibility for the overall communication system? Who is responsible for setting communication policy? For implementing it? If different units (public information, legislative affairs, freedom of information, and the like) exist, what are the roles and responsibilities of each? How will the efforts of different communication functions be integrated? Although each agency must find the answers appropriate to its own situation, several broad principles do exist. Communication is too important for agency heads to divorce themselves from the process. They may delegate broad authority for directing communication activities to a communications director or public information officer with whom they must work closely, but agency heads and their top management team must remain involved in setting, implementing, and evaluating communication policy and performance. It is up to an agency's entire management team and work force to make the communication system effective. Effective communicating involves more than policies, procedures, and media. It also involves attitudes and behaviors that reinforce the importance of sharing ideas, information, and feelings, rather than hoarding them.

This chapter has described techniques for improving internal downward and upward communication and provided guidance for organizing an effective agency communication system. Like the book as a whole, the chapter is consistent with the trend in organizations and in organization theory toward *lateralism:* it emphasizes lateral, collegial relationships and concepts rather than vertical ones, with the aim of making public organizations more open, egalitarian, adaptive, and learning-oriented, as opposed to control-oriented. I have been stressing ways to avoid or overcome the problems inherent in vertical communication by recognizing the realities of bureaucracy and hierarchy while utilizing concepts and techniques from lateral communication that make it generally more open and accurate than vertical communication. The next chapter focuses more fully on lateral communication among colleagues, whether in the same or different agencies. As we have seen in previous chapters, much of the advice for communicating with this audience—colleagues and organizational peers—applies to other audiences as well.

6

Improving Relationships with Colleagues and Other Agencies

Most of the gap-filling subformal lines of communication are horizontal, connecting peers rather than subordinates and superiors. Even when subformal channels link officials of different ranks, the informality of the messages exchanged plays down variations in status. This is important because men are more prone to speak freely and openly to their equals than to their superiors.
—*Anthony Downs, 1967, p. 113*

Good, the more communicated, more abundant grows.
—*John Milton,* Paradise Lost, *Book V, verses 70–72*

Communicating with organizational peers differs from communicating with elected officials, superiors, or subordinates but is also instrumental in managerial effectiveness. Communication among peers tends to be more open, informal, and accurate than is communication among organizational unequals. In addition, certain kinds of information are best obtained from peers. Task-related information, information relevant to the principal work of an agency, gets shared primarily through lateral communication—engineer to engineer, teacher to teacher, traffic controller to pilot, caseworker to caseworker. Peers, whether in the same or a different agency, also provide much of the information for handling technical matters and problem solving. ("This is how we handled the situation.") Peers similarly tend to be the best sources of empathy when the need to commiserate arises. Despite the obvious task-related and morale importance of lateral communication, such communication is often discouraged in favor of more formal, vertical communication. This chapter emphasizes ways of improving lateral communication among peers within the same agency and across agencies.

Purposes for Communicating with Colleagues

Communicating with colleagues typically accomplishes several different managerial purposes. Among them, the most important are coordinating tasks, sharing professional knowledge, solving problems, and providing mutual emotional support.

Coordinating Tasks

Achieving administrative integration or coordination has been likened to the search for the philosophers' stone (Seidman and Gilmour, 1986). Despite some new variations, only a handful of basic approaches have been used for achieving administrative coordination. These include hierarchical command from superiors; rules, plans, and procedures specifying who will do what, when, and how; and communication among participants. All three approaches can succeed under particular conditions. Government has traditionally emphasized the first two coordinating methods, methods probably more appropriate when government was smaller, less complex, and slower paced. While hierarchy and procedure have worked in many instances, increasing technological and policy complexity, increasing pluralism, and a faster pace often show these forms to be less flexible than necessary. Management practitioners and scholars increasingly appear to understand that the rational model—emphasizing hierarchy and plans and procedures developed in advance—often fails to implement government strategies and policies effectively (March, 1978; Peters and Waterman, 1982; Peters, 1987; Campbell and Garnett, 1989; Thompson, 1984). These scholars contend that environmental complexity, uncertainty, and change make it extremely difficult, perhaps impossible, to anticipate all changes that will inevitably occur when implementing policy. This body of knowledge therefore stresses the need to experiment and make adjustments. It also emphasizes the need for communication and cooperation among a range of actors to increase learning as the policy evolves. Coordinating through communication is consistent with this newer approach to policy development and implementation and is increasingly necessary to supplement or replace reliance on hierarchy and procedure.

Effective program or project coordination generally requires sharing information on agency, program, or project plans; the roles of different staff members in those plans; and how communication and coordination devices are to be used.

Agency, program, or project plans include objectives; time, budget, personnel, and other resource constraints and needs; schedule targets; technologies utilized; geographic factors; political nuances; and other germane factors. For coordination, it is important that staff colleagues understand underlying strategy and goals, not just their specific duties. Colleagues with this larger picture can better improvise constructively if specific tasks or schedules fail.

Know *how different staff members fit into those plans,* that is, knowing the role each staff member is to play, allows colleagues to assist rather than interfere with each other's work. Sharing information about roles can also avoid the suspicion that one colleague is encroaching on another's job. If actual encroachment occurs, of course, it needs to be dealt with, especially if it causes staff tensions. Clarifying roles may be required if there is no need for overlapping roles. Depending upon the situation, however, overlap and duplication of effort may be necessary to reduce the likelihood that some tasks will "fall through the cracks." In this situation, staff members need to understand the reasons behind assigning duplicate or overlapping roles. Staff members who understand why redundancy is important are more likely to accept this condition. They may even find it reassuring to have a backup and may welcome the chance to compare ideas.

Knowing what and how *coordination and communication devices are to be used* is essential to project or program participants. This includes knowing what information needs to be reported and when; what reporting channels must be followed; the nature and role of coordinating committees, task forces, or other devices; and preferred communication media. It also helps participants to know the names and roles of any special coordinators besides project or program managers who typically are responsible for coordinating all phases of work. Liaisons or "linking pins" are emissaries to another unit who serve as conduits of information between units. "Fixers" or troubleshooters are individuals assigned to intervene in cases where emergencies arise, conflict among participants occurs, or generally when coordination breaks down (Bardach, 1977). Both liaisons and fixers have often proved to be effective in aiding coordination.

Sharing Professional Knowledge

Public employees more likely will learn professional or task-related knowledge from peers than from superiors, unless those superiors share the same profession and have previously held subordinate positions. Budget examiners compare notes and learn tips of their craft from other budget examiners. Instructors usually learn about teaching from other instructors rather than from deans or college presidents.

Several guidelines make sense for enhancing such sharing of knowledge. Staff members need to find colleagues who are knowledgeable about one or more facets of the job they need help with or are interested in. Public administrators may be in a better position to arrange such matches since they probably know more staff members and their strengths. Rarely is one colleague "the" expert to consult about all matters, and it often works better if colleagues have a symbiotic rather than a dependent relationship. One can advise the other on writing grant proposals and get help on office politics in return. A more balanced exchange has a better chance of lasting than does a one-sided relationship.

In my experience, most true professionals are willing to help a colleague if that colleague shows genuine interest and appreciation. In practical terms this means paying attention when the requested knowledge is imparted, thanking the colleague for information or help, and showing the colleague that his or her ideas are actually being used. Being able to provide information in return, even if occasionally, also strengthens the professional relationship. These guidelines apply to mentoring relationships as well, even though they are often not strictly horizontal relationships. More information on learning from mentors and coaches is provided in Chapter Ten.

Solving Problems

Lateral communication is crucial in all phases of problem solving. The traditional model of problem solving includes identifying the problem, weighing options and choosing a solution. Valuable recent work by Bolman and Deal (1991) stresses the importance of *reframing,* deliberately looking at a problem or situation from a variety of vantage points or frames of reference. According to Bolman and Deal, situations can be viewed through four major frames or perspectives. The *structural* frame emphasizes establishing and maintaining formal goals, roles, and relationships related to task. The *human resources* frame focuses on motivating employees to make full use of their ideas, skills, and energy. The *political* frame concentrates on issues of power and political competition for scarce resources. The *symbolic* frame helps managers see broader issues related to organizational mission and culture.

Decision makers need to recognize that reframing, seeing a problem from different perspectives, can lead to breakthroughs in solving it. For example, a situation I experienced involved a government employee who exhibited rebellion to authority, high absenteeism, and poor performance. Several managers perceived the situation as a disciplinary problem requiring agency disciplinary action. Despite oral and written warnings, the counterproductive behavior continued. One colleague finally applied a different frame. By looking at the situation with a structural frame, as well as a human resources frame, he identified the problem as one of faulty job design. The employee felt frustrated and unfulfilled in her job. Restructuring the job to include more challenging tasks and a more collegial operating style improved her outlook and performance. Lateral communication fosters visualizing a problem with different frames of reference. This is especially the case when different professions and specializations are brought to bear on the same problem. Such pooling of knowledge and frames of reference tends to avoid prematurely identifying a problem narrowly and inappropriately.

Collegial exchange also increases the number of viable solutions to be considered and the odds that the chosen solution is sound. In seminars I conduct on managerial decision making, groups with diverse composition and high interaction usually solve problems requiring creative solutions more quickly than do homogeneous groups and groups with little communication. In the diverse, interactive groups one comment will often spark an idea by someone else that leads to a viable solution. More systematic research generally supports the problem-solving superiority of functioning groups over individuals because different group members usually raise options or concerns that any single individual would not consider.

In less traditional conceptualizations of problem solving, lateral communication also plays a crucial role. March and Olsen (1979) basically reject the idea that decision making is predominantly rational and systematic. They believe a more realistic sense can be gained by viewing decisions as *garbage cans*. Each can has its own mix of people, opportunities, problems, and solutions. Problems and decisions rarely come neatly and orderly packaged. In such cases where precision and consensus are missing, gaining insights from a range of colleagues and frames of reference is even more essential.

Providing Mutual Emotional Support

Employees are more likely to commiserate with, complain to, and confide in equals than superiors because employees often fear letting their superiors know their vulnerabilities or inner thoughts. Lateral, collegial communication, therefore, is the predominant channel for the emotional support essential to an employee's psychological well-being, physical health, and continuing productivity. If superiors discourage collegial communication except about obviously task-related matters, they paradoxically risk jeopardizing task attainment. Employees need a work support group with whom they can talk over anxieties about the job, personal problems, career aspirations, and other matters they feel are too sensitive to tell superiors. If collegial communication of this kind is squelched, counterproductive complaining and small talk tend to replace it.

In fact, research shows that employee satisfaction with support level, trust, and openness is related to the quality of interpersonal communication (Jablin, 1979; Goldhaber, Yates, Porter, and Lesniak, 1979). In turn, increased "trust appears to increase the amount of information communicated and to reduce the tendency to filter unfavorable information" (Kirmeyer and Lin, 1987; O'Reilly and Roberts, 1974). Improved emotional support therefore improves communication for task-related matters as well. It should be noted that collegial exchange needs to be more than brief pleasantries or small talk if it is to provide emotional support or task performance. Kirmeyer and Lin (1987), in their study of communication and social support among sixty police officers and civilian dispatchers, found that only longer nonwork conversations were associated with supportive ties. Short conversations did not show such support, since they were too brief to convey more than social small talk.

This is not to say that superiors can ignore the emotional support of subordinates. Research indicates that a superior's tolerance for openness (Burke and Wilcox, 1969) and social visiting or companionship between superior and subordinate (Cohen and Wills, 1985) relate to employee social support. Public administrators who are highly effective in the long run typically take strong personal interest in their colleagues and subordinates. They also work toward providing a supportive emotional climate for staff members. Superiors must realize, however, that much of this emotional support is better provided by peers. Superiors can foster such collegial support by (1) setting an example of concern for the "whole person," not just what an employee produces on the job; (2) encouraging expression of feelings as valid and important to agency success; (3) providing opportunities at retreats and social gatherings for staff members to discuss more than shoptalk or small talk; and (4) initiating training that encourages greater employee awareness of self and others. A number of useful diagnostic tools and group process methods exist for aiding self- and group awareness. These include the Myers-Briggs Type Inventory, Interpersonal Adjective Check List, Managerial Grid, Leadership Grid, and other instruments.

Providing Incentives

It is important for administrators to motivate employees to communicate with one another directly. To do so, superiors may have to overcome certain natural reservations of their own about lateral channels for sharing information.

Encourage Lateral Communication

Administrative superiors who discourage staff members from talking with each other instead of reporting information to those superiors thwart lateral communication. Walton (1962) reports research showing the inhibiting effect on navy engineers and scientists who learned that administrators valued vertical more than lateral communication. As a result, important collegial communication diminished.

There are several reasons that superiors might want to restrict lateral communication. For example, superiors may think that lateral communication counterbalances their power by providing an alternative and sometimes competing source of information to the formal, vertical channel they control. Subordinates who can get key information from peers need not rely so heavily on their boss and may get information that conflicts with the boss's version. Public executives who feel threatened by lateral communication and attempt to restrict it risk becoming isolated, confined to one view—their own. Again paradoxically, such administrators usually end up losing information and control in an attempt to hoard them. As Chapter Five emphasizes, healthy organizations foster multiple sources and channels of communication.

Moreover, administrators may fear being left out of the communications loop and worry that *their* superiors will demand immediate answers. Several measures can help with this problem. Administrators themselves should be allowed to seek information from staff members instead of being expected to know everything when called by their superiors. Administrators should be assessed by their superiors and elected officials on the quality of their communication and performance within their unit rather than on their instant command of everything that happens. Administrators and staff should periodically consider what kinds of information both administrators and staff members need to do their work intelligently. Often a constructive balance can be reached so that administrators get the information they need to satisfy superiors without insisting on knowing everything. And administrators learn what staff professionals need to know from them.

Furthermore, some public administrators fear that subordinates will waste time socializing, gossiping, or complaining about agency matters if collegial communication is encouraged. Katz and Kahn (1966) do note the tendency for a group of peers to talk about matters that are unrelated or counterproductive to their work *if the group lacks involvement in task coordination.* In other words, employees without actual work—tasks to coordinate, problems to solve—find other things to occupy their time and their communication. Staff members will communicate with each other no matter what superiors do to restrict such communication. The lesson here is to encourage constructive lateral communication that supports task attainment and emotional health.

Public administrators can also motivate staff members to communicate laterally by taking certain steps. (1) They can refuse to answer a subordinate's questions that could be handled just as well or better by that subordinate's peers. (2) Administrators can refer a subordinate to the staff member best able to answer such questions. In some instances, referrals can be made on a case-by-case basis. Where many and repeated questions exist, a staff directory keyed by functions or questions handled helps staff members contact their colleagues directly. (3) Administrators can encourage staff members to work out problems themselves and report on the results. (4) Administrators can praise examples of effective collaboration among colleagues. (5) Public administrators can put other staff members in contact with exemplars of collaboration to learn from them. (6) Administrators can bring examples of dysfunctional lateral communication (mixed signals, information hoarding, and the like) to the attention of offenders.

Reward Group Performance

Realizing that much truth lies behind the adage "knowledge is power," some public administrators and officials seek to augment their power by hoarding information. Such hoarding often leads to communication breakdowns and performance failures. Vital political, task-related, or other information fails to get to those who need it to function effectively. Experience and research show that incentive systems that emphasize rewards to individuals increase competitiveness and hoarding behavior, while rewards for group performance tend to motivate lateral communication and information sharing (Zander, 1982).

Totally replacing incentives for individual performance with rewards for group performance may be too drastic since individual incentives themselves are insufficient in many public agencies. Yet a more constructive balance could be achieved by basing more merit raises, agency commendations, or other rewards on how well the entire unit performs. A sound incentive system that motivates lateral communication and overall performance should include both individual and group incentives. To be most effective, the formal incentive system and informal rewards and sanctions discussed above should complement rather than undermine each other. A formal incentive system that rewards group communication and performance can be undermined by a public administrator who sends signals that direct communication with the boss will be rewarded and communication among peers punished.

Empowering Subordinates to Communicate with Colleagues

Motivating subordinates to communicate laterally will accomplish only marginal results if subordinates are poorly equipped to do so. Subordinates need to be empowered; they need status and ammunition to communicate. They need specialized knowledge or information they can impart in exchanges with colleagues so that their contribution will be valued. Empowering subordinates by supplying them with vital information or knowledge is one way of building their confidence. Praising the subordinates directly and to their peers is another.

Subordinates can be empowered with *substantive knowledge,* what Yehezkel Dror calls "policy issue" knowledge, and *procedural knowledge,* Dror's "policy making" knowledge. Subordinates need substantive knowledge about public finance, special education, mental health, military defense, or other policy areas to be effective in their work. This kind of knowledge is often obtained laterally— from one expert to another. Superiors can impart some of this knowledge, and they can also provide subordinates with the time, access, and authority to acquire specialized knowledge in a particular field. Doing so increases subordinates' ability to communicate.

Superiors are more likely to possess procedural knowledge about who holds power or information, whom to contact or avoid, what other actors are involved, how decisions are made, and the like—in other words, how the system works. This kind of procedural knowledge can be invaluable to subordinates in equipping them to work effectively with each other. Public administrators should realize that many technically knowledgeable professionals lack schooling in bureaucratic politics and procedure and make efforts to guide them by means of briefings and example. As with substantive knowledge, subordinates can become expert in some specialized procedural area, thereby boosting their credibility and ability to communicate with peers. This expertise can involve bill drafting, protocol, the workings of another agency, and the like. I once worked with a man in New York State government whose claim to fame was being the only person at that time who knew the entire process of assembling, producing, and distributing the state budget document. This procedural expertise gave him status, power, and something to communicate about.

Subordinates also need to be equipped with *communication knowledge*—how to communicate effectively with each other. Initiating communication training that emphasizes lateral, professional-to-professional communication helps sensitize and educate staff members. Helping subordinates learn from agency examples of good teamwork and communication breakdown is also important. Further discussion of ways to learn communication skills is included in Chapter Ten.

Sometimes staff members need status that cannot be conferred through knowledge or overt praise. Especially when relating to counterparts in other units or agencies, staff members may need an upgrade in rank or authorization to communicate as equals. Even when an official increase in rank is impossible, creative superiors can devise special assignments or temporary titles to boost a subordinate's status. Strong endorsements and official authorizations also help.

Expediting Opportunities for Colleagues to Communicate

However important collegial communication is to government agencies, colleagues may lack opportunities to talk with each other. Effective managers find or make such opportunities.

Provide Contexts and Reasons

Communication among staff colleagues can also be facilitated through specific contexts and reasons for communicating. Staff meetings, departmental and interdepartmental task forces, joint projects, training sessions, retreats, site visits, business trips, conferences and professional activities, parties, receptions, and ceremonies typically provide the necessary context and reason for bringing staff members together so that increased communication can take place. Some staff members will take the initiative to seek colleagues in their own or another unit to exchange information or feelings. They have learned how valuable such contacts can be. Other staff members may not see the benefit or may be reluctant to take the initiative. In such instances, public managers can expedite lateral communication by deliberately creating appropriate contexts. This can include assigning a joint project to two staffers who do not know each other yet, sending a staff member to a meeting where she will gain information and contacts, organizing staff luncheon discussions of mutual interest, or holding an informal gathering to celebrate an agency or program success. As director of the Michigan Department of Commerce, Doug Ross turned around that state's capacity to attract and deal with businesses. One of the changes he instituted was the Monday morning informal coffee that allowed all members of the economic development staff to "compare notes, socialize, and raise any issues they wanted to with Doug or with each other, without the usual stiffness that bureaucracies impose" (Linden, 1990, pp. 150–151). These regular, informal exchanges improved agency communication and results, according to participants.

Initiating contact between staff members is only the first step. If these colleagues sense that their information or ideas are useful to each other, conversation and writing between them will increase in frequency and duration, thereby triggering greater exchange.

Staff members can enhance this process by showing acceptance and support of what colleagues have to say. When colleagues sense that their ideas are valued, they will likely contribute more often and take greater risks in communicating. Public managers can likewise assist by indicating in words and behaviors that they value a staff member's ideas. Unless poor rapport exists between manager and staff, getting recognition will increase a staff member's credibility with peers.

Provide a Conducive Physical Environment

Staff peers also need a physical environment conducive to communication. Having rooms available for scheduled meetings and spontaneous gatherings aids lateral, collegial communication. It also helps if each room is equipped with one or more devices for recording ideas that can be shared by all group members. Keeping a common, group record of what is discussed enhances information and agreement among members. Recording devices can include chalkboard, message board, overhead projector and screen, computer and large display or screen, flip chart, and video or audio recorder. New technology allows computers to be controlled by handwriting instead of by keyboard. Since handwritten records or minutes are more accepted and less obtrusive, this new system makes computers more common in formal and informal meetings. As always, the devices should be appropriate to the objectives, user, audience, and management situation. For example, a flip chart may be superior to "higher tech" devices such as a computer or video recorder if both users and others in the group feel more comfortable with the flip chart and are less constrained in their discussion.

A physical environment conducive to lateral communication requires more than good meeting rooms, however. A growing number of agencies and companies are coming to recognize that much valuable conversation occurs informally and so are providing lounges and dining rooms designed for more than a short break or quick bite. An increasing, healthy practice is integrating dining areas so that employees of different rank and specialization can eat and talk together. Public administrators may need to tolerate more socializing by staff members than they are used to. Instead of a knee-jerk reaction about "nobody spending enough time at his desk," public administrators should deal individually with staff members who abuse this greater informality and interaction. The bottom line is group and individual performance, not appearance.

Building layout also influences communication patterns. Staff members with the greatest need to interact should be located close to each other, with enough privacy to enable conversation. Proximity tends to improve existing communication and stimulate further interaction. Traffic patterns, too, make a difference. Employees whose paths rarely cross are less likely to communicate with each other. Hallways, tunnels, connecting ramps, and lobbies can be places for conversation.

At one state college where I worked, I discovered that the best staff interaction occurred in the main hallway just before lunch. Much task-related as well as informal conversation occurred. These gatherings often took the place of staff meetings since official decisions were frequently made there. I learned to be in that hallway or be left out. Many decisions can be made informally as long as those who need to be involved are present and prepared to make them. The problem with my situation was that not everyone present was prepared to discuss some issues intelligently on the spur of the moment. Also, staff members were sometimes absent and learned what happened only later, if at all. By encouraging informal decision making, however, my dean facilitated faculty interaction. A concern arises if most real business is conducted informally. This can turn previously informal gatherings into ritualistic meetings that employees feel compelled to attend. If this occurs, the importance of official meeting is diminished and the amount of needed informal personal contact is reduced.

Where colleagues are necessarily separated by distance, phone systems with messaging capability, electronic mail and bulletin boards, fax capability, messenger service, audio- or teleconferencing, and other approaches can keep lateral communication flowing. As emphasized before, some cues cannot be conveyed as well when not done face-to-face. Occasional site visits or face-to-face meetings can help reduce this problem.

Invest Time

Employees can be so busy with routine tasks that they have little time to talk with peers. Some superiors may think this state of affairs is desirable, but subordinates in these circumstances run a greater risk of becoming out of touch, demoralized, and less productive. Enlightened public administrators do not only tolerate contact with colleagues. They view healthy lateral communication as a good investment, so they actively identify reasons, places, and times for such exchange to occur. Collegial conversation can occur during scheduled or impromptu meetings or during lulls in the workday. Agencies where the work load prevents much collegial contact should either rethink the work load or find other time for collegiality.

Breakfast or lunch (bring-your-own or otherwise) discussions can be used to good advantage if they introduce colleagues to each other, provide benefits in the form of acquired knowledge and contacts, and respect employees' time and work load. The Rotary Club, Toastmasters, and similar organizations have achieved enormous success in many areas by following this formula. Members attend sessions at times that fit their regular working schedule, hear talks containing information of interest or benefit to them, and meet members in the same field or different fields with whom they can interact professionally or socially. This creates a network that allows members to contact other members for information, advice, or mutual business. Attendance is normally voluntary rather than mandatory and depends on motivating members with worthwhile programs. In some areas such organizations have predominantly government memberships and may even meet in public buildings.

Agencies can accomplish many of the same benefits by encouraging a comparable colloquium, discussion series, idea exchange, or the like. Chapters or sections of the American Society for Public Administration, International City Management Association, National Association of County Officials, National Association of College and University Administrators, National Association of Secondary School Principals, National Association of Elementary School Principals, National Association of School Superintendents, and similar professional organizations often hold such sessions in or

near government centers and benefit those who attend. Enlightened
public administrators encourage their subordinates to be active
professionally. Care should be exercised, however, to avoid turning
such occasions into official or unofficial business meetings that staff
members feel compelled to attend. This merely places more time and
work demands on employees without giving them added benefits or
change of pace.

Taking time out to celebrate a favorable evaluation, successful project, budget increase, employee honor, or other event stim-
ulates lateral communication because normal status or other barriers tend to be relaxed. The staff is in a positive mood and more
likely than usual to risk interacting. Such celebrations also usually
improve motivation and staff teamwork. Celebrating big and small
"wins" is an integral part of the *transformational leadership* that
Burns (1978), Kouzes and Posner (1987), Peters and Waterman
(1982), and others advocate.

Handling the Need for Confidentiality in Agency Communications

By encouraging lateral communication among colleagues in the
same or different agencies, there is a greater opportunity for information to leak. The need to maintain confidentiality is one reason
some officials give for restricting downward and lateral communication. Evidence exists, however, that confiding in colleagues and
subordinates often helps maintain confidentiality better than trying
to keep them in the dark. By explaining the situation and the need
for confidentiality, public administrators express trust in peers and
subordinates. Making them aware of the consequences if information is disclosed frequently motivates employees, whether colleagues or subordinates, to keep the faith. They now have more
ownership in maintaining confidentiality than they would if they
had learned this information on their own. Astronomer Clifford
Stoll learned this principle while pursuing an international computer spy.

Meanwhile, one of the Lawrence Berkeley Laboratory
computer masters described the whole incident to a

programmer at the Lawrence Livermore Lab. He, in turn, sent out electronic mail to several dozen people, saying that he was going to invite me to give a talk on "how we caught the German hackers." Dumb.

Ten minutes after he posted his note, three people called me up, each asking, "I thought you were keeping this hush-hush. Why the sudden publicity?"

Terrific, how do I undo this? If the hacker sees the note, it's all over.

John Ehrlichman observed that once you squeeze the toothpaste tube, it's tough to get the stuff back in. I called Livermore; it took five minutes to convince them to erase the message from all their systems. But how do we prevent this kind of leak in the future.

Well, I could start by keeping my officemates better informed. From now on, every week I told them what was happening and why we had to keep quiet. It worked remarkably well . . . tell people the truth, and they'll respect your need for secrecy [Stoll, 1989, p. 246].

In my government experience, the tactic of "leveling" with subordinates and colleagues usually proves more effective for keeping legitimate confidences and secrets than do more conventional approaches such as security classifications and providing information only on a strict "need to know" basis. Often, if superiors cannot convince staff subordinates that the benefits of keeping certain information confidential outweigh the costs, the secret is perhaps better divulged. This advice is again more appropriate for the general case of domestic policy agencies than for the special case of military and intelligence agencies. Chapter Seven covers disclosure and the public's right to know in greater detail.

Communicating with Peers in Other Government Agencies

Much of government's business requires the involvement of more than one agency. Our governmental system, characterized by federalism, separation of powers, proliferation of agencies, and policies that assign responsibility to multiple agencies, increases the likelihood of interagency communication. Increasing technological complexity also brings multiple agencies together since no single agency has a monopoly on technological expertise. The recurring financial stringency that many federal, state, and local government agencies are currently experiencing also causes more agencies to cooperate to pool their diminished resources.

Public managers communicate with their counterparts in other government agencies through official correspondence, official publications such as the *Federal Register,* interdepartmental task forces, commercial news media, and other channels. Some of the most crucial and most complex communication often occurs among departments.

Learning About Procedures, Norms, and Cultures of Other Agencies

Because of the greater flexibility, speed, and accuracy discussed in Chapter Five, subformal communication among government agencies has considerable benefits. As Downs (1967, p. 116) points out, however, an official in one government agency rarely is familiar with subformal communication networks or ground rules in another agency. One way that administrators can overcome this obstacle is to know even one person in the other agency who can direct them to the correct official or give advice about his or her agency's informal communication norms and practices. Building and maintaining their own subformal network in other agencies helps administrators communicate more effectively with those agencies. Only if intense rivalry and conflict exist between agencies are these subformal networks restrained or closed. Even under these conditions, contacts in other agencies with whom administrators have good rapport and credibility will likely provide some communication link. Other sources of information on an agency's communication practices include former employees of that agency and contacts in other departments who deal regularly with that agency. What these sources lack in terms of "insider" knowledge, they often compensate for with the greater candor allowed an outsider.

Government directories, operations manuals, agency rosters, and other documents provide useful information about whom to call for which purposes. Such official directories and manuals typically convey the formal organization chart and communication flows. Rarely do they provide insights into the subformal system, such as who is likely to be more cooperative and who is the actual expert on a topic despite her or his title. For those public administrators who deal regularly with an agency, acquiring that agency's internal telephone roster can often supply more information about who does what and who reports to whom. Making notations on directories or telephone rosters can be useful for reference later. Completing an audience profile (Chapter Three) for target units or individuals in another agency can also help consolidate knowledge about that agency's practices and preferences.

Public administrators communicate with their counterparts in other agencies for a numbers of reasons. Many policies or projects require the cooperation of several agencies. Other agencies request information needed for their work. Law requires other agencies to be sent official reports or to be notified in the event of some plans or actions. The support of other agencies is required to enable an agency to do its job. Public officials can request that departments intervene on behalf of a constituent, or department clients can request direct intervention. Of the many reasons for interagency communication, the most central are discussed in the remainder of this section.

Spanning Department Boundaries

A key purpose of interagency communication is *boundary spanning*—gleaning intelligence about what is happening in the external environment. Since other agencies are a key part of that environment, much formal and informal boundary spanning is directed at those agencies. Public agencies continuously need to know what cooperating and competing agencies are doing, how other departments have solved problems comparable to their own, what procedural and political changes are occurring, and many other essential pieces of intelligence. Agencies can span boundaries by being part of a coalition, as discussed below; by linking administrators; or by communicating through professional specialists.

Links Among Administrators. Administrators who are effective boundary spanners actively cultivate their network to maintain existing ties and make new contacts. They do this through professional association activities, links with former colleagues, organization membership, interagency committees, and the like. School ties comprise a valuable network as do colleagues from professional training. Federal Executive Institute alumni make a formidable network in federal government, as do certified public managers in some states and International City Management Training Institute participants in municipal governments.

Effective administrative spanners typically follow at least two principles. First, they keep others informed of their activities and keep abreast of what others are doing. For example, a new director of one public agency I worked for spent the first three days of his tenure calling his contacts, letting them know about his new position and plans. This also gave him the opportunity to find out what they were doing and how they might help each other. At the time, I thought he was just socializing. Now I see the value of what he did. Second, effective administrative spanners work to maintain a mutually beneficial relationship. If a contact in another department continually provides information and advice without receiving any in return, he or she is likely to stop supplying them. At the very least the contact may provide less valuable information than given earlier. When an opportunity to reciprocate without compromising agency confidentiality arises, good boundary spanners follow through.

Links Among Professional Specialists. Professionals can complement the role of administrators as boundary spanners. Throughout government, professionals communicate with each other via telephone, correspondence, electronic bulletin board, conferences, and other media. Physicians talk to other physicians, school guidance counselors consult other counselors, scientists correspond with other scientists. These relationships are built on shared knowledge and interests, on mutual loyalty to a profession, on mutual respect for other professionals, and often on personal relationships that have developed credibility between the communicators. Such ties often transcend formal authority and convey communication more accurately and responsively than do official channels. In my experience, even when government officials in different agencies are not communicating with each other because of official prohibitions or because official channels are slow, professionals are communicating subformally with other professionals. I can remember when the New York City Department of Human Services wanted to obtain an advance copy of a New York State audit report of New York City human services programs. Official channels failed to get that advanced copy, but a city caseworker got it from a fellow caseworker working for the state.

In his fascinating account of tracking down the computer spy known as the Hanover Hacker, Clifford Stoll relates the problem of getting the FBI to supply German officials with information to justify a search warrant and arrest of the spy.

> Time to call [FBI agent] Mike Gibbons. "The Germans haven't received anything from the FBI," I said. "Any idea why?"
>
> "We're having, er, internal problems here," Mike replied. "You don't want to know."
>
> I did want to know, but there was no use asking. Mike wouldn't say a thing.
>
> "What should I tell the Bundespost?" I asked. "They're getting antsy for some kind of official notification."
>
> "Tell them that the FBI's Legal Attache in Bonn is handling everything. The paperwork will come along." "That's what you [FBI] said two weeks ago."
>
> "And that's what I'm saying now."
>
> Zip. I passed the message back to Steve at Tymnet, who forwarded it to Wolfgang [Hoffman, Datex network manager in Germany]. *The bureaucrats might not be able to communicate with each*

other, but the technicians sure did [Stoll, 1989, p. 196; emphasis added].

Some administrators discourage the professionals on their staff from forging links with professionals in other organizations. These administrators perhaps fear that increasing ties with other professionals outside the agency and increasing commitment to their profession will diminish the loyalty of professionals to their own agency. Such administrators fail to recognize the enormous benefits of professional linkages. Agency professionals benefit by increasing their access, knowledge, and status. Agencies benefit from having more motivated, productive professionals and wider access to information and other resources. If the interest and commitment of professionals are being drawn away by outside involvement, perhaps the agency is failing to motivate professionals to do its own work.

Coordinating Cooperative Action

Environmental health hazards necessarily involve health, environmental protection, law enforcement, and other agencies. Promoting regional economic development typically requires cooperation from the legislature, chief executive, and agencies of economic development, transportation, public and higher education, housing, recreation and cultural affairs, tourism, law enforcement, and other departments and business organizations. In anticipation of possible terrorist actions growing out of the war with Iraq, security for the January 1991 Super Bowl in Tampa, Florida, involved the Tampa Department of Public Safety, the mayor's office, stadium officials, the county sheriff's department, the Florida State Police, the governor's office, the Federal Bureau of Investigation, the U.S. Customs Service, the U.S. Immigration and Naturalization Service, the National Security Agency, the National Football League commissioner's office, and other public and private organizations. Public administrators, particularly at middle and higher levels, spend much time trying to coordinate cooperative efforts.

Several patterns of interagency communication exist (Seitz, 1978; Gortner, Mahler, and Nicholson, 1987). In the *hierarchical* pattern, one agency has authority over subordinate agencies that report to it through a chain of command. Orders flow from the top agency, and requested reports flow back to that agency. This hierarchical pattern generally functions in a superagency structure like the U.S. Department of Health and Human Services, where many sizeable but subordinate agencies report up the chain to the department secretary's office.

In a variation of the hierarchical pattern, a lead agency serves as project manager, coordinating multiple agencies' efforts on a particular project or program. Communication flow typically forms a *wheel* pattern, with the lead agency being the center or hub, and the cooperating agencies being the spokes. Communication flows primarily between the hub and the spokes. Communication between cooperating agencies must be channeled through the lead agency or at least be reported to the lead agency. With U.S. space missions, NASA has been the lead agency coordinating the efforts of dozens of federal agencies and hundreds of contractors and subcontractors. As with the hierarchical model, this wheel pattern can aid central coordination, but it can also have some adverse affects. Those at the top or in the hub can become overloaded, while agency employees at the periphery can lose morale and the initiative to communicate with agencies other than the lead agency.

Whenever one agency lacks the official or financial power to coordinate other agencies, other patterns occur. The *coalition* model consists of a complex network of channels that directly or indirectly link agencies belonging to the coalition for a common purpose. Coordination in this pattern results more from joint planning and the exchange of information than from hierarchical direction. Councils of governments in many metropolitan areas and intercollegiate associations typically follow a coalition pattern. In the *broken-channel* pattern, direct links exist among some agencies, but no agency is linked directly to all others with control over the others.

Coordination in the coalition and broken-channel models can take different forms, depending on how participant agencies work out power relationships among them. Three options exist. "First, agencies might agree to accept the current balance of power and to respect the turf of the other bureaus. Second, bureaus may agree to actively coordinate their activities and facilitate others' activity. This would imply more systematic coordination, usually to accomplish more complete and better quality service delivery to clientele. The third approach is active competition among bureaus" (Gortner, Mahler, and Nicholson, 1987, p. 170).

Even competition among agencies tends to produce some coordination. Agencies in the same set—affiliated by jurisdiction, function, policy arena, or funding—seek intelligence about what other agencies in their reference group are doing. Changes or improvements by some members tend to be emulated by other members in order to keep pace (Seitz, 1978). Interagency task forces or committees are common coordinating devices that can reflect these three positions: truce, cooperation, or competition.

In their monumental study of NASA, Sayles and Chandler (1971) observed various techniques used to improve interagency coordination. Coordinating meetings—some small, some involving hundreds of representatives of agencies and private contractors—allowed for the continuous updating of targets and procedures, gave participants a firsthand feel for what was happening, allowed specialists a "chance to express both their concern and anxiety about various aspects of the project," and enabled adjustments after a give-and-take process (pp. 220-224). Most of these meetings were open to representatives even when discussion did not directly relate to their work. These information-sharing and problem-solving meetings worked because they emphasized direct, collegial communication and minimized superior-subordinate relationships. As noted in Chapter One, problems with NASA's later *Challenger* mission occurred substantially because of a lack of openness and a refusal to recognize and correct problems. In that mission, lateral communication was hampered by faulty communication upward and downward.

Another coordinating device that NASA used was the chartroom technique. The agency established chart rooms where officials and contractors could monitor progress on all phases of the *Apollo* project. Being able to monitor progress visually was one key to this system, but it went further. Officials stressed the concept of visibility, making the results and problems of any contractor accessible to other contractors. Contractors were encouraged to report problems before they became worse rather than hide them.

Securing External Agency Support

The same basic guidelines that apply for acquiring support from superiors and elected officials (Chapter Four) also apply for securing support from external agencies. When seeking support of any kind from any source, one should address at least three questions. (1) What types of support—financial help, additional workers, logistical support, added expertise, authorization to act, political support, or something else—are needed? (2) Which agency or agencies can supply the needed support? (3) How would a request for this support fit with the agencies' other priorities?

Assessing needs helps one determine what resources to seek from other agencies. To be realistic, no assessment can identify all department or program needs. Opportunistic public managers often acquire space, equipment, position lines, or general pledges of support without having a specific use in mind. They usually do have a general idea of how these extra resources might fit with present or later overall strategy. Acquiring resources merely because they are available frequently provides only marginal support and expends valuable political and financial capital.

After crafting a "shopping list" of needs, it pays to scout around to see which agencies can supply these resources. Contacts in other agencies can help locate these resources. Some public administrators officially or unofficially fulfill the role of broker, matching needs and resources among agencies. Such brokers are worth getting to know. Government publications provide other clues to help public managers locate resources—clues such as which agencies perform similar functions and might therefore have appropriate expertise, equipment, and so on; which agencies have lost budget or programs and might have available personnel, equipment, or space; which agencies are getting new equipment, space, or other resources and may no longer need what they are using now; and which agencies have the designated authority to authorize needed actions.

The logic of the audience profile is relevant to the question of how a public manager's request fits the other agency's priorities. Assessing the impact of a request on the audience—the agency from which support is sought—provides insights into what will motivate the agency to respond positively. It pays to show another agency how providing the requested support will aid that agency as well as the requesting agency. Will providing authorization for another agency to take action get a department "off the hook" on a lingering problem? Will supplying surplus used furniture give an agency much-needed space? Will undertaking a joint project enhance an agency's reputation with legislators for being willing to cooperate for the good of the team—and the budget? If a request can be shown to benefit the granting agency, it is more likely to be made. Finding out what other agencies need helps in making this case and in knowing what resources might be acceptable in trade. If the other agency demands an exchange for the needed resource, does what will be acquired outweigh the cost?

These and other interagency communication strategies deserve significant attention. At least one research study shows that an agency's communication strategies (formal and informal communications, linkages between programs) better determine that agency's influence in interagency networks than do environmental constraints such as mandates and degree of administrative autonomy (Boje and Whetten, 1981).

Chapter Seven further addresses external communication, but with government's external publics.

7

Communicating with Government's Publics

A riot is the language of the unheard.
 —*Martin Luther King, Jr., address in*
 Birmingham, Ala., Dec. 31, 1963

We tell the public which way the cat is jumping. The public will take care of the cat.
 —*Arthur Hays Sulzberger, 1950, p. 77*

As public servants in our democracy, federal, state, regional, and local governments have a fundamental obligation to inform their publics and be informed by their publics. This two-way communication is vital to government legitimacy and effectiveness. Polls, voting, and other citizen behavior, however, indicate that many citizens lack confidence in their governments and the information various governments communicate to them (Heise, 1985). On the other hand, research also shows that many citizens are basically satisfied with the performance of specific government agencies with which they have had business (Goodsell, 1983). Other research underscores the general ambivalence of citizens about government communication by showing that government advertising and publicity are supported in some circumstances, reviled in others (Yar-

165

wood and Enis, 1982). The fundamental nature of the government-citizen relationship and the credibility gap many citizens perceive make government-citizen communication one of the most necessary and most difficult managerial tasks. This chapter attempts to help public managers be more credible and effective communicators with their various publics. Government publics have been conceptualized in different ways. One key distinction is between constituent publics and client publics. Constituent publics are groups and individuals who exert influence over an agency and to whom an agency must answer. Interest groups, political parties, and political officials are typically constituent publics. Client publics are groups and individuals to whom government agencies provide services, products, and programs. Social services clients, highway and transit users, and public university students usually act as client publics, although they can also exert influence through political activity or through interest groups comprising people with common service needs. Most guidance for communicating with government's publics is directed toward constituent publics—legislative bodies, key interest groups, and the like. Chapter Four focuses on elected officials as a key constituent audience. This chapter emphasizes communication with client publics—how to convey important messages to agency clients and how to gather user perceptions about service delivery. Constituent publics are also discussed in this chapter—especially those who serve as intercessors.

Chapter Seven begins with a discussion of the situational nature of communicating with publics and proceeds to explore the nature of publics as audience segments, address the key purposes for communicating with publics, and describe both direct and indirect ways for communicating with client and constituent publics.

Communicating Strategically with Governments' Publics

As with other key audiences, the most appropriate way to communicate with clientele groups, taxpayers, civic associations, protest groups, and the like depends on the objectives for communicating, the nature of the audience, and factors in the management situation. Choice of message, media, format, length, and other elements depends on the diagnosis of these strategic factors. The crucial audience factor is examined first.

Use Audience Segmentation Strategies to Target Specific Audiences

Thinking of the "general public" may make sense philosophically, but it makes little sense for most communications. In communicating strategy, as in marketing strategy, it pays to think in terms of audience segments. As Chapter Three emphasizes, audiences that vary by goals, educational level, occupational mix, and other characteristics typically communicate with government differently. Right-to-life groups typically have a more graphic and aggressive communication style than do associations of trial lawyers. Parents who have lost a child in combat or military operations need a different message conveyed by a different medium than do reporters who also need to know about that casualty. The guidelines suggested below are drawn from research and experience in audience segmentation.

Audience segmentation involves disaggregating a mass audience into different, smaller, more homogenous audiences and targeting those audiences through appropriate media and messages. Segmentation avoids the shotgun approach of sending the same message to everyone via the same medium, a tactic often inefficient, ineffective, or both. For example, drowning a town in leaflets was found to be effective in reaching most citizens but ineffective in reaching the elderly, homebound, and other priority audiences (Rogers and Storey, 1987, p. 840). Careful segmenting of these audiences would have indicated use of different media. Telephone, television, radio, or door-to-door interpersonal contacts are better suited to reaching a less mobile audience.

Segmentation can also help avoid information gaps caused by selective attention. For instance, audiences better informed about and more favorably inclined toward AIDS prevention are more likely to be reached by public health education campaigns than are those less informed, less favorable, and less likely to seek out, receive, or retain AIDS information. Public health education campaigns can therefore widen the information gap unless the uninformed are segmented and specific media and message are tailored for them.

Make Direct Appeals to Audiences

Research generally shows that public information campaigns that try to change people's behavior by remote appeals to "conserve our nation's energy" or "improve our public schools" will likely fail (Rogers and Storey, 1987). Most audiences are more likely to change their behavior if the problem or change is shown to affect them directly. For example, research shows that effective law enforcement campaigns to involve U.S. citizens in crime prevention (the "Take a Bite Out of Crime" mass media campaign, for instance) must communicate to groups and individuals that they too are vulnerable to crime and can do something to prevent it (Mendelsohn and O'Keefe, 1981).

Apply Marketing Concepts When
Communicating with Audience Segments

Governments now make more extensive use of marketing concepts and techniques than they used to, especially in those areas where government can charge users—parks and recreation, postal service, and public transit, for example. Because the social or nonprofit marketing more common to governments is generally regarded as more difficult than for-profit marketing, however, not all marketing knowledge is applicable. Nevertheless, some concepts are highly useful. The *degree of involvement* a message requires is one important variable. Generally, the greater the involvement government asks of a citizen or group, the greater the perceived benefit to that audience must be relative to costs. For example, responding to local government appeals to recycle paper, glass bottles, and aluminum cans requires more effort from householders than does responding to appeals to use the public library more often. The benefit to householders of recycling must be clear enough and strong enough to outweigh the costs involved, both *monetary costs* (extra trash cans and bags) and *nonmonetary costs* (extra time and work for sorting and disposal). Nonmonetary costs typically include time, inconvenience, and psychic costs (for example, the fear of getting an AIDS test) (Rothschild, 1979). The benefits of recycling communicated to householders can be in the form of *positive reinforcement* (better conservation, cleaner environment, feeling of civic-mindedness) or *reduction of negative reinforcement* (householder savings on sanitation fees).

Governments can improve the appeal of a message and its likelihood of success if they make the "product" more attractive by increasing benefits and lowering costs to clients. In the case of recycling, municipal governments or regional sanitation authorities might supply trash cans and bags to households and businesses, make sorting easier, and give rebates to recyclers. This point cannot be overemphasized. A tendency in public information is to repeat or magnify the message when the appropriate public fails to respond. This tactic may have some value, but only if the "product" government is promoting (fire prevention, prenatal care, voting, college education, and so on) is attractive enough to have public demand.

The armed forces have certainly made effective use of media advertising in recruiting personnel and recognize the importance of using multiple media. Advertising attracts people to recruiters, who play the major role in persuading recruits to enlist (Martin, 1988). Advertising alone has a marginal effect on enlistment, but it augments the effectiveness of recruiters. A more important factor in enlistment success has probably been improvement of the "product." The armed forces have made enlistment more attractive than it used to be. Benefits now typically include signing bonuses, money for college tuition, choice of training, full health coverage, housing, paid vacations and retirement plans, in addition to the psychic rewards of being part of winning, highly regarded armed forces. Recruitment and retention have been so successful that the armed forces will now have to scale back in a less threatening world. The lesson is clear, however: slick communication and public relations cannot compensate for inferior or unwanted government goods or services. Government agencies have the responsibility of first providing quality services and goods that meet public demand. Doing this will make them more effective communicators with their publics.

Recognize That Audience Segments Are Groups of People

Even though it is useful to think in terms of audience segments
when planning communications strategy, public managers must
always remember that they are fundamentally dealing with people,
not some lifeless abstraction. Treating people as numbers or profiles whose voting, economic behavior, program support, or policy
compliance can be manipulated through adroit communication vi-
olates the spirit of democratic government. Adolf Hitler (1933, p. 77)
recognized this potential for influencing audiences: "The receptive
ability of the masses is very limited, their understanding small; on
the other hand, they have a great power of forgetting. This being
so, all effective propaganda must be confined to a very few points
which must be brought out in the form of slogans until the very last
man is enabled to comprehend what is meant by any slogan. If this
principle is sacrificed to the desire to be many-sided, it will dissipate
the effectual working of the propaganda, for the people will be
unable to digest or retain the material that is offered them."

In some ways, the potential for public persuasion is greater
now than in Hitler's time. The attention span of many American
citizens has been conditioned by television commercials, political
advertising, music videos, and headlines-only news to grasp primarily short, simple messages. Moreover, the sophistication of today's
communication technology and knowledge far surpasses that available in Hitler's era. Poverty, homelessness, crime, illiteracy, and
other conditions in the United States augment the climate for propaganda and persuasion. In light of these conditions, public administrators must exercise even greater caution to communicate
responsibly with government's publics. Hitler practiced audience
segmentation, but he targeted audiences with one-sided messages
rather than the many-sided, more balanced messages he feared
would undo the impact of his propaganda. It requires judgment
and courage for American public administrators to balance the political and social forces calling for short, simple messages with the
need to supply more complicated and realistic messages. Further
discussion of the ethical issues involved in applying communication knowledge and technology can be found in Chapter Nine.

Recognizing that audience segments are comprised of people

also has implications for program effectiveness and responsiveness. Public administrators should try to understand and empathize with citizens who attempt to communicate with government. It helps to remember that all government managers, even mayors, governors, and presidents, are also citizens. As government managers, we also need to communicate as citizens with some government agencies. Even Internal Revenue Service officials must communicate with the IRS as taxpayers. Few, if any, public administrators are immune from dealing with motor vehicle registration lines or forms. Thinking of how we would want to be communicated with as citizens can help us as government managers or specialists communicate more responsively with other citizens.

A number of government agencies deliberately expose employees to the special needs and interests of agency clients. One dramatic and effective effort is that of the U.S. Department of Health and Human Services' Health Care Financing Administration (HCFA). HCFA employees primarily have contact with computers, printouts, cost analyses, policy papers, and other sources involved in the HCFA's administration of federal Medicare and Medicaid programs. Realizing the lack of contact with actual recipients of health care, HCFA organized "reality-based training" to help employees better empathize with patients and clients and better understand the nature of the services being financed. One such reality-based training program "began at a home for the disabled where people with cerebral palsy, multiple sclerosis, and traumatic injuries spend their days in wheelchairs. It ended at a home for severely retarded children and adults who need to be fed and changed and cared for 24 hours a day. In between, the government workers shared a lunch of macaroni and hamburger with homeless women, and they trekked in a cold rain with AIDS outreach workers through the worst of the city's housing projects. They came face-to-face with drug addicts, prisoners, and a baby whose only hold on life was the respirator that breathed for him" (Fitzgerald, 1990, p. 1B).

Such personal contact can accomplish several things. First, it can show employees how what they do makes a difference in the lives of other people, thereby helping to motivate these employees. Second, exposure in the field gives headquarters staff greater understanding and appreciation for what field staff must do to implement agency policy. This can lead to increased cooperation and perhaps wiser policies. Third, government employees better recognize that they are employed to serve people, not nameless cases or statistics. This recognition can be part of an agency's culture, emphasizing enhanced or renewed commitment to public service, meaning service to people.

Purposes for Communicating with Government's Publics

Central purposes for communicating with government's publics include keeping publics informed about government policies, procedures, requirements, and conditions; gleaning citizen feedback about their government; and complying with citizen requests.

Keeping Publics Informed

Federal, state, and local government agencies provide public information through written reports; public meetings; cable network programming; press conferences; public service announcements; newspaper, magazine, radio, and television news coverage; and other media. Much of this public information is required by law. Government agencies at all levels are routinely required to issue annual reports and make them available to legislative bodies and members of the public, for example. Public meetings are often required before environmental or transportation projects are approved or major decisions affecting land use or public education are made.

Many of our laws affect government-citizen communication. Some have such widespread use and impact that they deserve attention here; particularly relevant are federal government policy laws that involve freedom of information, privacy, open meetings, and the use of advisory committees.

Freedom of Information Policies. The Federal Freedom of Information Act (FOIA), passed in 1966 and amended in 1974, provides general access to information possessed by any federal administrative agency except information in the following exempt categories:

National security
Internal agency rules
Material specifically exempted by other statutes
Confidential business information
Internal government memoranda
Personal privacy
Law enforcement investigations
Regulation of financial institutions
Oil wells

More details about the exempt categories can be found in Title 5 U.S. Code, Section 552, and Marwick (1985). Unless an agency judges that requested information is covered by one of these exempt categories, law requires a written response within ten days. This response can either supply the information, state that a ten-day extension is needed to comply, or specify under which exemption(s) the request is being denied. Public administrators need to remember that the FOIA "segregable portions" provision requires the release of nonexempt portions of a document even if the entire document cannot be supplied. FOIA policy deserves competent attention because information access is crucial to democratic government and because public administrators and their agencies can suffer adverse consequences if they handle requests improperly. Public administrators or employees can be disciplined for withholding information arbitrarily and capriciously. Courts can require agencies to pay court costs and attorney fees if a requester has "substantially prevailed" in a case brought under the Freedom of Information Act.

The Freedom of Information Act does not apply to records of the Central Intelligence Agency or to law enforcement agencies. The act does not generally apply to information possessed by Congress and congressional agencies such as the Library of Congress, General Accounting Office, Office of Technology Assessment, and Congressional Budget Office. These agencies have adopted regulations, however, that closely follow the Freedom of Information Act but usually with additional, specific exemptions. When dealing with congressional agencies, public administrators should consult the records management office of the particular agency. State and local government agencies are not covered by the federal Freedom of Information Act, but most have comparable policies of their own. Public administrators (and others) can obtain information about such policies by contacting a state attorney general's office, secretary of state's office, city corporation counsel, or legal counsel for a specific agency.

Privacy Acts. The federal Privacy Act of 1974 and corresponding state privacy acts also affect public information practices. The federal Privacy Act allows citizens to request and inspect *personal* records held by a federal agency or a contractor who handles covered records for a federal agency. These personal records can be requested only by the subject of those records or his or her legal guardian. Such records can be amended or expunged if they are found to be not "accurate, relevant, timely, or complete," according to the act. The Privacy Act also places restrictions on how agencies use personal information and provides penalties for misuse. Public managers need to exercise caution when considering the discretionary release of personal information such as health and tax records.

Open Meetings Policy. The federal government, in compliance with the Sunshine Law of 1976, allows citizens to attend meetings of the governing boards of about fifty federal agencies and to have access to the records of those meetings unless they are exempt. According to the Sunshine Act, federal meetings may be closed to citizen access when national security issues are discussed; when internal agency rules or policies are discussed; when trade secrets or commercial or financial information is involved or discussion could lead to financial speculation or instability; when sanctions are being considered against an individual or corporation; to protect personal privacy, although in some cases individuals can waive their right for privacy to allow public access; when law enforcement records are being discussed; when privacy rights of government officials may be threatened; and when open meetings may jeopardize a proposed agency action. All of these possible exemptions are of concern to public administrators, especially the last two.

While agencies may close meetings to protect the privacy of public officials, federal law applies a "balancing test." Agencies or committees must weigh the public's need to know against an official's right to privacy. The legislative history of the government in regard to the Sunshine Act also suggests that "high government officials may have fewer privacy rights than lower officials and private citizens" (Marwick, 1985, p. 181).

The last exemption listed above (when open meetings may jeopardize a proposed agency action) also affects many agency meetings. If an agency judges that an open meeting would prematurely disclose information that would likely frustrate or jeopardize the implementation of proposed policy, it may close that meeting unless the agency had already disclosed its intended action or is legally required to disclose its intent before taking action. Public administrators should exercise this exemption carefully if policy on open meetings is to have any meaning. The courts have usually upheld this exemption in cases where premature disclosure would nullify proposed action over contract negotiations or trade policy, for example. A federal court denied efforts to keep the Nuclear Regulatory Commission's budget deliberations closed under this exemption, however (Marwick, 1985).

Laws in almost every state establish a comparable right to citizen access to state and sometimes local government meetings. In other cases, local ordinances apply. Some governmental bodies fulfill the letter of the law on open meetings rather than the spirit of the law by providing minimal notice and by holding meetings at times and places difficult for citizens and reporters to attend.

Use of Advisory Committees. The federal Advisory Committee Act of 1972 gives citizens the right to attend meetings of federal advisory committees. This act enumerates exemptions identical to those for the federal government (listed above), according to the Sunshine Act. The federal Advisory Committee Act, however, is generally considered to have less influence on how federal agencies communicate with their publics.

While the foregoing policies are the major ones that affect the federal government's dissemination of information to publics, they are certainly not the only policies. Since law affecting agency communication differs somewhat among levels of government and even among agencies, public administrators may need to expend a considerable amount of effort to become knowledgeable about such legal requirements. Consulting with an agency's public information office and its legal counsel's office is a good way to start. Reviewing the agency's authorizing legislation, compendium of agency regulations, and relevant policy and procedures manuals also can be rewarding.

The need for governments to communicate with their publics transcends legal requirements. Democratic ideals, administrative professionalism, and the need for citizen compliance with agency policy make it necessary to communicate effectively with citizens even without laws requiring such communication. The following sections discuss some of the major ways that governments communicate with citizens directly and indirectly.

Direct Communication with Government's Publics

Direct communication ranges from face-to-face discussion to phone calls to television programs.

Face-to-Face Contact. The most common type of direct personal contact with citizens occurs during the provision of service. This contact whether by school principal, police officer, or other public servant often occurs when citizens feel anxious or harassed (for example, when parents are worried about their child's educational progress or when victims are waiting for news about their stolen car). A newspaper article about the Bridgeport office of the Connecticut Department of Motor Vehicles included this description of clients: "Imagine, though, standing behind a counter day after day facing a few hundred faces numb from waiting and harboring hair-trigger tempers. 'People get upset at us because they don't bring the papers the state requires,' [senior examiner Brenda] Kennerly said. 'American Express we don't take as an I.D.' And some of those faces want fake I.D.'s or they present fake I.D.'s. Or they can't figure out the new written tests, which are presented on 'touch-the-screen' video machines. Or they just feel like whacking somebody" (Bravo, 1990, p. B1).

Tom Peters himself would be hard-pressed to maintain his posture of the-customer-is-always-right in this situation. And yet an informal audience profile of motor vehicle clients would suggest that diplomacy, friendliness, and attentiveness are the order of the day when dealing with people who typically feel hurried, harassed, or even dehumanized.

Some public officials and administrators observe a "visitors" day or period that allows citizens personal access. Jimmy Carter held a monthly visitors day when he was governor of Georgia but concluded that it would be difficult to continue the practice as president. This format can work for many administrators, however. Preplanning is needed for security, for registering citizen input, for taking warranted follow-up action, and for giving citizens feedback on that action.

Face-to-face contact may also involve visiting individuals or groups in their workplace, home, meeting place, or other locations. To be most effective as communications channels, such visits should be more than the whirlwind press opportunities that presidents and governors sometimes make to some farm, urban, minority, or other family who serves a public relations purpose. Consistent with a strategic approach to communicating, administrators should consider which audiences and locations are likely to enable the most accurate and useful communication and which formats (one-to-one, informal small group, open meeting) will serve most effectively. Another issue is whether to announce a visit in advance or to visit spontaneously. If fact-finding is the aim, advance notification might prompt more preparation and therefore more information. If hearing citizen attitudes and positions is the objective, a spontaneous visit often generates more accurate information.

Public hearings and meetings constitute yet another method for communicating face-to-face with segments of the public. Some hearings and meetings are legally required as part of a rule-making or policy-formulation process. Other meetings and hearings are held at the discretion of agency leaders. Whether required or optional, such meetings and hearings too often become pro forma exercises, frustrating citizens and public administrators alike. The following guidelines are intended to improve the usefulness of public meetings and hearings.

1. Clarify meeting objectives, target audience, and management and political context. Is the meeting or hearing required or optional? Is the objective to disseminate or gather information, solve problems or make decisions, launch or assess initiatives, or encompass a combination of these? Consistent with the strategic situational approach advocated here, meeting objectives should influence the choice of meeting participants, agenda items, logistical arrangements, and other factors. If the purpose is primarily to disseminate information to citizens, oral and visual presentations (videos, filmstrips, poster displays, resource tables, and the like) can be arranged with appropriate opportunities for questions to clarify information. On the other hand, if the purpose is to solicit citizens' ideas, attitudes, or cooperation, agendas and formats that allow greater citizen participation (roundtables, discussion groups, nominal groups) are more appropriate. The choice of participants also depends on the objectives. Information-sharing meetings call for experts who can communicate technical information clearly. Meetings or hearings to elicit citizen reaction should involve citizens who are affected or potentially affected by a policy or program and officials should be able to act on citizen advice. Citizens can justifiably become frustrated if they believe that no one of sufficient authority is present to hear their opinions and ideas.

Clarifying objectives, audience, and situation can also help prevent unnecessary discretionary meetings or hearings. Public school administrators who want to elicit citizen reaction to an experimental curriculum, for example, may discover after assessing these factors that other media may be more appropriate to their purpose than a public meeting. Detailed interviews; surveys of students, parents, and teachers; or meetings of small reaction groups usually provide more specific, useful information than an open public meeting. A thorough assessment of communication strategy factors may also show that a meeting or hearing would be counterproductive now and should be reconsidered later. Eliminating unnecessary or poorly focused meetings will avoid much citizen frustration and make those meetings that are held more credible and useful.

2. Select the date, time, and place of a meeting or hearing in light of the objectives, audience, and context. Public hearings and

meetings often exclude people who work during normal business hours. Evening or even weekend meetings make sense for some audiences. The meeting place should be within a reasonable distance, safe to get to, and accessible for those with handicaps. Also plan meeting places appropriate to the meeting objectives. A meeting to explain the need for budget cuts would likely generate criticism if held in an expensive hotel conference room. A public meeting to dramatize the need for library renovation could be held in the existing, inadequate library—as long as it is safe, of course.

3. Notify target audiences of a meeting or hearing via appropriate, multiple media. Letters, television and radio announcements, posters, fliers, and announcements at other meetings, on computer bulletin boards, or in phone calls are some of many notification methods. Using a combination of media increases the chances of reaching target audiences. Some media are particularly appropriate to objectives and audience: notice of a hearing on utility rates sent with utility bills, notice of a meeting on funding for the arts included in concert and play programs. Notification should include this basic information: who the meeting affects and why (to motivate attendance); purpose of meeting (so citizens will know that their role is—listener, speaker, reactor—and can plan accordingly); action (what is likely to result from this meeting—a decision, more meetings); date, time, place, and directions (if necessary); financial implication of proposal being discussed (unless including this would be misleading or would bias deliberations); and any other appropriate explanatory material (Cogan, 1992).

4. Make sure the meeting site is ready. Among other actions, this includes ensuring that on-site directions to the actual meeting room are visible and clear, on-site access exists, audiovisual equipment works and is in the right place and backups (spare bulbs, chalkboards, and so on) are available, table and seating arrangements are appropriate to the size of audience and the nature of meeting, staff members know their roles, and news media are notified (if appropriate). It also pays to check on contingency arrangements. Select an alternative room in case the audience is too large or small for the first room or in case of sound, lighting, heating, or other problems.

5. Use agenda strategy. This involves making sure that the

agenda does not exceed available time or attention span. Two or more meetings may be more productive than one marathon session. Agenda strategy also involves careful sequencing. If certain information is essential for enlightened deliberations, make sure that gets shared first. If the purpose is to develop cooperation among different interest groups, begin with areas where agreement can be reached and build from that instead of tackling the thorniest issue first. For more extensive treatment of agenda strategy see Garnett (forthcoming).

6. Clarify meeting ground rules and procedures. Whether running a meeting or hearing or participating in some way, public administrators need first to clarify ground rules and procedures for themselves. Leaders then need to clarify ground rules for others at the beginning of the meeting or hearing. The following issues typically need to be addressed: Why is this meeting being held? What is its purpose? How does this meeting relate to other managerial or political activities? Who is to speak at this meeting? In what order? Are there time limits for presentations? Will questions be taken during presentations or at the end? Are written transcripts of remarks or testimony being accepted for the record? Will votes be taken at this meeting or at another time? Will Robert's Rules of Order, modified Robert's Rules, or some other set of procedures be followed? Will a transcript be made available to reporters and to other citizens? Clarifying ground rules at the beginning avoids problems later. For example, if someone calls for a vote late in a meeting and only then is it mentioned that no votes are to be taken, it may seem that the leader fears the outcome of a vote. The meeting may degenerate into a discussion of whether a vote is appropriate and which rules to follow. If ground rules are clarified up front, such problems are avoided or minimized.

7. Run a meeting or hearing in a way that is consistent with the objectives, audience, and management situation. These three elements influence the proper choice of meeting format, as indicated earlier, as well as an appropriate meeting style. Rigorous adherence to Robert's Rules of Order may be appropriate for keeping control of an agency meeting with many speakers for and against a controversial proposal. The same complicated rules would likely inhibit participation in a meeting where interest group representa-

tives and public officials are attempting to solve mutual problems. Likewise, a control-oriented leadership style is more appropriate for an information-disseminating meeting than for a meeting intended to let citizens speak their mind. In the latter case, strict rules and time limits may make citizens feel that they are not really being given the opportunity to be heard. Of course, some control must be exercised to allow those who want to speak to do so.

8. Follow through after a meeting or hearing to ensure that results and feedback are forthcoming. Meetings and hearings are tools used as part of an ongoing public management process. Public administrators must therefore take steps to ensure that a meeting or hearing is an integral part of that process rather than an isolated event. Important steps usually include scrutinizing meeting minutes or transcripts to identify promises, requests, or issues that require follow-up; assigning follow-up tasks to staff members (see Chapter Five for guidelines on delegating); sending minutes, transcripts, and other information to meeting participants (as appropriate) and to other relevant actors; and providing direct feedback to citizen leaders and meeting participants about what was accomplished as a result of the meeting. Where possible, this last step adds a nice touch that can improve future credibility and rapport with citizens.

Telephone Calls. There are several ways to communicate directly with citizens by telephone. Presidents, governors, mayors, legislators, and department administrators have used call-in programs to get advice and hear complaints from citizens. These programs vary in length from about fifteen minutes to several hours. Many such programs are radio broadcast, and some are televised. Less formal are efforts of officials to "reach out and touch someone" by directly calling individuals who are either selected at random or who have special knowledge or characteristics pertinent to a particular issue. Many executive and legislative offices and administrative agencies have established telephone hot lines that citizens can call to get information or action. These hot lines are usually staffed by aides, public advocates or ombudsmen, or volunteers. In addition to the preceding guidelines for handling citizen requests, the following pointers also apply. Those staffing telephone request lines or hot lines should be able to speak the caller's language and relate to callers because of similar experience or direct knowledge of callers' problems. Those staffing telephones should also use common telephone courtesy: avoid putting callers on hold unless absolutely necessary; give name, position, and affiliation; explain hot line procedures, if necessary; be civil and professional in manner—even if provoked—and let callers know what steps will be taken and what results they can reasonably expect from their call. Telephone courtesy also means avoiding the tactic of two-timing callers: having two (or more) government officials on the line without clarifying who they are and who is talking when. This confuses, frustrates, and alienates callers. These guidelines also apply to citizen information centers and to complaint bureaus, which also allow face-to-face contact.

New programs are now available to help one communicate via telephone with citizens who speak a language other than English. For example, in 1990 the American Telephone and Telegraph Company announced the expansion of its translation services to provide telephone interpreters who can help with 143 languages and dialects, twenty-four hours a day (Sims, 1990). Such services can help citizens communicate with police and fire departments, schools, and other public agencies. The subscription and usage fees are the necessary price for providing viable access to all citizens.

Written Publications. Much government communication with its publics occurs through written letters, reports, forms, informational bulletins, rules, orders, and other documents. Citizens' image of government often stems from their reaction to government writing. Imagine the reaction of a taxpayer who received a letter from the U.S. Office of Management and Budget containing this concluding paragraph: "Since data is central to the issue of refined implementation guidance and legislation defers implementation, we believe it is advisable to examine the data that your organization is assembling to preclude any such intended effects" (Lutz, 1989, p. 201).

As taxpayers and citizens, how would public administrators feel about getting a letter like this? Pompous bureaucratese often has the opposite effect to that intended. By raising the complexity and jargon level of writing, a public manager actually "talks down" to the reader by depersonalizing the relationship with that reader. Since much government writing has become stuffy and bureaucratic, efforts by the U.S. Air Force, the General Accounting Office, the Internal Revenue Service, and other government agencies to simplify and humanize writing are steps in the right direction. Consistent with the strategic situational approach advocated here, however, I reject the position taken by some writing experts that simpler, more conversational writing is necessarily better. Strategy factors in a particular situation may call for pompous style and jargon because that is what is expected and understood by a particular audience. Of course, jargon and bureaucratese should not be deliberately used to confuse or put off citizens so that they do not have to be dealt with. When writing to citizens, public administrators should assess their readers by using the audience map to determine audience role and use the audience profile to estimate readers' information level and needs, the likely impact of the message on readers, and other pertinent factors. Similarly, public administrators must target the content, wording, organization, length, and tone of their writing at their audience and their purpose for writing. When in doubt, it is best for public administrators to assume that the external publics to whom they write are intelligent but may not understand technical or bureaucratic jargon.

Television Programs. The presence of television in almost every American household and television's tangible, visible impact make it an effective medium for many messages. The success of the commercial program "America's Most Wanted" in assisting in the arrest of numerous criminals demonstrates this impact. The combination of visually reenacting the crime, showing pictures of criminals, and providing viewers an easy, nonthreatening outlet for action (toll-free telephone call) has stimulated many citizens to provide valuable information leading to arrests.

Government or social agencies can raise consciousness and transmit information through a single television program or even a series. One CBS program, the "National Driver's Test," asked viewers to test their driving knowledge and skills. By allowing people to take the test in a nonthreatening, home environment, this program stimulated exceptionally high citizen involvement. The program did more than raise public awareness about what constitutes good and bad driving; it also gave viewers a specific mechanism for improving their driving by directing them to driver education programs. As a result of this creative combination of a nonthreatening environment, audience involvement, and a specific outlet for action, about 35,000 people enrolled in driver education programs (Rothschild, 1979). The soap opera series "Cancion de la Raza" has provided the Los Angeles Chicano community with information and insights about social and legal problems faced by members of that community (Rothschild, 1979). The ongoing, attractive nature of this series gives it more impact with its target audience than would a single television documentary.

Public service announcements can also tap the power of television to dramatize a cause or provide information. Despite use of free air time, the cost of producing and distributing a professional public service announcement can be expensive. For a program or cause with strong interest, however, celebrities, musicians, and technical crews may donate their services. In spite of the interest and impact celebrities can generate, public agencies are advised to choose spokespersons for their announcements carefully. Name recognition alone is not enough. Effective spokespersons should also support the cause and be identified with it. Bill Cosby possessed these qualities when doing public service announcements on child labor. Actor Ted Danson is likewise well-known and regarded as a strong advocate of environmental conservation. Some skeptics of public service announcements note that these "free" announcements are not usually aired during prime time and therefore advocate buying air time for priority causes. Cuccia (1981) provides useful pointers on government public service announcements.

Films and Videos. As with television, sound and visual movement make film and video forceful media. In addition to a variety of training and other films for internal use, government agencies have produced some notable films for public viewing. As early as 1936, the U.S. Department of Agriculture's exceptional film *The Plow That Broke the Plains* was shown in 3,000 theaters and dramatized the dust-bowl consequences of poor soil conservation practices. The award-winning film *The River* vividly presented New Deal issues such as flood control and hydroelectric power (Herold, 1981). State and local governments have also been in the motion picture business, producing films promoting economic development and other causes.

The videotape format allows films to be viewed conveniently by small groups or individuals at a place and time of their choosing. This versatility makes videos appropriate for many uses. Public health clinics now give patients videos to instruct them in personal health practices or disease prevention. These videos can reach patients who are unable to travel or who are embarrassed about learning about venereal disease or AIDS in a public setting. A public school teacher can check out a video of the training session he or she missed. Departments of economic development can send promotional videos to individual businesses interested in locating in their jurisdiction. Uses of video can be as creative as public administrators can devise. Northern Michigan University's 1991 student recruiting video emulated MTV music videos with rock music and flashy dancers. Although criticized by some educators, others have lauded this video for being contemporary and appealing to the target audience—current high school seniors attracted to the short, fast-paced, rhythmic, colorful messages of MTV. Potential users should recognize that films and videos can be expensive to produce, especially films, and both can become quickly dated.

Computers and Computer Disks. Census, economic, and other government information has been available on computer tape for years. Now increasing amounts of information are available on-line or through the sale of disks. Computers can reach audience segments other media may fail to reach. Targeting a different student group than does Northern Michigan University, Drexel University, a technology and engineering-oriented university, has had considerable success providing information about courses, campus life, and so forth on computer disks sent to science-oriented high school graduates. Many of these graduates prefer to acquire no-frills information and feel comfortable interacting with a computer. Government agencies offer weather, tax, and other information on-line to businesses and individuals. Citizens of Santa Monica, California, hold town meetings via electronic bulletin board. These on-line town meetings identify the location of potholes, organize crusades to help the homeless, and address other community concerns (Reitman, 1991).

Actions and Decisions. As emphasized in Chapter Five, actions do speak louder than words in government. This also applies to communicating with government's various publics. The Internal Revenue Service communicates via mail, printed documents, television and radio, computers, and other media to more citizens than do most government agencies. When it comes to communicating to actual and potential tax evaders, the IRS knows that merely warning citizens about the penalties for evasion is an insufficient deterrent. The IRS, therefore, has harnessed state-of-the-art technology to detect tax evaders, particularly drug dealers, money launderers, racketeers, and other criminals. The IRS's Criminal Forensic Laboratory can "wire" undercover agents, detect voiceprints, reconstruct documents or computer disks, enhance fingerprints with lasers, and unleash other technological weapons to catch and convict tax evaders. Directly, through investigation and convictions, and indirectly, through media coverage of this sophisticated technology's impact on convictions, the IRS communicates its message: evade taxes at your own risk. Between 1980 and 1989, the number of drug and money laundering cases recommended for prosecution rose 337 percent, while the comparable number of tax evasion cases against legitimate business people fell 31 percent (Hershey, 1990).

Indirect Communication with Government's Publics

Besides the direct communication just discussed, government makes use of several indirect means of relaying information and perspectives.

Communication Via News Media. Governments also communicate indirectly with their various publics via news media—newspapers, magazines, radio, and television. Training in relations with the news media was not included in the professional preparation of many public administrators. They discover later, however, how crucial relations with the press are to their administrative goals and to their careers. The top-ranking air force officer was fired in September 1990 for what Defense Secretary Dick Cheney said was "poor judgment" in disclosing to reporters possible air strikes against Iraq's capital that would also target leader Saddam Hussein. General Michael Dugan told reporters that if war broke out the Pentagon planned to use air strikes to "decapitate" Iraq's leadership by targeting Hussein, his family, and his mistress (Thompson, 1990, pp. A1, A12). Secretary of Defense Cheney afterward had to tell reporters that it was improper to talk about future military operations, especially the targeting of officials. That might violate a presidential executive order barring U.S. involvement in assassinating foreign leaders. General Dugan survived three hundred Vietnam combat missions, enormous competition for promotion on his way to the top of the air force ladder, and many administrative challenges, but he made inappropriate disclosures to the press. He was known to be particularly open and friendly with reporters, in itself no failing. But he went too far, according to his superiors. Getting media attention, being considered "in-the-know," and being able to divulge key information are all tempting to public administrators, especially those who labor in relative obscurity. Public administrators must possess self-discipline to balance the need to inform citizens and get media attention that might aid their program, agency, or own career with the need to avoid irresponsible disclosures or comments.

　　A necessary first step in achieving constructive rather than destructive relations with reporters and editors involves knowing *their* objectives and knowing news professionals as an audience. The basic responsibility of news professionals is to cover and report stories deemed newsworthy. What reporters consider newsworthy varies but usually includes some or all of the following: (1) something that affects many people or important people—military operations, tax hikes, medical breakthroughs, and the like; (2) a story or information that concerns something new—new policy, technology, program, leader, or the like; (3) something that involves a departure from the norm—scandal, corruption, bureaucratic snafu, differential treatment, interagency conflict, and so on; (4) something of human interest—the plight of certain people or animals, government employees "putting themselves in their clients' shoes."

　　Reporters rely heavily on public administrators and information officers to supply them with information and leads for stories that fit one or more of the above criteria. What public managers deem newsworthy often differs from what a reporter deems newsworthy. It therefore pays to recognize the reporter's perspective when making something appear newsworthy (or unnewsworthy, if coverage is not desired). What reporters do with information stories they receive depends in large part on the kind of news medium they represent and on their own professional style. Exhibit 7.1 compares requirements and procedures for leading types of media.

Public administrators must recognize that the needs and styles of news media and of reporters vary so tactics for dealing with them must also vary. Public administrators should therefore find out who the reporter is, what news organization the reporter represents, what type of story the reporter is working on, and what the deadline is. Most journalists will identify themselves before being asked because this is established professional practice. Yet many government managers and professionals have answered sensitive questions without establishing the identity of the questioner, only to find their remarks quoted in the next day's paper or in an interest group publication. The best policy is to ask for name, affiliation, type of story, and deadline. The answers to these questions will indicate what kinds of information the reporter needs, for what purpose, and how quickly.

Next, administrators should find out what specific questions are being asked. Unless a reporter is trusted, the best advice is to answer only the questions asked. If doubt exists about what a question means, an administrator should ask the reporter to restate the question. This not only protects against misperception, it also gives an administrator extra time to formulate an answer.

Many questions can be answered quickly and easily by telephone. If, however, administrators are uncertain about facts or their authority to answer a specific inquiry or if they need more time to think out a response, they should ask the reporter when the information is needed and arrange to call the reporter back. Some interviews are too complex to handle by telephone, particularly if the reporter has no prior knowledge of the problem or subject. In these cases, administrators should suggest a face-to-face discussion and set up an appointment.

Exhibit 7.1. Newsgathering and Reporting Styles and Requirements.

1. Basic components of news research involve:
   - Locating reliable information
   - Cultivating and protecting news sources
   - Observing and recording information
   - Organizing and maintaining records
   - Evaluating and verifying information gathered

   Reporters typically seek out information about:

   Details—finding out names, facts, figures and verifying this infor-mation with other sources

   Controversies—seeking differing points of view, checking sources against each other, checking official records to verify claims

   Policy decisions—learning who is affected by the agency's corpo-rate decision, factors influencing the decision, how the decision was reached.

2. Different Approaches to Newsgathering and Reporting

   a. *General Assignment Reporting*
      - Requires broad knowledge of current issues and quick study of any topic on short notice.
      - Editor defines subject or event and specifies data to be collected.
      - If time permits, reporter begins by reading references in old news files (the "morgue") and talks with background sources (e.g., public information specialists, interest group representatives).
      - News release, news conference, event, or key interview produces leads the general assignment reporter pursues to construct story, usually within the time and interest constraints set by editor.
      - General assignment reporter needs brief statements, releases, fact sheets, sources for verification, background or quotes, names of officials and experts who are available for comments and questions.

   b. *Radio and Television Reporting*
      - Aims for immediate and capsulized coverage of many different stories.
      - Assignment editor decides who will cover stories and how much time is allowed for coverage.
      - Background research usually occurs by telephone.
      - Unless a major event is being covered, official statements, inter-views, or on-the-scene reports will be edited to 10 to 30 seconds of air time. The central idea must be communicated in first 10 seconds.
      - Television needs alternative times and locations for interviews, if possible, to maintain hectic schedules.
      - Radio and television reporters also need brief statements or re-leases, fact sheets, names of officials or experts available for

Exhibit 7.1. Newsgathering and Reporting Styles and Requirements, Cont'd.

questions and will sometimes ask for leads to acquire background information and verify other information.

c. *Beat Reporting*

- Involves coverage of issues and events within a given environment or subject area (e.g., legislature, consumer issues).
- Objectives are to develop in-depth knowledge of topic, sources that will provide continuing leads, or new angles, and perspectives that will place current or narrow issues within a broader context.
- Editor allows more freedom to develop stories, but will reassign reporter or impose limits if material fails to draw interest or fit in with editorial objectives.
- Beat reporters obtain information through daily observations, meetings, conversations, review of official notices and publications, and briefings.
- Beat reporter needs background materials, professional and interest group publications, official agency or company documents, access to officials and experts for briefings and in-depth interviews, leads for verification, background, or contrasting views.

d. *Investigative Reporting*

- Investigative reporters conduct in-depth research into a problem or situation, usually with intent that highly visible coverage will result in official action to remedy the situation.
- Editors either assign a team to pursue the investigation or reporters develop a proposal, based on preliminary research, which must be approved by the editorial board, editor, or news manager.
- Investigation of records and leads often proceeds for several weeks before a story appears. Key interviews are scheduled only after the foundation of the probe is well established so these interviews can obtain official reaction to the evidence developed thus far.
- Investigation usually involves more than one reporter so that different leads and findings can be compared and evaluated.
- Investigative reporting requires knowledge of official records and communication systems, use of records, and freedom of information laws to obtain public records to build documentation and protect sources, and investigating and interviewing skills.

e. *Feature Writing*

- Takes a human interest approach to an issue, problem, topic, personality, or event.
- The reporter usually has considerable latitude in developing the story and is allowed more time than for covering hard news.

Exhibit 7.1. Newsgathering and Reporting Styles and Requirements, Cont'd.

- Information is gathered through personal observation, interviews, and background research.
- The feature writer needs background materials, opportunities for observing the featured person(s), photographs, and time for more relaxed interviews.

f. *Editorial Writing*

- Editorial writing is based on stories carried in news sections or regular newscasts or on information presented at editorial board meetings. It is important for managers to correct factual errors in news stories before editorials are written.

Source: "Newsgathering and Reporting Styles and Requirements." Copyright 1983, Barbara Wallace. Reprinted by permission.

Agency executives or authorized public information specialists should usually be the people to answer policy and personnel questions. Technical and professional staff should respond to inquiries in their areas of expertise. The following policies prevail in many government agencies.

1. Except during emergencies when special procedures are in effect, professional and technical staff need not clear every contact with the media or seek advance approval of statements. They should proceed to answer questions related to their own work and expertise.

2. All staff members should be extremely careful to give completely accurate information, and they should exercise discretion. This is essential because a comment made public in the media usually cannot be withdrawn if it proves to be inaccurate or indiscreet.

3. Staff members should not answer questions on agency policy unless they have been given policy statements and clarification, and staff members should never discuss personnel issues or confidential data. Likewise, plans or recommendations that have not yet been acted upon should be withheld unless cleared in advance by management.

4. Agencies should establish a reporting system to alert top managers about who is talking to the media and what is being said. (This is not a "gag rule" because it imposes no advance permission to speak with a reporter. It is simply an information system that informs administrators about the types of information going out of

the organization.) Top administrators especially need to know about in-depth questions since these may indicate that a reporter is preparing a major story about the organization.

Another decision involves what information should be provided. Facts or statements readily available in published form should be provided without hesitation. Consistent with research reported earlier about inoculating against opposing views, it also pays to provide reporters with adverse information if they can easily obtain it from other sources. Public administrators damage their relationship with reporters if they plead ignorance about information reporters know they have. Lying is professionally unacceptable and tactically foolish.

It also pays to know and respect the conventions and norms of journalism. Public managers should establish the ground rules for an interview or for the disclosure of sensitive information before answering questions or offering observations. Sometimes it is helpful to invoke special conventions. For example, a reporter may be making wrong assumptions about a situation, or an organization may need to give reporters confidential information to protect innocent employees from unfavorable publicity. In such cases, editors and reporters may be willing to protect sources and information in order to obtain valuable background data or to confirm the observations of unofficial sources. The two major protective conventions are "off the record" and "deep background."

If a reporter agrees *before* the interview that the information will be *off the record*, that reporter may not publish or broadcast that information in any form, even if its origin is kept secret. It is considered a breach of journalistic ethics to publish or broadcast information given off the record. The reporter is free to verify it, however, through other, independent sources. Journalists also consider it bad faith on the part of government or business officials to invoke the off-the-record convention to force reporters into silence, perhaps later giving the story to another reporter. Many journalists, for this reason, never agree to off-the-record interviews. They believe such conditions undermine news accuracy and accountability. Therefore, public administrators should always use this convention sparingly and carefully.

If public administrators ask a reporter to treat information as *deep background,* the reporter can publish or broadcast it but cannot quote or attribute it to a specific source. It is as if the reporter arrived at the information independently. Deep background has the same effect as "not for attribution."

Even invoking these journalistic conventions sometimes gives insufficient protection. President John Kennedy's practice was "to say comparatively little to a newsman in confidence, even 'off the record,' that he could not afford to have published" (Sorensen, 1965, p. 314). Savvy government, business, and nonprofit managers observe comparable caution. This is not to say that being effective with the press primarily involves shrewdness in "how to play the game." Knowing the game is important, but as with marketing discussed above, public administrators must have a good product to sell to be effective in the long run. Reporters, editors, and their audiences can usually distinguish hype from results. One key to good media relations, then, is to achieve sound management and agency performance. Another key is to be honest. Public administrators and agencies with a reputation for competence and for leveling with the press and public are less likely to be impaled by the press for the occasional snafu or crisis that will surely come.

News media also serve as holders of information that governments need. Officials actively scan media coverage to learn citizen reaction to government services, to assess the consequences of government actions, and to learn what important publics (and other governments) are doing. For years federal bureaucrats have read the *Washington Post* each morning to learn what is happening in their agency and others. Government leaders worldwide watch Cable News Network (CNN) to keep track of news developments such as the abortive coup d'état in the Soviet Union of August of 1991. This feedback to governments occurs through normal media coverage. Increasingly, however, media organizations themselves are fielding complaints from citizens and pursuing remedies from the government agencies involved. In the news media, citizen advocates, ombudsmen, and others with similar titles and roles can be sources of information to government agencies. Others outside the media also can serve as intercessors.

Communication Through Intercessors. Legislators, citizen advocates, and interest group representatives serve as conduits for communicating with government's publics. Strategy factors, as discussed in Chapter Three, may indicate that communicating via these intercessors would be more effective than direct communication in some circumstances. Public administrators should consider involving intercessor *immediate* audiences to help reach *primary* audiences under the following conditions: (1) when the credibility of the intercessor is higher than that of the agency with the target audience, making communication more convincing than if it came directly from the agency; (2) when it is necessary or desirable for managerial or political reasons (leaving powerful legislators or lobbyists out of the communications loop often triggers retaliation); and (3) when it serves the agency's and public's purpose to broaden the policy arena, bringing additional actors and insights into play. Intercessors can also provide citizen feedback about government performance.

Gaining Publics' Insights on Government Service and Performance

Merely waiting for citizen feedback about government performance is not enough. To get a real picture of how citizens feel, administrators can actively encourage contact, put themselves in their clients' shoes, and make better use of surveys and opinion polls.

Promote Contact Between Agency Employees and Citizens. Officials should promote direct, continuous contact between citizens and their public servants. In business, Du Pont CEO Edgar Woolard has instituted an Adopt-a-Customer program at a number of his plants. This program "encourages blue-collar workers to visit a customer once a month, learn his needs, and be his representative on the factory floor. As quality or delivery problems arise, the worker is more likely to see them from the customer's point of view and help make a decision that will keep his 'adopted child' happy" (Dumaine, 1990, p. 128). Adopt-a-citizen programs obviously could help an agency get a better sense of what its clients need and want.

Experience the Client's Perspective. Another way to elicit citizen reaction is for public administrators and officials to gain a sense of the citizen's situation: ride public transit, stand in line for college registration, call the posted number for agency information, read some replies to clients. Acting as a client provides valuable insights. While in line or on the bus, administrators can also observe verbal and nonverbal reactions of other "customers" and informally talk with them about their assessment. Many government agencies have adopted the practice of some hotel and restaurant chains by sending inspectors or auditors in the role of customers to experience agency treatment firsthand.

Utilize Surveys and Opinion Polls. Surveys and opinion polls are a useful and underutilized source of information from agency clients and citizens (Kaufman and Couzens, 1973). In a useful handbook—*Obtaining Citizen Feedback: The Application of Citizen Surveys to Local Government*—Webb and Hatry (1973, pp. 16–17) demonstrate that surveys can provide the following:

> 1. Citizen perceptions of the effectiveness of public services, including the identification of problems and gaps in services. 2. Factual data such as the numbers and characteristics of users and nonusers of community services. 3. Reasons for dislikes, or for nonuse of services. 4. Pretests of citizen demand for new services. 5. Perspective of community opinion on a wide variety of issues. 6. Data on citizen awareness of local government programs and the avenues or media by which citizens become informed. 7. A form of citizen participation that can be expected to be representative of citizen viewpoints in the community. (Surveys also might be used to help reduce a sense of isolation or alienation from government.)

These broad uses also apply to regional, state, and federal governments as well. According to Webb and Hatry (1973), effective surveys usually involve the following steps.

1. Decide on topics to be covered, desired degree of accuracy,

and allowable cost. Once an agency has determined that a survey will fulfill one or more of the above uses, it needs to identify relevant topics. Surveys can focus narrowly on a single service, program, or policy issue or can measure attitudes or information on a range of topics. Some governments, such as those of Los Angeles County and Dayton, Ohio, regularly survey citizens on a broad spectrum of topics to keep abreast of public opinion. The desired degree of accuracy depends on information usage. Data used to shape policy, for example, need to be more accurate than data assembled to get a broad gauge of citizen reaction. Cost will also depend on accuracy required, sample size, and the type of survey taken.

2. Determine the type of survey. Major forms of survey include face-to-face, telephone, and self-administered (mailed or returned by those being surveyed). Face-to-face surveys typically achieve greater accuracy but also cost more than telephone surveys. Self-administered surveys typically cost the least but have the poorest response rate. Combining survey types can help overcome some of these limitations. Nonresponders from a self-administered survey can be telephoned to improve the response rate. A small sample of face-to-face interviews can be used to verify the accuracy of telephone interviews.

3. Plan the survey. Survey planning primarily involves deciding on sample size and method for selecting the sample, devising questions, recruiting and training interviewers, and getting necessary clearances for conducting the survey. It also pays to develop a coding scheme at this stage rather than wait until survey data have been collected only to find that they are uncodable or unusable. Sampling and survey construction require technical knowledge. Unless public administrators possess such knowledge, they should consult staff specialists, public opinion consultants, or specialized sources. DeMaio (1983) emphasizes survey techniques for federal application. Webb and Hatry (1973) target local government but their guidelines also apply to other levels. Isaac and Michael (1981) target public education, but their suggestions have broader relevance as well. Converse and Presser (1986) provide a useful general manual.

4. Pretest survey questions and procedures. Where time,

money, and political feasibility allow, pretesting with a smaller sample comparable to the actual sample usually pays. Pretesting can detect biased or confusing questions, faulty interview procedures, problems with coding data, or errors in choosing the appropriate target audience. When pretesting, it makes sense to control as many variables as possible. Letting inexperienced interviewers test untried questions, for example, may leave doubt about the source of pretest bias. Public administrators should allow enough time for incorporating necessary changes into the final survey.

5. Conduct the actual survey. The actual survey can be taken by government employees, university researchers and students, outside public opinion consultants, volunteers, or a combination of these. The kind of help needed depends on survey difficulty, sensitivity, and necessary accuracy. Outside consultants often give the image of greater objectivity and accuracy. Solid firms do provide these qualities, but at considerable expense. Some fly-by-night consultants in this mushrooming field supply only the expense. University researchers, supplemented by trained student interviewers, can provide accuracy and outside objectivity at less expense. Sometimes university researchers and students can be persuaded to undertake a survey as an unpaid public service that has educational value. Most state universities and many private schools have research bureaus, political polling centers, or academic departments of public administration, political science, or communications that are equipped to conduct government survey research. With training as interviewers, government employees can usually do a proficient job of surveying. Care must be exercised, however, that survey results are not called into question because government personnel are directly involved in sampling, question design, or interviewing. In times of fiscal constraint, many governments have turned to volunteer interviewers including members of the League of Women Voters, high school students, borrowed business employees, and others (Webb and Hatry, 1973). Generally, volunteers are more appropriate for occasional low-impact surveys than for regular or sensitive ones.

6. Review and analyze the data and interpret the findings. It pays for agencies to review data from the pretest and survey to see that they fall within sensible limits and are not artifacts of question or interviewer bias. Anomalies deserve closer scrutiny. When inter-

preting findings, outside personnel should be encouraged to consult with agency administrators and specialists unless a totally independent survey is critical to credibility. Outsiders, even professional consultants or academicians, often lack detailed familiarity with the issues covered, the nature of the target audience, and the specific context surrounding a survey. This lack of familiarity can lead to misinterpretations that insiders would likely catch. Likewise, in interpreting findings it helps to have different perspectives from outsiders not caught up in agency affairs.

7. Incorporate the findings into decision making. Survey results can indicate the need for changes in service delivery, structural reorganization, or even a change in how governments relate to their publics. A well-conducted, credible survey provides ammunition for legislative or administrative decisions. Its value does not stop there, however. It can redirect government thinking in the longer term in some cases. Whenever possible, public administrators should let citizens surveyed, those involved in conducting the survey, and the general public know how citizen opinion has been genuinely incorporated into actions. This reinforces citizens' understanding that their attitudes and opinions are taken seriously by the governments that serve them. Such credibility building makes additional surveying and relations with citizens all the more effective. More fully understanding what citizens need is a crucial step in responding to their requests.

Responding to Citizen Requests

Citizen requests for information or action reach governments daily through letters, petitions, phone calls, meetings, press releases, news programs, editorials, and other media. Important to success in handling such requests is the perceived capability of those receiving the requests and the degree to which citizens, both the requesters and the general public, are informed about follow-up results. If citizens doubt that those taking the requests can help them or have influence with those who can, citizens are less likely to request information or action. Likewise, without follow-up on results, government efforts to handle citizen requests via information center, public advocate, complaint hot line, citizen response unit, or some other mechanism lose credibility. Keep the following guidelines in mind when responding to requests.

First, identify as accurately as possible what is being requested. This may involve reading a request letter twice, marking up a letter to highlight the request, asking a caller to summarize what he or she wants done, or occasionally making a follow-up call to seek clarification. Such effort is often worthwhile, however, in reducing citizen frustration over replies that respond to the wrong request or to only part of the actual request.

Second, maintain an appropriate tone when responding. In general, use the positive, polite, sincere, responsive tone you would want if you were the receiver. An aggressive or condescending tone may put off citizens, violating the spirit of public service. Occasionally, the situation will require a different tone if the request is illegal or offensive. It may still be necessary in such cases to be civil, even if not warm and supportive.

Third, provide specific information in your reply. As a rule, public administrators should give specific information unless that is prohibited or tactically unwise. Specifics typically help citizens far more than do generalities. This often means supplying names, dates, addresses, even technical information. When feasible, instead of referring to a particular regulation or document, agencies should supply it. This eliminates citizen frustration over having to make another request for the document mentioned.

Fourth, be sure that the language of the reply reflects reasonable assumptions about the citizen's knowledge, vocabulary, and interest. Jargon-filled replies will confuse and frustrate most citizens, as will replies that are unnecessarily technical and complicated. Such replies are typical of inexperienced or insecure public servants. It is generally sound practice to assume citizens are intelligent but lack specialized knowledge or vocabulary related to the subject.

Fifth, comply with the request or provide a tangible avenue for action. Citizens deserve responsiveness from their government. If it is legally, economically, and administratively feasible to comply with a citizen's request, administrators should do so. If they cannot comply, they owe citizens a clear explanation of why their request cannot be met. Such explanations should address real reasons rather than solely resort to the cop-out "Your request is denied under regulation 30-12." If compliance is not feasible, follow the explanation with a tangible avenue for action. This helps citizens and gives cause for optimism. The avenue for action may involve telling citizens who can help them, when they should reapply, how their application may be corrected, or what alternative courses of action would accomplish their aims.

Finally, whenever feasible, administrators should follow up to find out whether the citizen found the reply helpful. Some agencies handle replies that are so numerous and so routine that follow-up is impractical and unnecessary. Often, however, administrators can follow up with a call, a letter, or even a personal visit to see whether the citizen is satisfied or further action is required. Such follow-up becomes particularly important when the citizen request involves severe consequences (leaking toxic waste, for example), when many citizens are affected or potentially affected, or when requests were previously mishandled. (A sense of fairness would indicate extra attention to requests that have been ignored or mishandled previously, whether by the administrator's agency or another.)

This chapter has covered the essential reasons for communicating with government's publics: to keep citizens informed, to gain citizens' insights and preferences, and to respond to citizen requests. The chapter has advocated an audience segmentation approach and has described media and tactics for receiving information and ideas from citizens as well as communicating to them. Part Three, the concluding section of this book, examines crucial issues in government communication germane to public managers. Chapter Eight focuses on the vital issue of how to communicate during crisis—the time when communicating is most difficult yet most essential.

PART THREE

Crucial Issues in Government Communication

8

Communicating
During Crises

Do not let us speak of darker days; let us speak rather
of sterner days.
>   —*Winston Churchill, address at*
>   *Harrow School, Oct. 29, 1941*

History is a vast early warning system.
>   —*Norman Cousins, 1978, p. 13*

Because of government's need to be open and responsible and because of the frequently great complexity of issues addressed, communicating in government is generally more challenging than
communicating in business, as Chapter One explains. Some communications tasks are particularly difficult, however, requiring
even greater care and sensitivity. This chapter deals with perhaps
the most difficult communication task—communicating during
crisis. While crises are unlikely to occur often, managing during
crisis situations profoundly affects agency morale and performance.
Some topics addressed here, such as delivering bad news and coping
with the grapevine, also apply to noncrisis situations.
  Public and business administration texts typically admonish
readers to avoid crises by planning ahead and staying on top of

things. The adage holds that too many crises indicate poor management. I generally concur with this adage but want to note that some
crises are unavoidable even by the best management. And some
highly effective managers have even been known to precipitate crisis
so that they can exert leadership, strengthen authority, and enhance
their reputation as leaders. This last strategy obviously entails high
risks and is inappropriate for most management situations. Public
admininistrators, especially during the turbulent 1990s, will confront enough financial, political, administrative, or other crises,
without having to induce them. Among the types of crises governments periodically face are natural disasters, transportation and industrial accidents, war or military operations, terrorism and
sabotage, major service or performance breakdowns, corruption and
scandal, hostile changes in leadership, major misinformation or
miscommunication, and severe citizen dissatisfaction.

Communicating During Each Stage of Crisis

Sociologist Theodore Caplow (1976, pp. 43–47) has identified seven
key stages to crisis situations. Even though all stages do not always
occur or occur in order, Caplow's stages highlight some of the crucial managerial and communications issues crisis involves. It needs
to be emphasized that appropriate government and private sector
responses to crisis should not be seen in terms of some rational,
lock-step framework. Instead, response needs to be *contingent* on
external factors such as the nature and severity of the crisis and
internal factors such as an organization's technological capacity to
detect and respond (Kouzmin and Jarman, 1989). Communication
during crisis should therefore be contingent upon the situation as
this book advocates throughout.

Stage 1: Recognition of Crisis

Natural disasters, civil disorders, military threats trigger crises that
involve many government and private organizations, communities,
and sometimes entire nations. Government agencies can be hit with
such drastic, unmistakable crises or with less obvious administrative
or political crises. An agency undergoes *organizational crisis* when

unforeseen events or circumstances forcibly change its normal priorities. As Caplow (1976) points out, a fire is not a crisis to a fire department since fires and similar emergencies constitute fire department routine. A fire *is* a crisis for a university, hospital, or public transit system. A fire department experiences crisis when accused of failure to respond—leading to unnecessary loss of life or property—or when found guilty of misusing public funds. Key communication at this stage involves getting news of potential crisis and interpreting that information.

Formal channels and news media typically convey the message about major crises such as natural disasters. An increasing number of public administrators and agencies continuously monitor cable and network television news, wire services, or computer information services, enhancing their ability to learn about crises. Subformal and informal channels are often superior for learning about political and administrative crises, especially those limited to one or a few agencies. A public manager's network of contacts in other agencies, interest groups, party organizations, and the like becomes crucial for learning about potential crises of this type. The pointers covered in Chapter Six for cultivating and maintaining interagency information networks and for boundary spanning apply here. An increasing number of government agencies conduct periodic analyses of their environment to determine which issues might develop into crises. The *crisis audit,* or *crisis scan,* is one form of systematic scanning. Figure 8.1 shows a crisis scan patterned after General Electric Corporation's environmental analysis tool.

This first crisis-recognition or crisis-warning stage is perhaps the most crucial one of crisis management. If warnings are missed entirely or substantially, as was the case in the Bhopal chemical spill, "the acute crisis can strike with such swiftness that so-called crisis management after the fact is, in reality, merely damage control" (Fink, 1986, p. 21). The space shuttle *Challenger* explosion was predicted by a number of experts whose messages were never heeded by top officials. One warning memo even started with the plea "Help!" (Mitroff, 1988).

Once information about a potential crisis is received, public managers need to decide whether a crisis actually exists or will likely occur and whether to mobilize their agency's resources to cope

Figure 8.1. Crisis Scan.

Step 1: Systematically scan issues, developments, trends, and events in key areas, including the following:

- Opinions and attitudes of the general public and of service clients, organizations, and individuals who serve as opinion leaders
- Activities and actions of clientele groups, political parties, interest groups, and the like
- Changes in the economy—markets, currencies, shortages, and so on
- New technologies, theories, or developments of knowledge
- Changes in the physical environment—weather patterns, water levels, atmospheric conditions, biological systems, and so forth
- Legal changes due to legislation, court decisions, agency regulations or rulings, and the like
- Significant actions by other government agencies

Step 2: Evaluate these issues, developments, trends, events in terms of probability factor, impact factor, and timing factor.

Assess the probability factor (probability that the event or trend will produce a crisis) on a scale of 0 percent to 100 percent by consulting expert advice, comparing to previous experience, and so on. Assess the impact factor (consequences or impact if a crisis actually develops) on a scale of 1 (virtually no impact) to 10 (monumental impact). Assessing the impact factor also involves consulting experts and considering what happened in previous situations.

Step 3: Plot the issues, developments, trends, events on a crisis barometer.

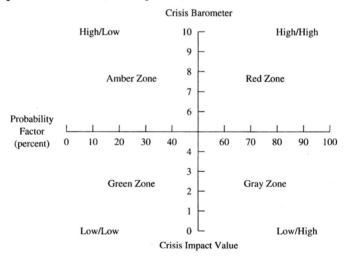

Source: Fink, 1986, p. 45.

Figure 8.1. Crisis Scan, Cont'd.

Step 4: Assess timing factors for those issues, developments, trends, events crucial enough to land in the red zone and for important amber or gray zone entries on the crisis barometer.

Assess timing factors by estimating the time when a crisis is most likely to occur, to peak, and to dissipate. Expected time of arrival, expected period of peak crisis, and expected duration period provide a sense of how much preparation time is available, when to expect the worst, and how long a crisis to prepare for. Depending upon the nature of the crisis, time frames can be estimated in years, months, weeks, days, or hours.

Step 5: Develop government responses to potential crises.

Start planning organizational responses for those issues, developments, trends, events estimated to have high probability and high impact (red zone) and those with low probability but high impact (gray zone). Both indicate potential crisis.

Note: Excerpted by permission of the Publisher from CRISIS MANAGEMENT ©1986 Steven Fink. Published by AMACOM, a division of American Management Association, N.Y. All rights reserved.

with crisis. In making such decisions, it is important to communicate with those members of the organization closest to the scene and those most involved in any efforts to combat the crisis. Bypassing the formal chain of command may be necessary in some situations to get a more direct feel for the *nature, level, scope* and *potential consequences* of a crisis and the *appropriate response* to it. Consulting multiple sources via multiple channels helps prevent misdiagnosing a crisis and misjudging the appropriate level of response. Communication during the crisis-recognition stage should occur quickly, however, since inaction from "paralysis of analysis" often allows a crisis to become more serious. If the possibility of a crisis exists, public managers would be well advised to err on the side of mobilizing to meet that crisis. As Caplow (1976, pp. 44–45) observes: "There is very little danger in wrongly identifying a noncrisis as a crisis; it will give everyone concerned an interlude of pleasurable excitement and probably be remembered as a crisis surmounted. There is always a grave danger of responding too slowly or too feebly to a crisis announcement. By morning the situation may be irretrievable."

Public administrators can often detect political crises by assessing the kind of political attacks on their agency. If an agency's goals and its means of achieving those goals both come under attack, that agency is probably experiencing political crisis (Thompson and Tuden, 1959).

Stage 2: Appearance on the Scene

As soon as the crisis is recognized, it is usually important for the public administrator to get on the scene, even if better facilities exist elsewhere for a command post. A leader's presence often helps calm anxieties and rally the forces coping with the crisis. A leader who sits in his or her office far removed from crisis can be viewed as uncaring, afraid, or indecisive. If such perceptions occur in the minds of subordinates and citizens, the authority and credibility of that leader can be severely damaged. Of course, citizens did not expect President Bush to be present in Saudi Arabia to rally American troops. Secretary of Defense Richard Cheney, Chairman of the Joint Chiefs of Staff Colin Powell, and Operations Commander General H. Norman Schwarzkopf were on the scene at various times to glean intelligence and boost troop morale.

For many other crises, emmissaries are inappropriate communicators in light of the situation. One of the criticisms of former New York governor Nelson Rockefeller was that he never went to the scene of the Attica prison revolt in 1971 when forty-three inmates and guards were killed. He felt strongly about not negotiating under threat and about not legitimizing inmate actions with his presence. Yet fragmentation of effort on the scene and absence of a recognized figure of authority with whom inmates could negotiate contributed to the disaster. Former New York mayor Edward Koch knew the value of being on the scene when subway, bridge, or other crises occurred. If a crisis is more of a political crisis than a disaster or emergency, the leader may deem it appropriate to avoid confronting critics, thereby aggravating the situation. Direct involvement of top officials may escalate the situation, whereas downplaying it may be more appropriate. The leader's presence at the scene of crisis is important in maintaining the motivation of employees on the front line.

Receiving information about the crisis remains a key form of communication during this stage. The need arises, however, to send key messages as well if they have not been sent previously. Crucial messages to be communicated during this stage are that the crisis is judged important enough to deserve the attention of the highest levels, that government cares about what has happened to people because of the crisis, that efforts are under way to cope with crisis, and here is what the public needs to do to minimize damage and help government efforts. Articulating these messages widely and clearly helps minimize damage and improve cooperation with recovery efforts. The Kemeny Commission, while investigating the 1979 nuclear accident at Three Mile Island, found that "the quality of information provided to the public has a significant bearing on the capacity of people to respond to the accident, on their mental health, and on their willingness to accept guidance from responsible officials" (Fink, 1986, p. 93). The nature and severity of a crisis influence decisions about how much information to communicate and to whom. Crises threatening human safety and health obviously require quicker and more widespread communication than do internal agency political crises.

Many of the communication channels discussed in Chapter Seven are appropriate during crisis, especially radio and television announcements and press briefings. Once again, using multiple channels is important in reaching public and private organizations and individuals affected by a crisis. Not only do different channels reach different audiences, but multiple media also provide backups. A killer tornado in 1979 caused principal communication systems to fail in Wichita Falls, Texas. Fortunately, city officials had foreseen the need for backup systems and had practiced using them. Ham radio sets provided needed communication between the command center and mobile units. Trained individuals also visually tracked the tornado and events (Kellar, 1983).

Since distortion-resistant messages are particularly crucial during crisis (see Chapter Five), media best able to convey such messages deserve consideration. The National Oceanic and Atmospheric Administration (NOAA) uses flying laboratories and satellites with multisensor collection systems to gather data on storms and other weather conditions and to transmit those data intact to NOAA headquarters for analysis (Chartrand, 1985). Military and emergency management command centers increasingly utilize computers to receive and transmit information directly in its original form.

Stage 3: Recruiting a Crisis Council

Whether on the scene or directing operations from a remote command post, the leader will need to form a crisis council. Because of crisis, the leader can name virtually anyone to such a council, regardless of rank and affiliation. This ad hoc group usually advises the leader and assists in implementation for the duration of the crisis. A crisis council of about fifty people of varying rank and function advised President John Kennedy during the Cuban missile crisis of 1962.

A recent trend in government and business is to establish permanent crisis management teams. Ronald Reagan, in one of his first official acts as president, formed a crisis management team consisting of the vice president, secretary of state, secretary of defense, national security adviser, and director of the Central Intelligence Agency. This team assessed the Falkland Islands crisis involving Britain and Argentina in 1982 (Littlejohn, 1983). Most crisis councils are temporary, however.

Public administrators should consider at least two factors when recruiting members for a crisis council. Some members of the crisis council should provide knowledge of the specific crisis situation or the subject of the crisis (for example, expertise and experience with oil spills, impeachment procedure, or the psychology of terrorism). Without relevant expertise, any crisis council is handicapped. Other members of the crisis council should be selected to provide immediate and smooth access to resources needed for mobilizing to cope with crisis. If financial analyses are needed to meet legislated spending cuts, having the budget director on the crisis council assures access to financial analysts. In other situations, members of a crisis council can provide direct links to emergency communications, civil defense, medical, police, transportation, or other resources. Some members of the crisis council supply both knowledge and access. In the 1971 Attica prison uprising, the commissioner of corrections supplied both knowledge of prison conditions and access to corrections guards and equipment.

In most governments the chief executive has authority to command the resources of administrative departments. It still makes sense to include the directors of needed departments in the crisis council, however. Including the directors gets the departments more psychologically involved in the crisis than they would be if the directors were summoned only as needed. By being present when decisions are made, directors commit themselves and their agencies to those decisions. Also, having a director integrally involved in crisis deliberations gives his or her department an inside liaison. Directors can communicate directly to their staffs without having messages filtered through intermediaries. Although rapport among members of the crisis council may aid working relations under the strain of crisis, rapport should not be a primary criterion for an individual's inclusion, particularly if rapport is confused with thinking alike. During a crisis, it is particularly important to avoid groupthink and hear different views of what happened and how to resolve the crisis (Janis, 1989; Rosenthal, Charles, and 'T Hart, 1989). Most crisis councils should include public information specialists, especially the person who will give most of the press briefings. Having communication and public opinion expertise helps this person gauge public reaction, important to handling the crisis. Being included in the crisis council also helps the briefer become informed about the crisis and efforts to handle it. If the individual briefing the press is obviously cut off and uninformed, reporters will likely turn elsewhere for information. This risks rumor or misinformation, perhaps handicapping emergency efforts.

Several key communication issues need to be recognized when dealing with crisis councils. Selection of crisis councils on the basis of contribution (knowledge or access) rather than strictly on rank means that lateral communication among peers will produce more cross-transfer of knowledge, more viable ideas, and more honest reactions than will adhering to normal vertical communication. Stratifying crisis councils and maintaining formal, vertical communication often defeats their purpose. In large councils such as that convened during the Cuban missile crisis, smaller inner councils may be needed. Whenever feasible, however, maintaining an egalitarian attitude tends to bring out the best in members, particularly those who might otherwise be reluctant to contribute. Even if members recognize inequality of status, equal right to speak and equal judging of ideas on their merits must be maintained to preserve the integrity, morale, and success of the crisis council.

Another issue involves the problem of compartmentalizing. Including or excluding participation on a crisis council by compartmentalizing on the basis of present role may omit some needed expertise, as occurred during the Bay of Pigs crisis (see Chapter Five). Compartmentalizing can also lead to closed loops, or relying unduly on the same officials and agencies who contributed to the crisis in the first place, as occurred in the Centralia mine disaster (see Chapter Five). If problems are pigeonholed, other people and ideas may not be heard to supplement the ideas already found wanting.

Stage 4: Mobilizing Resources

An early task of the leader and crisis council is to mobilize to meet the crisis. This may involve alerting one agency or hundreds, as occurs with national emergencies. Mobilization has practical and symbolic purposes. It readies people and equipment if action is needed. It also symbolizes the urgency of the situation and the temporary suspension or downgrading of other organizational functions (Caplow, 1976). Communication during this stage revolves around alerting agencies and people of the seriousness of the situation and how their help is needed. It is generally better to alert agencies and people who may never be utilized than to leave out actors who may be needed later. Delayed communication can cause the loss of preparation time, momentum, and motivation.

Stage 5: Implementing a Crisis Plan

Police forces, hospitals, military units, and many other organizations have plans for dealing with natural disaster, civil disorder, military, or other kinds of crisis. Other agencies may be less likely to become involved in major crises like these, but they need to be prepared in case they are needed in such crises and in other, less drastic but still crucial administrative or political crises. These agencies should have a plan for who will do what and how employees will communicate with each other and with the public. Crisis plans should embody the principles outlined below.

Crisis plans should provide for contingencies, including the worst-case scenario. What is the worst that can go wrong in terms of the crisis and efforts to deal with it? Many lives were saved during the tornado in Wichita Falls because emergency plans anticipated the worst and people acted accordingly. Even though crisis plans should account for contingencies, plans should not be hesitant or ambiguous. The agency's resources should be put into implementing the crisis plan. If the situation changes, the agency's weight should be thrown behind the plan that accounts for those new contingencies.

Having some kind of clear but flexible plan is usually better than "moment to moment improvisation" (Caplow, 1976, p. 46). Robert Littlejohn (1983), who has been deputy director of emergency management for New York City, maintains that a crisis plan should contain the following parts: (1) an overview of the crisis situation (events, actors involved, time frames, places); (2) plan objectives (clear and measurable, if possible); (3) assumptions on which the plan is based (assumptions about conditions and reactions that may be beyond control, but need to be taken into account—for example, assumptions about weather conditions or degree of political opposition); (4) trigger mechanisms that state conditions under which the plan will be activated (trigger mechanisms can be set to activate in phased escalation if the crisis worsens or to trigger contingency plans if conditions change); and (5) action steps (detailed plans for implementing the crisis plan, including personnel, assignments, technologies to be used, timetables, target audiences and communication channels, signals, and the like).

Merely having a crisis plan is not enough. The plan must be clearly communicated to those who have to use it and it must be rehearsed periodically. An April 1991 fire at the Maine Yankee nuclear power plant burned dangerously for hours without the governor and officials of the Maine Emergency Management Agency knowing about it. A veteran police dispatcher failed to alert other officials of the seriousness of the accident as required by state emergency procedures. When the officials did learn about the fire, they assumed from the police dispatch that it was minor. No one informed the local police chief and civil defense director either during the crucial stage of the fire. Local news media, who according to the emergency plan were supposed to be notified immediately so that they could alert citizens in the danger zone, only learned of the fire the following morning. Fortunately, the fire was brought under control, but a major disaster could have occurred. The emergency plan specified communication procedures, but public officials failed to follow important steps (Stecklow, 1991).

During the crisis intervention phase, communication is primarily oriented to *task*—giving orders and instructions, monitoring developments. Increasingly, however, government officials managing crises recognize the equal importance, during this stage, of communication oriented to the *emotional health* of crisis victims, their families, and other participants. During the rush hour transit disaster reported in Chapter One, emergency service workers from the Philadelphia Office of Mental Health and Mental Retardation joined hospital physicians and social workers in counseling victims at the scene and en route to the hospitals. During the crisis, a hospital administrator said, "People are going through pangs of massive fear and fantasies of death. They just need someone to talk to, so you just listen." A social worker emphasized how crucial it was in the early stages of trauma to provide a relief valve for stress. "You've got to open lines of communication," she said. "You've got to let people know it's OK to talk about this terrible thing that's happened to them" (Paolantonio, 1990, p. 17A).

Informal or professional counseling is often necessary for trauma victims, their families, and friends, but it may also be necessary for bystanders and others who are shocked by what has occurred or feel guilty that they were spared while others were not. Public school administrators, teachers, and counselors increasingly recognize the importance of helping children who suffer from posttraumatic stress, blocking, or nightmares work through their feelings after a school tragedy such as the April 1991 air crash that killed two children who were playing on their elementary school playground and Senator John Heinz.

Employees often need emotional support and counseling, too. The victims of reductions in force frequently need counseling to help them preserve their self-esteem and allow them to begin a constructive job search. But employees who remain may also need emotional support to assure them that their jobs are secure, they were not responsible for colleagues being dismissed, and they have no reason to feel guilty about what happened.

Immediate communication with crisis victims is obviously crucial. Continued communication with these victims is also important, however; some studies show that as many as 40 percent of crisis victims remain psychologically disturbed sixteen weeks after the crisis (Raphael, 1986).

Stage 6: Announcing the Outcome

After the crisis plan has been implemented and the crisis surmounted or endured, it is important to announce the outcome. Again, this message has both practical and symbolic values. It signals the suspension of the crisis council, the end of crisis intervention, and the demobilization of forces. It also signals the beginning of a return to normalcy. This is important because people cannot psychologically cope with crisis for an indefinite period. A clear signal that the crisis is over, or at least that its acute phase is over, helps people recover sooner emotionally. President Bush signaled a victory for Operation Desert Storm after a quick ground campaign in February 1991 even though the war was not officially over until April. This clear message triggered celebration and relief that the war was essentially over and that troops would be returning (although some not for months).

Some experts believe that winding down a crisis properly is almost as difficult as mobilizing for one. Once danger is past, those managing a crisis may disband the crisis council and return to business as usual without communicating clearly to their employees, volunteers, and citizens what the result of the crisis was and what the aftermath involves. Failure to announce resolution can lead to confusion, which prolongs the chronic phases of crisis or complicates recovery.

Stage 7: Distributing Rewards

Following a crisis, leaders should thank those who served faithfully and also those who stood ready to serve but were not called on. If thanks go only to those who served, morale among those who were prepared to help but didn't get the opportunity may suffer, and as a result, they may be less willing to stand by next time. After a January 1978 snowstorm paralyzed Charleston, West Virginia, the administrator of the largest hospital in the area sent a memo thanking all employees—even those who wanted to get to work but could not—for keeping medical services functioning. With this stroke, the administrator helped make stranded employees feel part of the hospital team that deserved satisfaction in coping with crisis. Since crisis management is predominantly a team effort, rewards— whether praises or raises—should be primarily be team rewards. (See Chapter Five on communicating to motivate.) Some individual rewards may be warranted for those making extraordinary efforts during the crisis.

Communicating during this phase, then, primarily involves using rewards to motivate—to reinforce the performance of those who performed well during the crisis and to encourage others to rise to the occasion next time. These rewards also convey the message that crisis management, not brushfire management, is as much an organizational priority as leaders said it was when mobilization occurred. If employees are mobilized for crisis without being later told what resulted or without being rewarded for extraordinary effort, they are less likely to be motivated to cope with the next crisis.

Stage 8: Learning to Improve Crisis Performance

Another stage, one missing from Caplow's framework, is a crucial learning phase. Of course, learning from successes and mistakes and adjusting accordingly should be occurring during all stages of crisis management. A specific period is needed, however, after the acute phase is over and recovery is well under way, to bring major participants together for a postmortem. By assessing how the crisis developed, what efforts succeeded, and where shortcomings occurred, government and private sector organizations can improve cooperation and effectiveness in meeting future crises. Understandably, the nature and extent of the crisis will determine who participates in the postmortem.

Maintaining Good Rapport
and Working Relations During Crisis

One of the several paradoxes of government communication is that rapport among people is most necessary during crisis, precisely when rapport is most likely to be stretched thin or missing altogether. During crisis, those most affected tend to feel threatened, overworked, and perhaps even isolated or manipulated, depending upon how the crisis is being handled. Certain guidelines exist for helping to maintain solid rapport.

Show employees that management supports them and is willing to share in the sacrifices that crisis usually requires. During a sensitive period of protecting a mob informant, Klaus Rohr, head of the FBI's Organized Crime Squad in Philadelphia, gave up Christmas with his family in order to guard the informant so that his agents could have a needed break. This action communicated to his agents that Rohr was concerned about their welfare and was willing to share in the necessary dirty work. This was one instance of the kind of support that earned Rohr the affection and loyalty of his subordinates, who were all the more willing to do their share during emergencies.

Be especially sensitive to the feelings and behaviors of others during crisis. A crisis situation is likely to affect the feelings and behaviors of victims of a crisis and people trying to resolve it. Tension, frustration, fatigue, worry, and even grief can be expected, especially during severe or long crises. Tempers tend to flare more quickly than usual, and feelings may be hurt more easily. Public administrators can help in such situations by exhibiting at least the impression of calm and by avoiding remarks or actions likely to threaten or antagonize subordinates or colleagues unnecessarily. Of course, public managers will still need to criticize poor performance, which can be even more damaging during a crisis. However, criticism should concentrate on what went wrong and how to correct it rather than on personal attacks. This kind of descriptive feedback (see Chapter Ten) will more likely keep the employee functioning during the crisis than debilitate him. Social amenities are often casualties of crisis. Yet informal social contact is even more necessary during times of crisis to relieve tension and boost morale.

Gathering the "troops" for social contact in the hall, during meals, or after work often helps them survive a crisis.

Public administrators must realize that anxiety over an impending crisis is often more difficult to deal with emotionally than is the actual crisis itself. For example, employees waiting to be dismissed because of government retrenchment often find the uncertainty of not knowing what will happen more debilitating than actually getting notice of dismissal. At least then they know what has happened and can take tangible steps to cope with it.

Utilize the value of humor. Humor has sprung up about wars such as those in Grenada and the Persian Gulf, nuclear disasters such as those at Chernobyl and Three Mile Island, and about other crisis situations. Some of this humor is offensive to certain audiences. We now know, however, that much of this so-called gallows humor is essential to preserving the sanity and spirit of those who suffer most from such crises. Public managers can utilize the benefit of humor in several ways. They can be tolerant about the use of humor by others. Instead of indicating a callous disregard for the severity of a crisis, an employee's humor may well mean that he takes the situation so seriously that he needs to express humor to relieve tension. Of course tolerance of humor, even during crisis, should not extend to tolerating racist jokes or jokes that demean other groups or individuals. This kind of humor sets a tone counterproductive to handling crisis or returning to normalcy.

Managers can also interject humor themselves. The FBI's Klaus Rohr gained a reputation as a funny man by continual joking and kidding with his staff. A sign on his office door showed Uncle Sam warning visitors, "THIS PLACE IS BUGGED." His homespun mixed metaphors and malapropisms became known as Klausisms to his agents. "When an agent isn't performing up to Rohr's standards, for example, Rohr might warn the agent to stop 'skating on thin water.' Such remarks were especially soothing to the agents when times were tough—such as when [Nicodemo] Scarfo and other mobsters were acquitted of murder charges in late 1987. And when they were acquitted of murder charges the following spring. 'A lesser man would have maybe caved in under that kind of pressure,' [Agent Mike] Leyden said of Rohr. 'We were all under tremendous pressure after those two losses. He hung in there [and helped us hang in there]' " (Lounsberry, 1991, p. 4B). This example shows that humor can even be used constructively to prod subordinates. Sarcasm, however, is almost always risky because it is likely to be interpreted adversely. Humor, so important to effective morale under normal circumstances, is even more necessary during crisis to add levity and a sense of proportion. Humor counteracts the tendency for people to take the crisis and themselves too seriously.

Coping with the Grapevine

Grapevines and rumors require the attention of public administrators during organizational normalcy, but they are especially important during a crisis. Rumors fly among employees and members of the public in the absence of information about how bad the crisis is and how they will be affected. Internal agency grapevines and their counterparts in other organizations tend to be especially prolific during a crisis or an impending crisis be it a proposed layoff, transition in leadership, teachers' strike, or something else.

Grapevines can convey *personal* communication—unofficial messages transmitted by persons outside their capacity as officeholders—and *subformal* communication—unofficial messages that flow through formal or informal channels. In either case, grapevine messages tend to spread more quickly than others because attempts at verification are typically minimal or nonexistent. Grapevines exist because people have a psychological need to talk about their work and related issues that affect them. Although grapevines and rumors usually have negative connotations in management circles, grapevines can be useful sources of intelligence. Moreover, because grapevines convey subformal and personal messages, grapevines in healthy agencies can often be faster and more accurate than official channels. Receiving or sending communication via grapevine depends on the health of the agency, level of distortion, type of rumor, level of information, and other variables. Understanding these variables and the characteristics of grapevines, rumors, and rumor spreaders increases a public manager's ability to respond appropriately.

Different Types of Rumors Require Different Responses

As many as seventy-five different types of rumors have been identified. Some types important to managers are discussed here (Esposito and Rosnow, 1983). *Pipe-dream rumors* involve wishful
thinking, anticipating a bigger raise or greater authority, for example. *Wedge-driver rumors* divide loyalties by accentuating differences among individuals, groups, or organizations. *Bogies* are rumors expressing fear of present or anticipated situations or events.
Of these three main types, bogies and wedge-driver rumors are potentially the more damaging to public agencies and deserve quicker
and more energetic responses. Concerns by employees about rumors
of a crisis situation deserve immediate and continuous attention.
Even if employees first hear about the crisis from the news media
or other source, agency officials need to brief employees as soon as
possible about the crisis and keep them informed on a regular basis.
There is little more demoralizing than to find out about matters
affecting one's agency and job from outside sources. Keeping employees informed also lessens the need to rely on grapevines for
information. Pipe dreams when burst may disappoint those spread-
ing or relying upon rumors, but they are easier to get over—unless
a succession of disappointments occurs.

    Subcategories of rumors include those typed as self-fulfilling,
premeditated, and spontaneous. *Self-fulfilling rumors* can change
perceptions, causing a new perception to occur. Rumors of bank or
savings and loan instability or of the power of a government official
tend to be self-fulfilling. Whether a public manager squelches or
expedites a self-fulfilling rumor depends on whether he or she
agrees with the new perception being spread. *Premeditated rumors*
are those circulated deliberately to gain personal or organizational
advantage. Trial balloons floated to news organizations and other
officials for reaction can be useful tests of policy. Leaks are another
form of premeditated rumor. (Refer to the discussion of secrecy in
Chapter Six.) Of course, what is a trial balloon to one administrator
may be considered a leak by another. Premeditated rumors are often
difficult to prove unless the instigator is traced. If tracing is impossible, the rumor may be countered with contrary information. *Spontaneous rumors* occur when people attempt to explain events they

do not understand (Esposito and Rosnow, 1983). For this reason spontaneous rumors often distort reality and need to be countered with reliable information, as indicated below.

Rumors and Rumor Spreaders Tend to Follow Patterns

Research by Gordon Allport and others (Allport and Postman, 1947; Caplow, 1976) shows that most of the distortion in a message occurs near the beginning of the grapevine chain (Caplow, 1960). Distortions take two forms: exaggeration and the invention of new elements. Exaggeration can turn "some personnel cuts" into "massive cuts" into "a bloodbath." Distortion also occurs because people invent new elements to fill logic gaps created by previous distortions (Caplow, 1976). A rumor spreader might supply what to him is a missing link: "Reorganization must be accompanying massive employee cuts to justify that many layoffs." Toward the chain's end the message has usually become so condensed and simplified that few distortions occur. Identifying exaggerations and inventions and correcting them quickly are ways of dealing with spontaneous rumors, for example.

Research also shows that only a small minority starts or spreads rumors. One study of state government agencies over a three-month period traced rumor flow through a grapevine of 169 managers. Nine percent of the managers were found to be "liaisons" (passed on the rumor), 69 percent were "dead-enders" (received the rumor but did not transmit it), and 22 percent functioned as "isolates" (neither got nor passed along rumors) (Esposito and Rosnow, 1983, p. 45). Other research found about 10 percent of rumor spreaders (liaisons) in the grapevine.

The small minority of people who spread rumors tend to possess certain characteristics. They tend to lack self-esteem and attempt to gain esteem and popularity by contributing sensational news. Rumor spreaders also tend to feel a great deal of anxiety and uncertainty about a situation and use rumors as outlets to relieve stress and uncertainty. The kinds of stratagems discussed in Chapter Six for building emotional support among colleagues and for empowering them as communicators apply in this situation. Building esteem and providing people with constructive messages to share

are two ways of reducing rumors. Reducing anxiety and uncertainty by keeping people informed is another.

Grapevines Generally Follow the Law of Supply and Demand

According to Caplow (1976, p. 77), "A grapevine is capable of transmitting a variety of messages on a variety of topics. What it actually transmits during a given period seems to depend on the supply of and demand for particular kinds of information. The grapevine is most active when information is scarce and the demand for it is high; it is least active when the information is plentiful and the demand for it is low."

If little official information exists about an impending retrenchment, reorganization, change in leadership, or other crisis, the grapevine will likely be active since demand for information on issues that affect employees is high. As more official information gets disseminated, grapevine demand is met and activity tends to lessen. One fairly dependable tactic for reducing counterproductive grapevine activity is *saturation*—supplying the grapevine with more information than it wants on the topics it demands. If it would be harmful to release the information expressly demanded, saturation with information on related topics can be effective in satiating grapevine demand. Grapevine demand for the names of the specific employees to be laid off can be at least partially satisfied with information about the criteria for layoffs, bumping procedure, timetables, and so forth. This provides tangible, useful knowledge to employees and may serve to alleviate some anxiety without prematurely constraining administrative discretion.

Accuracy of Rumors Varies by Organizational Climate and Cohesiveness

Research and practice generally show that grapevine distortions are higher in organizations with pathologies including nonsupportive organizational climate, confusion or conflict over mission, poor coordination, low morale, and mistrust between leaders and followers. A synthesis of research on cohesive, integrated organizations finds that healthy organizations have healthy grapevines. "Field studies of rumors in armies, political parties, factories, hospitals, and prisons, for example, have found that most of the rumors that circulate in well-integrated organizations carry substantially accurate information, flow through fairly reliable channels, and are subject to the cross-checks that discourage distortions. In a well-integrated organization [the grapevine] is remarkably quick and reliable" (Caplow, 1976, p. 77).

The best defense, then, against rumor distortion is having a healthy system of coordination and communication and sound morale in the first place. In fact, it works both ways. Effective grapevines help agencies identify problems sooner and serve as a check and backup system to formal channels.

Additional Guidelines for Coping with Rumors and Grapevines

Other pointers or guidelines also deserve emphasis. (1) Keeping vertical, lateral, and external channels supplied with constructive task and emotional support messages leaves less demand and room for counterproductive messages. Keeping employees, clients, and citizens informed reduces their need to manufacture information. (2) Informing employees or members of the public about the potential consequences of rumor in crisis or other situations can help prevent rumor or stop the spread of unverified mesages. (3) If distortions occur, the grapevine can be used to trace the reasons behind rumor. Asking members of the grapevine what their concerns are can help identify the type of rumor being spread and why the exaggerations and inventions got started. This gives one an advantage in setting the record straight. (4) Some agencies and companies have used a rumor line effectively. A hot line staffed by people from the public information or communications unit provides callers quick verification or correction about rumors (Esposito and Rosnow, 1983). People staffing the rumor line need to be kept informed about crisis or other developments about which rumors could start. (5) If distortion occurs, the nature and source of the distortion should be identified and corrected quickly since misperceptions take hold and are harder to overcome as time passes. No response may be interpreted as admitting the rumor is true. A late response often appears to be trumped up after the fact. (6) The communication or public information unit can informally contact employees, agency clients, or members of the public to learn a rumor's source and extent of circulation. If a rumor can be traced to a limited network, public administrators can visit or call those involved to correct the distortion. If a rumor is found to be widely circulated, more general responses such as direct television or radio announcements or press releases and briefings are indicated. (7) Public administrators may periodically want to start a premeditated but harmless or—better yet—constructive rumor to test the health of the agency grapevine.

Delivering Bad News

Most public administrators dislike bearing bad news. Responsible administrators realize, however, that this is often part of their job. Factors in the receiver and factors in the management situation become particularly important during times of crisis or personal rejection or in other situations where bad news is conveyed.

Assess the Audience and Probable Reaction

Audience analysis is more important when one is delivering bad news. Favorable news delivered poorly will still be well received. Bad news conveyed sensitively and artfully still may be difficult to accept. If conveyed poorly, bad news can be disastrous. A cardinal principle in relating negative news is for administrators to communicate such news the way they would want to get it themselves, with respect and sensitivity.

From the audience profile, it helps to determine, if possible, the likely impact of the message on the audience. A minor reprimand may be shrugged off by an employee with a good performance record yet be devastating to one with a flawed record, who might fear that the reprimand will lead to discharge. In the former instance, the task is first to reinforce the valued employee's overall performance, then get her to see how improving one aspect can improve her overall contribution. Because the employee in the second situation is more likely to feel threatened by the reprimand, an administrator should probably spend more time analyzing and discussing the circumstances behind the faulty performance, getting the employee's explanation, and reviewing what constitutes sound performance. Likewise, announcements of imminent layoffs will be more devastating to employees with little prospect of other employment than to free exiters, employees who can easily find other positions when times get tough. Knowing the probable impact of bad news on the receiver enables public administrators to gauge more carefully the degree of effort and amount of tact required to convey that news, the appropriate sender, and medium.

Choose Appropriate Senders and Media

The sender most appropriate to convey bad news depends primarily on the type of bad news (the message's objectives), the audience, and the management situation. For bad news that is relatively impersonal—grant or job rejections, denial of requested information, for example—the appropriate sender is usually the administrator with official authority for that activity, such as the grant program officer or personnel director. The audience matters less in such routine instances, although certain audiences and objectives may warrant particular senders. For instance, the job rejection of a particularly qualified candidate whom an agency might want to hire later may warrant a personal call or letter from the program manager. This occasion could be used to offer optimism to the candidate and encourage him to apply for other positions or for the same position at a later date. If the bad news is personal and nonroutine, the most appropriate sender is usually the person who has the most credibility and rapport with the receiver. An employee may accept rejection for promotion better from a trusted supervisor than from an unknown manager. On the other hand, if hearing bad news from the supervisor will likely jaundice their working relationship, the news should come from someone else.

The appropriate medium likewise depends on strategic factors. In many situations, laws or administrative policies require that certain kinds of bad news be delivered in writing—notification of dismissal, rejection of grant application, notice of contract suspension, for example. Even in these instances a personal call or visit may lessen the blow and facilitate a continuing relationship. In other situations public administrators have greater flexibility in their choice of medium or media. Highly personal messages usually require face-to-face communication or a telephone call. Officers specially trained in counseling and public relations were sent to break the news to those who lost family members in the Persian Gulf War. If the families heard the news through other channels first, personal support was still provided. A message this sensitive and personal might appear callous if only conveyed by telegram or letter.

Consider an Appropriate Location for the Message

Some bad news is best related in neutral, nonthreatening surroundings. Critical performance appraisal interviews should therefore usually be conducted somewhere other than the boss's office. Other bad news is more appropriately given in surroundings that provide privacy and emotional support. Hearing about the death of a family member is never pleasant, but I would rather hear about it in the privacy of my home with all of its familiar emotional supports than in some cold or neutral place. I learned about my mother's death while working in a state office, hardly a conducive place to experience grief.

Sequence the Message Carefully

Message sequence (as discussed in Chapter Four) depends upon the purpose and nature of the bad news, the audience, and the situation. For job, grant, or other types of rejections, the primary purpose is usually to inform the receivers that their requests have been denied. Other important purposes should be to maintain the receivers' goodwill and to offer help where possible.

Such rejections when made in writing are usually conveyed effectively if they follow the reasons-first pattern. This pattern starts with a brief introduction describing the *context* and *subject* of the message but avoids prematurely signaling rejection. The introduction should also work to establish *rapport* or some positive tone by mentioning the merit of the receiver's qualifications, request, and so forth. In most cases it works better to precede the actual denial statement with tangible *reasons* why the request is denied. If the reasons sound convincing, the receiver in most cases will infer the rejection and may even agree with the decision. To be convincing, the reasons must be understandable and plausible to the receiver. Citing code or regulations without specifying substance is rarely persuasive. "Your request has been denied under Article 2, Section 6" makes little sense to most readers. The actual *notification of rejection* should follow immediately. While diplomacy is desirable in conveying bad news, the actual notification statement should be unambiguous or the reader will be left wondering whether the request is denied or accepted. It is then typically sound practice to end by offering *alternative action steps* (for example, "apply again next fiscal year," "contact the following agency that handles these requests"). The ending should at least convey some grounds for optimism. "Your idea has merit, and I wish you success in finding grant support." Of course, if the writer is convinced that the idea lacks merit, it would be unprofessional to give false optimism. Others might find merit in it however. Using this pattern as a formula for mechanically manipulating people into thinking that they have been treated respectfully when they have been dealt with routinely would be an abuse of communication skills as discussed in Chapter Nine.

This pattern also makes sense for rejections conveyed orally. It should be used flexibly, however, rather than mechanically. The sequence may need to change according to objectives, audience, and situation.

For other kinds of bad news different sequences make sense. Conveying news of death or accident only after giving extensive reasons for its occurrence would likely prolong the receiver's uncertainty and anxiety. In such situations, telling what has happened first and going into details later may actually be more humane. Here again, the sender should observe cues from the receiver and the situation in deciding how to sequence the message.

This chapter has stressed the importance of communication during crisis, raising key issues for attention and providing guide-

lines for communicating during the stages of crisis. It has also examined ways to cope with grapevines and with delivering bad news,
essential tasks at any time. Many of the issues raised in crisis communication involve ethical concerns of the kind addressed in the
next chapter.

9

Communicating Ethically in Government: Issues and Guidelines

Evil communications corrupt good character.

—*I Corinthians 15:33*

Political language . . . is designed to make lies sound truthful and murder respectable, and to give an appearance of solidity to the wind. One cannot change all this in a moment; but one can at least change one's habits.

—*George Orwell, 1954, pp. 162–177*

That government communication and ethics are intertwined has long been known. Paul Appleby (1952), a guiding force in public administration, included communication skills as part of the prescription for a moral public administrator. The codes of ethics for both the American Society for Public Administration and the International City Management Association address communication issues. Violations of law or professional ethical standards usually involve communicating—falsifying government documents, testifying falsely in a judicial or administrative proceeding, or misusing government information for private gain. On the other side of the coin, communicating in government often touches on ethical issues. Are governments fulfilling their obligation to keep citizens informed? Do agency communication practices favor some audiences over others? Are superiors or subordinates being placed in administrative or legal jeopardy because information they need is kept from them? Despite the long-standing relationship between government ethics and communication, little direct attention has been given to this subject. This chapter attempts to partially remedy this omission by introducing and operationalizing the concept of *truth in communicating,* showing how this concept can be applied when communicating with government's key audiences, and using whistle-blowing as an example of communicating strategically and ethically.

What Is "Truth in Communicating"?

Truth in advertising has traditionally meant supplying accurate information about products. Yet technically accurate advertising falls short if it lacks useful information about the product or avoids responding to consumers' concerns. Correspondingly, I propose we pay attention to the concept of *truth in communicating.* Truth in communicating involves accuracy in communicating, avoiding falsehood or misrepresentation whether by including false information, deliberately excluding vital information, or deliberately allowing people to misinterpret a message. To have the most value, however, truth in communicating needs to include *usefulness, openness,* and *fairness* as well as *accuracy.*

Consider a common scenario. A state highway department wants to change the right-of-way for a secondary road. The department is communicating accurately if its notice of a public hearing appears in the required sources and contains correct information about the date, content, and time of the hearing. Such communication lacks usefulness and fairness, however, if the notice never appears in places where many citizens involved can use it or if it appears only in places where professional lobbyists are likely to respond. Likewise, the highway engineer who is sent to the hearing to explain department plans may provide accurate information, but information so technical that few can understand it. Such communication is hardly useful to citizens or responsive to their concerns about how the planned change will affect them. Such communication also hinders openness. One highway engineer confided to me that a way he used to reduce controversy (and his discomfort) at such public meetings was to bombard participants with so much technical and bureaucratic jargon that they acquiesced out of confusion, boredom, or frustration. Although this engineer's vocabulary rated high and his communicating strategy usually accomplished his intended purpose—to minimize criticism and resistance—he failed to communicate ethically. As a public servant, the engineer owed citizens a clear explanation of highway plans and a fair chance for those who did not understand jargon and technicalities to be heard.

Truth in communicating is not only good ethics; it is almost always good communication strategy as well. The highway engineer just mentioned and his department encountered opposition and delays on later projects because affected citizens and interest groups no longer tolerated the tactics of bureaucratic confusion.

An event in the international arena also demonstrates the utility of forthright communication. In April 1990, when the Soviet Union was attempting to prevent Lithuanian independence while trying to keep the United States from intervening, President Gorbachev's chief spokesman, Gennady Gerasimov, was sent to retain American support. An editorial captured the effect of Gerasimov's speech in one American city.

> The tenor of his remarks—and the audience's appreciative response—were a good indication of why the Kremlin crackdown has caused so little outrage in this country. Mr. Gerasimov was disarmingly frank. He said that the Soviet Union was in the midst of an "identity crisis." The dream of building a new society through socialism has failed, and there's no consensus over where to go from here. . . . Mr. Gerasimov's fear is that [planned market and free market] reformers will end up so at odds that the conservatives—the communist bureaucrats and die-hard believers in "cradle-to-grave socialism"—will win out. This danger, he said, is compounded by resurgent nationalism, of which Lithuania's drive for independence is a case in point. . . . This is a case where, in Western eyes, the stability of a relatively enlightened Soviet

regime is viewed as more important than imminent independence for a long-suffering "captive nation." For Americans, who cherish freedom foremost, that's an uncomfortable point of view. But we still found ourselves joining in the applause for Gorbachev's man ["A Painful Choice," Apr. 30, 1990, p. 6E].

As in this instance, being forthright and open about a situation is usually the best policy. Honesty builds trust, trust essential for any successful long-term relationship. Since most relationships in government—between countries, agencies, or individuals—must be ongoing to reap real results, risking a relationship by communicating unethically is counterproductive as well as wrong. Withholding vital information, misrepresenting data, and using news media unscrupulously to gain tactical advantage place long-term strategy at risk. Honest communication also respects the audience's intelligence and capability. Reporters, other government professionals, employees, lobbyists, taxpayers, and others are more sophisticated than ever and have contacts, tactics, and legal and technological tools to acquire information. Now it is generally no longer a case of *whether* a lie or withheld information will be detected, but *when.*

From a pragmatic standpoint, then, it pays, especially in the long run, to communicate accurately, openly, responsively, fairly, and usefully. Individual and agency performance depend on these qualities. Forthrightness of the kind Gerasimov displayed helped maintain U.S. support for Gorbachev through the 1991 coup attempt and the ultimate granting of independence to Lithuania and other republics.

Some government officials, managers, and professionals do not embrace the concept of truth in communicating. Richard Nixon was quoted in a 1982 *New York Times* article as saying, "[As a candidate] you have to dissemble. . . . There's a lot of hypocrisy and so forth in political life. It's necessary in order to get into office and in order to return to office." Ronald Reagan, testifying under oath about the Iran-Contra scandal was asked, "Even if you decided that there was some information that would not be revealed to Congress, you would not instruct your administrative people . . . to lie about it, you would simply tell them to withhold the information, is that correct?" Reagan replied, "Well, yes, I think that is a fair statement of what I would do" (Epstein, 1990, p. 10A). Such statements from public administrators of the highest rank indicate that ethics in communicating is hardly a universal practice. While various surveys show that citizens generally have confidence in government honesty, particularly when specific agencies are mentioned, part of the skepticism that does exist about government stems from suspicions that government is being misleading or unresponsive in how it communicates with citizens (National Commission on the Public Service, 1990, pp. 71–94).

The challenge to communicate ethically goes beyond the presence of unethical public officials and administrators, who constitute a small segment of public servants. A broader challenge arises because pursuing one or more of the attributes of ethical communicating may sometimes conflict with others of those attributes. For example, New York City's government discovered in the early 1970s that the more the city communicated to its citizenry that services such as trash pickups and police patrolling were distributed unevenly on the basis of perceived need, the more the city government received public criticism about its policy. More vocal citizens from affluent neighborhoods complained that they were being treated unfairly because other areas were getting more services. Mayor John Lindsay's administration faced the competing choices of better informing citizens about city policy or continuing to provide the South Bronx, East Harlem, and other neighborhoods with the extra services they badly needed. (The attribute of openness conflicted with the attribute of equity.) At about the same time, Governor Rockefeller's administration discovered that the more voters were informed about a statewide community development bond issue—a bond issue many public policy experts advocated for revitalizing many of New York's urban and rural areas—the less voters supported it. The administration's resolution: minimize public information about the bond issue. (It lost anyway.)

In these instances, leveling with publics hindered government's ability to respond to citizen needs as those governments perceived them. In a democracy, however, for long-term effectiveness, government officials and managers owe it to citizens to be open and aboveboard, educating the public and changing public attitudes, if necessary, rather than functioning as a professional elite that substitutes its judgment for that of the people.

Charles Goodsell (1989) emphasizes the difficulty public administrators face in trying to accommodate competing values: *means* orientation (a tool subject to higher authority), *morality* (a sense of moral values, what is "right"), *multitude* orientation (service to citizens directly), *market* orientation (adherence to market economic decisions), and *mission* (obeying agency mission). Goodsell contends that these values all have relevance for public administrators and are useful in different situations according to the circumstances. The highway engineer emphasized means and mission values when he communicated in ways he thought would benefit his agency and bosses. A multitude orientation emphasizes communicating a message in such a way that citizens can understand the message and act on it. A market orientation communicates primarily economic logic and terms. Goodsell's "Five M" framework can be useful for understanding a public manager's own value preferences and relate to the ethical values of truth in communicating, as noted in the case of the highway engineer.

In general, the four values that contribute to truth in communicating—accuracy, usefulness, openness, and fairness—reinforce each other rather than conflict or compete. Moreover, ethical communication generally improves government performance and credibility, especially in the long run. I will now examine each of these four ethical values in greater detail.

Accuracy in Communicating

Deliberately lying is unethical and often illegal, as John Poindexter and other public officials have discovered. Distorting communications to circumvent the law is also unethical. For example, Frederic Andre, a member of the Interstate Commerce Commission (ICC), said in 1983 that bribes in interstate trucking should not concern the commission because "bribes are 'one of the clearest instances of the free market at work.' When other members of the ICC insisted that bribes were wrong, Andre replied, 'Well, they are just discounts. . . . A bribe is a rebate, is it not?'" (Lutz, 1989, p. 212). Attempting to legitimize bribes by calling them discounts, rebates, or economic competition at work misrepresents the truth—to the public, to fellow government officials, and to the communicator himself.

Citizens, whether individuals or in organized groups, depend upon local, state, and federal governments for information that affects their health, safety, jobs, and life-styles. Citizens are realistic enough not to expect that all communications from government will be palatable, but they should expect that communication from government be honest and as accurate as possible. Omitting information important to citizens is as unethical as deliberately including false information. A draft press release from the Environmental Protection Agency said "a Los Angeles chemical dump has 'exploded and burned.' When the draft press release came back from EPA administrator Ann Gorsuch's office, the word 'exploded' had been deleted along with the names, descriptions, and possible adverse health effects of the chemicals involved" (Lutz, 1989, p. 215). Such miscommunication fails to protect the environment or citizens.

The making of unauthorized statements to citizens is a key, related issue. Many public employees are in the position of giving advice to citizens even though their advice does not have official agency authorization and backing. For example, taxpayers getting free tax preparation advice from the IRS and from state and local government tax departments sometimes get different advice from different tax advisers. Studies of the accuracy of tax advice in 1988 showed that taxpayers who called the IRS for advice were given inaccurate information 40 percent of the time. Yet taxpayers who receive incorrect advice can end up paying a penalty or risking legal action for following incorrect advice. Inaccurate advice about medical treatment, eligibility for social services, building safety standards, and so forth can harm citizens physically and economically. Public employees who have given inaccurate advice have rarely been held liable. The courts have generally followed the precedent set by a 1947 Supreme Court decision (*Federal Crop Insurance Corporation* v. *Merrill*, 1947). This decision held that a government agency cannot be held liable for damage caused by acting on inaccurate government information. The fact that public administrators and employees are unlikely to be held judicially accountable for incorrect advice makes it even more incumbent on them to (1) verify the accuracy of information they disseminate, (2) avoid giving advice when they are uncertain of its accuracy, (3) caution citizens that the advice being given is not necessarily official and cannot be completely relied upon, and (4) inform citizens whether binding advice is obtainable (for example, official, signed IRS opinions), and if it is, how they can acquire that advice. Following these guidelines can help improve the accuracy of information given to citizens.

Lying to news reporters or editors in an attempt to mislead the public is not only wrong but virtually doomed to fail in the long run. Reporters have contacts and ways of verifying information and are therefore likely to uncover falsehood. In addition, some reporters are as knowledgeable about certain public issues as are government professionals. Attempting to fool them rarely works. The unwritten code among news editors and reporters is to avoid government officials or professionals who lie to them, thus restricting crucial media access. A prolific grapevine among newspeople spreads the word about who cannot be trusted.

It is also important to be forthright with those in other government agencies. Obscuring meaning can reduce the understanding of a government policy and result in misguided policies or in policies that are resisted. For example, a National Security Council Planning Group issued National Security Directive 196 in 1985 recommending "that the U.S. Government adopt, in principle, the use of aperiodic, non-lifestyle counterintelligence-type polygraph examinations." President Reagan signed the directive, subjecting more than 100,000 government employees to lie detector tests at any time despite the legal and accuracy problems associated with such tests (Lutz, 1989, p. 213).

Likewise, using euphemisms to make certain government actions more palatable can desensitize senders and receivers about realities. In 1981, an assistant secretary of the Department of the Interior clarified the difference between killing and harvesting as "you kill rats, but you harvest game" (Lutz, 1989, p. 213). Harvesting involves killing even if that killing serves a legitimate purpose to protect crops or people or to protect game animals themselves from disease or starvation. To pretend that harvesting is not really killing is to ignore its fundamental nature. It then becomes more conceivable to harvest other animals—people. Inaccurate communicating, whether it falsifies or distorts, is almost always unethical.

Usefulness in Communicating

To be ethical, government communication should also be useful to receivers and senders. The usefulness value can be violated by sending a message inappropriate to the audience or failing to communicate needed information. Omitting any tangible outlet for action and communicating in ways difficult for the audience to understand also impair usefulness. Testimony from Arnold Aldrich, manager of the Space Transportation Systems Program, was hardly useful to the presidential commission investigating the *Challenger* disaster. Aldrich testified that the "normal process during the countdown is that the countdown proceeds, assuming we are in a go posture and at various points during the countdown we tag up on the operational loops and face to face in the firing room to ascertain the facts that project elements that are monitoring data and that are understanding the situation as we proceed are still in the go condition" (Lutz, 1989, p. 223).

William Lutz, collector of government "doublespeak," concludes: "While politicians often use doublespeak to avoid taking a position or accepting responsibility, or to lie and mislead, government workers often use doublespeak simply because it's the only language they know. They really think they are communicating a message with their doublespeak. Their audience, however, is just as bewildered and baffled as any politician's." (Lutz, 1989, p. 199). Pompous phrases and acronyms that obscure meaning are rarely useful to receivers unless they speak the same language as the senders.

Sometimes sound strategy requires a message that is ambiguous or uninformative. In such situations, senders are more concerned about pursuing their own objectives than they are about their receivers' benefit. One such situation occurred in early August 1990, about a week after Iraq's invasion and occupation of Kuwait. White House and State Department officials at that time "refused to characterize as hostages the Americans and other foreign nationals apparently held against their will for a week now in the two nations, saying only that they were 'stuck'" (Carroll, 1990, p. 1A). The decision to avoid the term *hostages* was part of a deliberate strategy. A senior U.S. official said, "We believe the best way of getting them out is to be cool. To sit tight. To not label them or try to single out [American] people from other [foreign] people (Carroll, 1990, p. 14A). In this instance using the somewhat ambiguous euphemism *stuck* was probably justified since officials thought the term *hostages* would inflate the value of held Americans to Iraqi leaders, endangering the lives of those held and further complicating resolution of the crisis. U.S. officials also pointed out that, technically, Americans held in Kuwait and Iraq were not hostages since no demands had yet been made. Using the term *stuck* rather than *hostage* was part of a deliberate strategy on the part of White House and State Department officials to improve their negotiating flexibility rather than primarily to enlighten viewers or readers. Even when the term *hostage* was used later, the overall strategy to devalue the hostage issue achieved results. The lack of emphasis on negotiating for hostages and public opinion against hostage taking were factors in Saddam Hussein's eventual release of American and other nationals held in Iraq and Kuwait.

Unless a public administrator works in military, diplomatic, or espionage circles, such situations are probably less common than situations where communicating to increase utility to the receiver also benefits the sender in terms of better relationships, increased compliance, and improved credibility. Inadvertent use of inappropriate jargon, inappropriate use of media, or information inappropriate to the audience's needs constitute bigger threats to making government communication more useful than does any conscious strategy.

Openness in Communicating

The Code of Ethics of the American Society for Public Administration charges members to "constructively support open communication." Likewise, the International City Management Association Code of Ethics charges its members to "Keep the community informed on municipal affairs; encourage communication between the citizens and all municipal officers." As these codes reflect, the value of openness applies generally to all major internal and external audiences of government—although to different degrees in different situations.

Public administrators should stress openness where freedom of information, privacy, open meetings, and related policies apply, as discussed in Chapter Seven. Yet such policies often lack the intended effect because of exemptions, direct or backdoor amendments that limit access, and countersuits to deny access. Openness, to be effective, must go beyond mere compliance with the letter of the law. Instead of merely reacting to Freedom of Information Act requests, public administrators should take a proactive position that openness and access are generally healthy unless they would likely produce harm.

In general, a public administrator should promote openness when other audiences have a legitimate right to know, when information is likely to be disseminated anyway, or when it is vital to assure others that he or she is acting openly and in good faith rather than being secretive. In April 1991 a citizen captured videotape footage of four Los Angeles Police Department officers beating a stopped motorist. That citizen first tried to inform police authorities of the incident. Because he was rebuffed by the police, the citizen took his tape to a Los Angeles television station. The tape was seen by millions of viewers across the country, resulting in controversy surrounding the police department and its chief. Because the police department took no action until publicity forced it to, the department's credibility suffered.

The widespread use of video cameras and television stations' encouragement of citizens to capture newsworthy events increase the chances that the facts of an incident will come out, making it better for government to be open in the first place. In a university reorganization in which I was involved, it was important to keep provosts, major deans, key department heads, and legislative representatives informed of each step taken. These were administrative or political actors who might resent being excluded or being surprised with a final proposal and actors who could block or weaken reorganization efforts. At several points during the process, a major actor was left out of the communication loop, invariably causing setbacks to our plans.

Chapter One shows how lack of openness on both the sending and receiving ends contributed to the *Challenger* and Ceausescu tragedies. As a rule, subordinates owe it to their superiors and elected officials to inform them, even of bad news, so that problems can be addressed. Superiors should be fair receivers of such information and not automatically condemn the bearer. Likewise, superiors owe subordinates enough information so that subordinates can do their jobs competently and avoid administrative or even legal trouble.

Openness carried too far can jeopardize sensitive negotiations or even the safety or welfare of government employees or citizens. Twenty-four carloads of police officers were about to arrest drug dealers in a June 1990 raid in Lancaster, Pennsylvania. The arrest was thwarted because station WGAL-TV camera crews arrived at the bust site before the police did. The snafu was blamed on "someone who 'out of ignorance . . . or self interest,' prematurely tipped the station to the raid, and thus 'violated the trust of every law-abiding citizen by releasing sensitive information'" (*Philadelphia Inquirer*, Apr. 29, 1990, p. 8B). Lancaster mayor Janice Stork estimated that about 80 percent of area drug trafficking could have been eliminated by this raid. In this instance the value of open communication conflicted adversely with the value of usefulness. The American Society for Public Administration Code of Ethics recognizes the importance of tempering openness with other values when it requires public administrators to "respect and protect the privileged information to which we have access in the course of our official duties."

Privileged and confidential information has a place, even in a democracy, but there is evidence to suggest that much information at all levels of government is classified more strictly than is actually warranted ("Keeping Secrets," 1990; American Library Association, Washington Office, 1988; Curry, 1988; Baumann, 1986; Robbin, 1986). Information policy reform efforts to declassify and reclassify information have made some headway, but they affect only a relatively small amount of information. Government communication could be more open in many agencies without jeopardizing security or protected interests. A change of attitude is needed to supplement formal reforms for openness. Administrators at all levels of government need to resist the tendency to withhold information except for valid reasons.

Governments should also be open *receivers* of communication from their publics. As discussed in Chapter Seven, this involves providing channels for citizens to make requests or complaints and equalizing access to those channels rather than restricting input to only those who can afford a lobbyist or who can supply formal briefs. If an agency sets up a citizen advisory board or a mayor's office initiates a citizen call-in program, the board or program should be treated seriously, not be just a community relations gesture. To make members of the public think that they have effective channels to government when they do not is unethical.

Fairness in Communicating

To be ethical, government communication should not take unfair advantage of audiences, especially those disadvantaged in some way. In light of this, government communicators should observe the following guidelines:

Avoid Using Media Others May Lack Access to or Be Less Skilled in Using

Primary reliance on formal written testimony at a public hearing usually puts less educated, less organized groups at a disadvantage. Using a variety of forums provides better opportunity to receive communication accurately just as relying on a variety of media enhances sending a mesage. Also, some citizens have the need to know government information but lack the technology or money to ensure access. The American Library Association Washington Office (1988, p. i) has noted this problem as regards increased government use of electronic communication.

> Another development, with major implications for public access, is the growing tendency of federal agencies to utilize computer and telecommunications technologies for data collection, storage, retrieval and

dissemination. This trend has resulted in the increased emergence of contractual arrangements with commercial firms to disseminate information collected at taxpayer expense, higher user charges for government information, and the proliferation of government information available only in electronic format. While automation clearly offers promises of savings, will public access to government information be further restricted for people who cannot afford computers or pay for computer time?

Public managers need to consider equity along with economic and administrative factors when selecting communication media for sending or receiving information, when pricing that information, or when contracting out information functions to private firms.

Avoid Using Knowledge of Language to Unfair Advantage

Deliberately using language or jargon that publics may not know to put them at a disadvantage, as the state highway engineer mentioned earlier did, treats those groups unfairly. Moreover, knowledge of how to manipulate language should carry with it the burden of doing so responsibly. This typically means avoiding language that obscures responsibility for public actions. For example, when President Bush in July 1990 made public his reversal of his campaign pledge of "no new taxes," controversy arose over how the statement should be worded. One draft statement started with a vague passive phrase—"it is clear that" [taxes, referred to in the statement as "tax revenue increases," would be needed]. Democrats who wanted President Bush to take personal responsibility for his policy reversal insisted that the introduction be reworded, "It is clear to me that. . ." This change clarified responsibility and broke one deadlock with Congress over budget negotiations (Balz and Devroy, 1990, p. 4A). Attempting to use language proficiency to cloud responsibility may have been good politics in this situation, but it was questionable ethics.

Avoid Using Knowledge of Persuasion to Unfair Advantage

Research on persuasion generally shows that less educated people are most susceptible to persuasion and propaganda techniques (Katz and Lazarsfeld, 1955; Miller, 1987). Such groups or individuals often lack the vocabulary, reasoning, and other skills that help one resist propaganda. Such audiences often need different sides of issues and counterarguments articulated clearly for them by government representatives or independent advocates. Once provided with relevant information about how an issue affects them, such groups can then meaningfully decide their preferences. Using knowledge of communication behavior to stack a case, omit key problems, or otherwise unduly persuade groups or individuals less educated because of poverty, homelessness, or immigration, constitutes unethical communicating.

Likewise, people who feel that their safety or economic security is threatened tend to be more susceptible than others to persuasion. Seizing on a subordinate's vulnerability to browbeat that employee into capitulating on an issue would violate the spirit of truth in communicating. Not only is the judgment of employees who feel threatened impaired (Asch, 1956), but their senses are overloaded or distracted, making them less observant when listening, watching, or reading. Making employees or clients feel threatened in order to put them at a disadvantage is unethical and foolhardy. Those threatened will more likely make errors in observation and judgment, causing problems and harming performance.

Research also shows that the person taking the most dogmatic position is likely to "win" a one-on-one debate or argument. Those with rigid positions tend to remain rigid while more reasonable, flexible people will more likely acknowledge the possible validity of other positions. Using dogmatic tactics to win debates or arguments may score points in some quarters, but such tactics will also likely reduce rapport and communication with those who have been beaten, adversely affecting the quality of decisions.

Communicating in Situations Involving Ethical Dilemmas

As emphasized in Chapter Eight, communicating in difficult situations or crisis requires more conscious attention to strategy and better use of oral, writen, and nonverbal skills. Some of the most difficult situations involve ethical dilemmas such as the following.

If public managers uncover improprieties within their agency, should they communicate this? The decision of whether to blow the whistle is a personal, moral one that public managers must make on the basis of the circumstances and their personal value system. Even before deciding to blow the whistle, however, it pays to consider communication strategy. Otherwise, the trauma and costs of blowing the whistle may accomplish little if the right message fails to reach the audience that can take action. A sound first step is to map and profile intended and unintended audiences carefully. Which primary and secondary audiences are likely to be sympathetic to the whistle-blowing message? How much credibility does the whistle-blower have with these audiences? If the whistle-blower lacks credibility, what evidence would make him or her more believable? Are there intermediaries with whom the whistle-blower shares trust and who could transmit the message more effectively to others?

As in implementing other kinds of strategy, it often makes sense to start with small, reversible steps (Etzioni, 1967). This often means first discussing the matter with colleagues to see whether they have other evidence and whether they support the charges. Next, it usually pays to take the matter directly to those suspected of being offenders. A private discussion with them might show them the error of their ways and get them to stop. It might also alert them of the intent to blow the whistle and either cause them to change behavior or put up their guard. Confrontation can also raise other issues and facts that may cause whistle-blowers to rethink their charges. Thus, direct but private confrontation may prevent an error in judgment, and allow whistle-blowers to claim later that they did indeed bring up the matter with those responsible and have demonstrated agency loyalty. If no satisfaction results from direct confrontation, whistle-blowers might look for others in the agency, preferably superiors, who support their case or who can better champion it.

In his efforts to blow the whistle on deliberately deflated body counts during the Vietnam war, Pentagon analyst Sam Adams not only encountered strong military and Johnson administration selective perception to ignore evidence that questioned the war's viability. In addition, Adams's own image as a fanatic on this issue diminished his credibility with military and administration superiors (Adams, 1988). Finding a champion with higher credibility with the primary audiences that needed to be convinced might have proven more successful at the time.

If all internal communications fail and whistle-blowers choose to persist in their charges, they will need to do what Sam Adams did, take the case to other agencies, legislators, and the news media. Going public with charges escalates the controversy and has made it difficult or impossible for many whistle-blowers to stay with their agency. Whistle-blowers should obviously think through this step thoroughly. As before, they need to select audiences carefully in terms of objectives and management situation. External audiences should be selected on the basis of their ability to correct illegal or unethical behavior (primary audiences) or their ability to reach those who can (immediate or secondary audiences).

Sam Adams and others finally convinced CBS's "60 Minutes" that their charges had merit, and that television program forcefully brought Adams's case to millions of viewers, albeit in 1982, long after the war ended. Adams's whistle-blowing did accomplish something, however. In the Persian Gulf War of 1991, Secretary of Defense Richard Cheney and top military officers, undoubtedly familiar with the Vietnam body-count controversy, refused to embellish troop or body counts. As emphasized in Chapters Seven and Eight, long-standing credible relations with reporters and editors help enormously in difficult situations such as this. The advent of a full-blown crisis is often too late to build such bridges.

When confronting whistle-blowing and other ethical dilemmas, it is especially important for public administrators to communicate ethically themselves by reporting accurately rather than embellishing information and by respecting the rights and careers of other employees rather than using them for personal advantage. Ethical communicating under such conditions of duress not only shows professionalism but keeps public administrators above reproach and enhances their credibility.

Obviously, this chapter cannot address all ethical dilemmas or how to communicate when confronting them. The case of whistle-blowing serves as an example of the importance of combining communication strategy and ethics when confronting other ethical dilemmas.

Communicating Through Ethical Actions

Previous chapters have stressed how strongly actions communicate. The need for actions to support rhetoric applies doubly for ethics programs themselves. Merely adopting an ethics code or even establishing procedures and penalties for enforcement does little to motivate ethical behavior from employees unless they perceive that the agency takes ethics seriously. All too often ethics codes or pronouncements are intended to defuse the ethics issue without having to tackle the tough but essential steps of actually implementing a workable program and continually evaluating its results.

Communicating to its employees, to elected officials, and to citizens that an agency takes ethics seriously usually involves the use of multiple media—briefings, regulations, statements, meetings, workshops, and behavior of top administrators—to convey that the agency does more than pay lip service to ethics. It also involves varying and repeating these messages as appropriate to the different audiences inside and outside the agency. The content of these messages evolves as the agency addresses such issues as why ethics affects the agency, individual employee, and the public to be served; what the relevant ethics policies are; what behavior is acceptable and unacceptable and under what conditions; who is responsible for fielding questions about what is acceptable behavior; how employees should report violations; how charges of violations are handled; what the real consequences of ethics violations are; and the agency's belief that ethical dimensions extend beyond illegalities or improprieties and that willful failure to communicate needed information or otherwise giving less than a best effort in serving the public is unethical. Finally, communicating through ongoing actions that ethics is an agency priority means penalizing violators, rewarding rather than crucifying whistle-blowers, and continually providing education for employees on the foregoing matters. If agencies communicate this message effectively to employees, as well as public audiences, many violations of ethics and of ethical communication may be avoided.

Much public distrust of government stems from government actions that speak louder than words: Watergate, the Iran-Contra affair, the Pentagon procurement scandals, the savings and loan crisis and bailout, the waste and corruption in some state and local governments. Illegal or unethical actions constitute a small minority of government actions yet shape the stereotype many citizens have of government. No amount of positive public information will significantly boost government's image unless government performance and ethics measure up to the rhetoric. To improve the credibility of public administration, the National Commission on the Public Service (1990) correctly recommends priority attention to improving public information, service performance, *and* honesty.

In closing this chapter, I want to emphasize that while advocating situational communicating, I recognize the danger in totally embracing situational ethics. Public administrators need core values and internal decision rules to guide their actions. The National Association of Government Communicators (1990) has developed a useful code of ethics that relates primarily to communicating. Provisions germane to our purpose are included below (reprinted with permission).

Members will:

- Conduct themselves professionally, with truth, accuracy, fairness, responsibility, accountability to the public, and adherence to generally accepted standards of good taste.
- Conduct their professional lives in accord with the public interest, in recognition that each of us is a steward of the public's trust.
- Convey the truth to their agencies' management, engaging in no practice which could corrupt the integrity of channels of communication or the processes of government.
- Intentionally communicate no false or misleading

information and will act promptly to correct false or misleading information or rumors.

- Represent no conflicting or competing interests and will fully comply with all statutes, Executive Orders and regulations pertaining to personal disclosure of such interests.
- Avoid the possibility of any improper use of information by an "insider" or third party and never use inside information for personal gain.
- Guarantee or promise the achievement of no specified result beyond the member's direct control.
- Safeguard the confidence of both present and former employees, and of information acquired in meetings, and documents as required by law, regulation and prudent good sense.
- Not wrongly injure the professional reputation or practice of another person, private organization or government agency.

For those who prefer guiding principles to a detailed code of ethics, my personal rule of thumb is this: if I am unwilling to tell my spouse, mother and father, children, clergyman, favorite teacher, and closest friend what I did, it is probably unethical. This chapter has introduced and defined the concept of "truth in communicating" to involve accuracy, usefulness, openness, and fairness and offers guidance for improving communication ethics. The following, concluding chapter addresses the challenge of improving communication skills in government.

10

Improving Communication Skills

Leadership and learning are indispensable to each
other.
—*John F. Kennedy, speech prepared for
delivery in Dallas, Tex., Nov. 22, 1963*

Perhaps nothing is more important to successful administration than successful communication. Yet one
rarely finds any systematic attempt to teach communication skills in schools of public administration.
—*Robert S. Lorch, 1978, p. 174*

Learning communication or other skills usually requires four key
steps: (1) acquiring the principles for using a skill, along with
guidelines for behavior drawn from theory, research, and the experience of effective practitioners; (2) recognizing how these principles
and guidelines are applied or misapplied; (3) practicing these principles and guidelines; and (4) getting feedback on skill performance
from an instructor, colleague, superior, mentor, or other (Whetten
and Cameron, 1984). Research on training effectiveness shows that
these four steps produce results superior to learning by lecture alone
(Whetten and Cameron, 1984; Porras and Anderson, 1981). Books
such as this one have a place in improving communication skills.
Books can discuss communication principles and fundamentals and
provide guidelines for applying those principles. Books can also

show in writing how certain skills can be applied or misapplied, although books can describe this only in terms of speaking and nonverbal skills. Acquiring and refining skills usually requires more than reading about them, however. The crucial practice and feedback steps require learners to go beyond the book. Much of the success of Operation Desert Shield and Operation Desert Storm in the Persian Gulf has been attributed to extensive practice maneuvers. Some U.S. military officers noted that their training exercises were harder than the actual battles to reclaim Kuwait. This chapter explores some of the most promising ways for applying knowledge gained from this book and for improving overall communication skills. As with other aspects of communicating strategically, the most appropriate approaches for developing skills depend upon one's purpose, audience, and management situation.

Learning from Formal Communication Training

Formal training in communication may occur in-house, at a central government location, or at a university.

Agency-Based Training

Many public agencies conduct in-house communication training. The mammoth U.S. Departments of Agriculture and Defense offer a range of courses on writing and speaking skills. Many smaller departments at all levels of government also provide at least some training. Agency-based training has many benefits. It can supply participants with skill instruction and practice within the specific context of that agency's task and environment. Participants within the same agency can get practice in communicating with colleagues about actual work-related topics. Actual agency communication barriers or problems can be addressed directly. Rapport within and among agency units can be improved.

The *relevance* of training has been found to be important to how well trainees learn and how much learning gets transferred to the actual job (French, 1990). Agency-based training has the potential for high relevance and direct transfer of learning if actual work situations are used. The success of the Defense Information School's

Public Affairs Officer course owes much to addressing questions that reporters might ask about actual military situations. Intensive grilling during practice military briefings prepares officers for similar questions from reporters and public officials later, although it takes more than relevant practice to reach the mastery of General Norman Schwarzkopf.

On the other hand, agency-based training may be less appropriate than other forms under certain conditions. Factors in the audience and management situation might be so sensitive that bringing agency employees together for communication training would heighten rather than reduce tension. Employees may perceive that the training is unnecessary or, worse, is being used to manipulate their behavior. The major strength of agency-based training stems from the opportunity to simulate and analyze actual work-related communication. Yet agency training programs that offer only general approaches to listening, speaking, reading, and writing without referring to agency problems or examples fail to utilize the relevance advantage. As noted before, however, some situations may dictate a more generalized, less threatening approach requiring participants to transfer their learning later to the actual job.

Centralized Training

Much communication training is conducted by central staff support agencies rather than by individual agencies themselves. U.S. Office of Personnel Management (OPM) courses in office and communication skills are attended by employees from dozens of agencies. Comparable training at state and local levels is offered by the departments of personnel or civil service. Sometimes these departments have specific training institutes such as the OPM's Federal Executive Institute or most of the state certified public manager programs.

Centralized training by support agencies typically involves participants from several agencies, although some support agencies also provide on-site training for individual departments. The interagency nature of the training audience offers some advantages. Participants get to know their peers in other agencies, thereby extending their professional network. Participants often learn that the communication issues and problems they confront are shared by peers in other agencies and can find out how those agencies address such issues and problems. Because of the audience and situation, however, it is usually less feasible to address extensively specific problems confronting any single agency. Since most participants will not be from the agency singled out for scrutiny, they may lack interest in that agency's particular problems. A reluctance also exists to showing an agency's "dirty linen" for other departments to see, even though mutual learning might result.

University Courses

Universities have conducted communication training courses for government employees for some time. The Institutes of Government of the University of Georgia and the University of North Carolina are among these. A growing number of colleges and universities are offering courses on government communication in their public administration degree programs. Sometimes courses such as the course I have taught at several universities—Communicating Skills for Public Sector Management—address a broad range of communicating skills. More often, courses deal with specific topics such as executive speaking or administrative writing. Sometimes these courses are taught by faculty trained in public administration, public policy, or political science. More often, they are taught by faculty trained in English, speech communication, or related subjects. Unless faculty from these fields are aware of the particular nuances of government communication, administrative realism may be missing.

Even though research has shown the importance of communication skills for public administrators (Corson and Paul, 1966; Murray, 1976; Cameron and Whetten, 1980; National Commission on the Public Service, 1990), courses in government administrative communication are not nearly as common to public administration programs as business communication courses are to MBA programs. The American Assembly of Collegiate Schools of Business (AACSB) strongly promotes the subject of business communication within business programs. Virtually every graduate and undergraduate business program has courses in business communication, organizational communication, or managerial communication. The National Association of Schools of Public Affairs and Administration (NASPAA) is the logical actor to stimulate more and better communication education in public administration programs. NASPAA does recognize the importance of communication training to prepare for government service. NASPAA's *Standards for Professional Master's Degree Programs in Public Affairs and Administration,* adopted in October 1988, states: "The curriculum components are designed to produce professionals capable of intelligent, creative analysis and communication, and action in the public sector" (p. 3). NASPAA goes on to specify that the general competencies that students of public administration and policy should acquire include "a demonstrated ability to . . . organize and communicate information clearly to a variety of audiences through formats including oral presentations, written memoranda and technical reports, and statistical charts, graphs, and tables" (p. 4). NASPAA's Commission on Peer Review and Accreditation looks for evidence in program reports and site visits that university programs are teaching communication skills.

Consultant Training

Consultants perform some of the agency-based and centralized training described above. Many consultants also provide individualized coaching or counseling for managers on public speaking, dealing with the news media, and the like. Such consulting may include videotapes and critiques of the manager's performance, tips on dress and mannerisms, and instruction on technique.

Psychologists and counselors are also increasingly being employed as consultants by government agencies and schools to help employees cope with the added work stresses resulting from increasing legal and technological complexity, periodic financial retrenchment, and rising citizen expectations of government. These forces place strains on human relationships that create communication problems at work. Using internal and external consultants is one way of addressing such problems.

Learning from Work Experience

Some of the best learning comes from the school of hard knocks—
the job itself. This section offers advice on learning from good and
bad on-the-job communication.

Making the Most of Existing Opportunities

The adage "experience is the best teacher" makes much sense for
improving communication skills. Every workday presents communication laboratories for public managers. Learning opportunities occur each time managers listen to complaints from
subordinates, write a memo, brief a superior, testify before a committee, or communicate in other ways. Merely practicing a skill
hardly guarantees improvement, however. Public administrators,
like poor golfers, can keep making the same mistakes unless they
learn from their experience.

Several conditions are prerequisite to effective on-the-job
learning. It is essential that an organizational climate exist which
tolerates mistakes and encourages learning from them. Heavy criticism and sanctions for an inept briefing or faulty report are more
likely to stunt the development of speaking and writing skills than
to improve them. Experience with learning shows that learners tend
to concentrate more on subjects and skills they feel positive about
and neglect those that have negative associations.

Learners need to receive sound feedback about their performance. Without a realistic assessment of performance, they are
either unlikely to change it or are likely to change it in counterproductive ways. Feedback can come from a superior, mentor, colleague, subordinate, or someone else. It can come through a formal
critique or from informal reactions by superiors or colleagues, such
as suggested revisions of a draft report, for example. Superiors and
subordinates share responsibility for feedback. Superiors are usually
in a better position to know whether a subordinate's communication was effective: how the boss reacted to a briefing, how agency
clients will likely perceive a letter. Superiors can therefore help
subordinates improve their skills through judicious feedback.

Yet superiors sometimes fail to provide feedback because they lack the time, do not want to be critical, or doubt their own skills. A number of government managers have told me that they rarely receive any comments from their boss, even when they sense that their performance is lacking. In such situations, subordinates should actively seek out their superior's reactions and consult others if the superior provides no or inadequate feedback. An informal network is a good consulting source.

The person or persons who provide the feedback should be skilled in doing so or be a relevant audience. Those providing advice should know the fundamentals of a skill and take interest in sharing that knowledge. Excellent speakers or writers do not necessarily give the best feedback. They may lack patience with less-than-outstanding performance and lack empathy with other people's problems. The best athletic coaches are rarely outstanding athletes, but they are usually good students of their sport and take satisfaction in helping others improve. Furthermore, the closer feedback providers are to the public administrator's intended audience, the more useful their reactions are. Some grants officers, for example, will critique a preliminary proposal before it is resubmitted to them. Such feedback is invaluable since it reflects the granting agency's priorities and requirements. Often, however, it is impossible or impractical to get feedback from the intended audience. For example, asking a legislative committee to critique an agency's draft report might engender resentment on the part of legislators, and showing the report in unpolished form would risk adverse reaction. Savvy administrators in such circumstances may seek feedback from individual legislators or staffers who are particular supporters of the agency, former legislators or staffers, or other administrators who have had considerable success with that committee. These proxy audiences can share insights about how the actual audience might react to that report.

The ideal source of feedback is people who possess good communication skills and are close to the intended audience. When administrators do not have access to such a source, they may need to find people who either are skilled communicators or are relevant for the intended audience. In the case of the latter, public administrators would do well to remember that not all of their target audience will be skilled speakers, readers, writers, or listeners either.

Effective feedback is usually descriptive rather than judgmental and is nonthreatening to the learner. Effective feedback on performance, whether from one teacher to another or from the secretary of state to an assistant secretary, concentrates on describing the characteristics of the skill involved in that performance. If the feedback is on running a meeting, for example, it should concentrate on fairly objective characteristics that the meeting leader and the coach discussed beforehand. Knowing the leader's agenda and objectives beforehand gives the person providing feedback a surer grasp of what to observe in the meeting and how to assess the leader's performance. Faulty feedback is more likely to result if the person giving it lacks understanding of the learner, the learner's purposes for communicating, and the management situation. After the meeting, the coach should concentrate on describing what he or she observed. Describing how many times the meeting departed from the agenda, for example, tends to be less threatening and more instructive than making a flat evaluation: "You lost control of the meeting and let it wander." The coach providing feedback can then ask the leader his or her reasons for allowing the departures. It may turn out that the meeting leader was unaware of the digressions or may have had tactical reasons for them. In either case a discussion centering on behaviors rather than judgments will more likely produce learning. Intelligent learners will draw their own conclusions. For example, "I allowed too many digressions, which dissipated momentum and focus" or "Most of the digressions I allowed made sense, but some will not be allowed again."

Feedback providers should acknowledge anything *they* learn from the situation. This turns the occasion into a mutual learning process rather than a critique. Such providers should also include points that help the "performer" (writer, speaker, and so on) see that he or she has done some things well. Without being reinforced, effective skills will likely be dropped or neglected.

Audio and video recordings of briefings, meetings, and other communication activities can provide revealing feedback to managers and employees. Some cautions need to be observed, however. Seeing themselves on video can be devastating to administrators who have not yet improved their communication skills or confidence level. Although managers and employees need not be fully polished communicators before they are taped (if they were, they wouldn't need this kind of feedback), they do need a minimum level of competence on which to build. Also, the video or audio recording needs to be of sufficient quality to reveal the behaviors being practiced. Faint audio recordings or videos focusing on the wrong people will not help much.

Seeking Communication Opportunities in Management

The foregoing guidelines can help public administrators make the most of learning opportunities on the job. Often, however, public administrators need to augment normal learning situations because they lack opportunities to improve some communication skills. When this is the case, they should deliberately seek assignments, tasks, or roles that will provide the learning experiences they currently lack. If conflict resolution skills need sharpening, an administrator may seek a position on the grievance committee. If a public administrator feels the need for a better grasp of the agency's overall communication system, volunteering to help with a communication audit would be helpful.

It takes dedicated, introspective public administrators to seek out experiences they find unsatisfying or even threatening in order to improve their skills. An opinion poll once showed that a higher percentage of people feared public speaking than feared financial problems, illness, or even death. There is no reason to believe public administrators are less afraid of public speaking than those surveyed. So, for example, if a public manager feels that more experience in public speaking would be valuable and therefore volunteers to brief citizen groups on policy issues, her dedication should be applauded. On the other hand, her agency would be ill-advised to place her in a situation that would damage her self-confidence and the agency's reputation. She could, instead, be sent to less threatening groups to explain less complicated issues, and thus build her skills gradually. In some situations, public administrators may be unwilling to tackle new or threatening situations. Superiors, colleagues, or mentors may then need to persuade these administrators of the ultimate value of such experiences to their overall effectiveness.

As this discussion indicates, public administrators can often learn just as much from situations fraught with mistakes as from dazzling displays of skillful communication. Some of my most vivid lessons about oral briefings occurred while I was witnessing a presentation that fell apart before completion. The presenter started strongly but got so distracted by questions during the presentation that he never finished what he had to say and never made his summary points. The lesson: establish ground rules in advance; if taking questions after the presentation, allow time for a summary statement after questions. The audience would have respected this presenter's request, but since he made none and since he started fielding questions indiscriminately, the briefing degenerated into a discussion that generated more heat than light. Other audiences, purposes, and situations might have called for taking questions as they arose. The point is that much can be learned from mistakes—our own and those of others. Instead of fuming inside about having to sit through an amateurish teleconference, for example, an administrator might well be analyzing how she would organize and deliver that teleconference more effectively.

Modeling the Communication Behavior of Others

Finding instructive learning situations is one way of improving communication skills, finding models to emulate is another. Such models can be superiors, colleagues, mentors, subordinates, or even adversaries. A former superior, Barry Van Lare, modeled much of what I now know to be effective leadership for meetings. A former mentor, Charles Levine, taught me by example how to organize a research article. In his book *The Charismatic Leader*, Jay Conger illustrates how leaders model behaviors and values through their actions as well as their words. "In another case, the leader's actions continually drove home the importance of being well prepared in one's work. At a conference, for example, a power shortage cut off lighting in the hotel's meeting room. The leader quickly went to his car and returned with a candle, matches, and a kerosene lamp. The meeting continued as if nothing had happened. 'He was prepared for that emergency. We couldn't believe it. The moral was "be prepared—anything can happen"'" (Conger, 1989, pp. 121-122).

Most professionals can think of similar examples in which their skills or values were molded.

Even though mentors are hardly the only ones who can model communication skills, their potential strength as role models makes them worthy of special attention. People in government, business, and the professions have had mentors since the original Mentor guided Odysseus in his journeys. Significant knowledge about the mentor-protégé relationship has emerged more recently, however. The following attributes of effective mentors as role models can be used as a checklist to help potential protégés judge who would make a good mentor and what their own role should be in the relationship. These attributes can also be used by mentors who want a clearer understanding of their role and that of protégés. In addition, the guidelines also provide direction on how mentors and protégés can better communicate with each other.

1. Effective mentors display substantial professional competence, including competence in communicating. Administrators and others who demonstrate professional competence and success in their own work and careers will be better able to tutor and guide the development of protégés, who typically are younger and less experienced. Unless mentors possess skill and savvy themselves, they will be unable to impart it to others.

2. Effective mentors engender trust through example and reputation. Despite an individual's substantial success and skill, a protégé would be ill-advised to regard that person as a mentor if little trust exists. A mentor-protégé relationship typically evolves over time and develops out of mutual trust and interest. If a person cannot be trusted to give sound advice and to avoid manipulating protégés for self-advantage, that person would make a poor mentor.

3. Effective mentors show enthusiasm for their profession and help instill that enthusiasm in protégés. Good mentors tend to enjoy their work so much that their enthusiasm is contagious. This passion for public service or administrative performance is often what attracts protégés to the mentor in the first place. This passion is also what helps motivate protégés throughout the relationship.

4. Effective mentors have a vision of professional and public service that they share with protégés. Good mentors usually have a well-developed vision of what government service involves; what forces are shaping government service; what the important issues, problems, and opportunities are now; and what will likely emerge in the future. Effective mentors, in other words, possess a firm grasp of the governmental system and their role in it without being unduly bound by that system. Their vision includes possibilities for improving the system as well as understanding how it works now. Good mentors not only have developed a vision through much forethought, but they are willing to share it with others, even protégés who are not yet at their level of understanding and mastery.

5. *Effective mentors impart advice, knowledge, and skill that helps protégés in their work and careers.* Mentors typically coach protégés on career strategy and how the system works as well as on specific job-related skills, including communication. In some cases mentors even hire protégés and take them along if those mentors leave the agency. In other cases mentors use their considerable contacts to help place protégés. Mentors also teach protégés. They impart substantive knowledge and skills that they have found essential to their own success. The teaching responsibility of mentors is more fundamental than their role as career strategist for protégés. Unless mentors help protégés to acquire substantive knowledge and skill of their own, protégés may need to rely too heavily on their mentors' influence. If that occurs, protégés embarrass themselves and their mentors. In performing their teaching role, mentors should observe the foregoing guidelines on modeling communication behavior and giving effective feedback. Mentors, more than others, are likely to have their example and feedback taken seriously by protégés.

6. *Effective mentors challenge protégés to achieve a higher level of performance.* By their example, instruction, and direction, effective mentors help protégés aim higher than they otherwise would. Protégés see firsthand how the mentor conceptualizes problems, relates to others, and is regarded by others. This cannot help but make protégés more aware of what superior performance requires. They desire to emulate the mentor's skills and success. They want to be held in the same esteem as their mentor. This motivation along with the mentor's personal tutelage and support usually make protégés perform at a level higher than they would without a mentor.

7. *Effective mentors protect protégés from administrators,*

politicians, and others unless criticism or sanction is necessary for their protégés' learning and growth. Managers in Japanese conglomerates are not the only ones who have benefited from a patron to sponsor, guide, and protect them during their careers. Managers at all levels of American government have likewise benefited from the help of respected superiors. Advancement in both the military and civilian branches of government tends to be enhanced by having a mentor or sponsor. Successful mentors have the clout and know-how to protect their protégés from at least some bad assignments, some criticism from above, and perhaps even from dismissal. Good mentors, however, recognize that sometimes having to take the consequences for a wrong move or faulty decision is the best learning experience for protégés.

8. *Effective mentors realize that mutual benefits are important to a mentor-protégé relationship but avoid exploiting their protégés.* Good mentors recognize that protégés typically need to reciprocate to maintain self-esteem and to repay previous help. It is therefore healthy for mentors to ask favors of protégés, particularly if complying helps protégés learn and grow in the process. True mentors, however, avoid manipulating protégés or placing undue demands on them, demands that monopolize the protégés' efforts and keep them dependent. Effective mentors also take an interest in protégés for their own development, not just because of what protégés can do to be of value to mentors. Administrators, teachers, and others who write off protégés they regard as no longer materially useful to them are not true mentors.

9. *Effective mentors guard against unhealthy protégé dependence upon them.* True mentors provide more guidance in the early stages of the relationship (typically also earlier in a protégé's career) but encourage protégés to exercise greater independence in decisions and actions as the relationship evolves. As they grow in skill and confidence, most protégés rely less on the mentor's advice and protection and see the mentor more as a colleague and friend. The relationship becomes less that of superior-subordinate and more one of equals. True mentors delight in seeing protégés achieve their own independence and success. Mentors will help protégés make other contacts that will help them and make them less reliant on mentors. If protégés remain dependent, mentors may have to

wean them from undue reliance by advising them to think more for themselves, refusing to offer them advice, or withholding help. Mentors may even have to sever the professional aspects of the relationship while attempting to retain a personal relationship. Maintaining friendship can be difficult. Recent research shows that even constructive mentoring relationships often end in "indifference or hostility" (Daloz, 1986, p. 33). A good measure of a mentor's effectiveness is how many of his or her protégés have become independent, contributing professionals in their own right. One star protégé does not necessarily reflect a mentor's success. The star would probably have risen anyway. A succession of successful protégés with different personalities and ability levels does indicate a good mentor. Potential protégés should avoid people who keep other protégés tied to their coattails.

As implied above, the mentoring relationship must be reciprocal to be effective and lasting. Protégés likewise have responsibilities.

1. *Effective protégés take a mentor's advice seriously without sublimating their own personality, values, and goals.* If mentors are willing to take time and interest in helping protégés, those protégés should live up to their part of the mentoring relationship by following a mentor's advice and instruction whenever appropriate. Protégés who regularly fail to learn what their mentors recommend or consistently ignore their mentors' advice risk alienating their mentors. Few mentors will keep giving instruction or counsel if they think protégés are not taking them seriously. This does not mean that protégés should automatically do whatever their mentors advise. Mentors' advice may typically be based on greater knowledge of how the system works. But because protégés are different people with different personalities, values, and goals their mentors' advice may sometimes be inappropriate for them. Protégés, for example, may be unwilling to make work their all-consuming priority to the extent that their mentors may have. Their mentors can counsel them about what it takes to reach the top, but protégés may be unwilling to pay the necessary price to do so. In terms of communication skills, protégés should temper their mentors' advice with awareness of their own personality and style. However much a protégé might want to imitate a mentor's flamboyant speaking style, for example, he might realize that such a style is inappropriate

for him given his personality, confidence level, and other characteristics as a message sender.

2. *Effective protégés help their mentors in appropriate ways.*
It is human nature for protégés to want to repay some of the help
their mentors have provided. Because mentors tend to be more advanced in their professional and career development, protégés rarely
can or need to reciprocate in full. To maintain self-esteem and a
spirit of mutual benefit, protégés do need to help mentors in appropriate ways. This may involve sharing contacts with mentors or
teaching mentors a particular skill protégés may have developed.
Many mentors at senior government ranks, for example, may have
less exposure to computer and quantitative skills than have their
protégés. Protégés can also serve as the eyes and ears of their mentors, keeping them informed on topics they are interested in. Much
of a mentor's continued effectiveness to himself and to his protégés
results from being a conduit of information from many sources.
One of Charles Levine's many qualities as mentor came from his
capacity as clearinghouse of information about public administration research and practice. He constantly received information from
his many former students and colleagues who would regularly report in, seeking advice or passing along information because they
knew of his interest. He was then able to pass along relevant information or leads to others. Protégés help their mentors remain effective in this way. Protégés should draw the line, of course, at helping
mentors in ways that are illegal or unethical. Mentors who are truly
concerned about their protégés' welfare avoid putting them in this
position.

3. *Effective protégés recognize that independence is the ultimate goal and work to achieve that.* Protégés share responsibility
with mentors for avoiding dependency. Protégés should talk with
mentors about their relationship and how they would like to see this
relationship evolve. Mentors and protégés talk about many things
during their relationship but too seldom talk directly about the
health and future of that relationship. Mentoring relationships, like
any relationships of value, need constant nurturing. Protégés
should also cultivate other professional relationships and should
increasingly "test their wings" as they increase their capabilities.
Such actions by protégés are necessary, especially if mentors fail to

cut loose the strings. Protégés too dependent upon one mentor run the risk of being too closely linked with that mentor. If this happens, protégés may be victimized by association if the mentor falls from grace or left stranded if the mentor leaves the agency.

4. *Effective protégés develop the capacity to become mentors to someone else.* Part of the often unspoken contract is that protégés reciprocate in appropriate ways. Another responsibility of protégés is to pay back some of what has been done for them by developing the capacity to be mentors to others. To do this, protégés need to develop their own knowledge, skills, and information networks. These will likely be enhanced as protégés make the transition to mentors for others. Teaching others and modeling skills and behavior for others often provide the best learning experiences for public administrators. It also pays for protégés to be introspective about the relationship with their mentors. This means paying particular attention to the strengths, weaknesses, and process of their own mentor-protégé relationship. Such introspection can enable protégés to emulate the mentoring behaviors they have found constructive and avoid behaviors detrimental to their future relationships.

Learning from Professional Activities

Professional association activities provide some of the best outlets for honing communication skills. Most professional associations sponsor workshops or seminars that relate to communicating skills. The American Society for Public Administration has conducted workshops on administrative writing and has had panel presentations dealing with speaking and writing skills. The International City Management Association provides comparable training and has published two books relevant to this matter: *Effective Communication: Getting the Message Across* (Arnold, Becker, and Kellar, 1983) and *Public Relations in Local Government* (Gilbert, 1975). The National Association of Government Communicators, a professional society comprising public information officers and others involved in communication activities, holds conferences and workshops and publishes a newsletter and the *Journal of Public Communication.* Professional associations can also foster better government communication by recognizing and honoring superior communicating. The Government Finance Officers Association makes awards to governments for communicating budget and financial information simply and appealingly. Comparable recognition by other professional associations would do much to increase the visibility and quality of government communication.

Professional associations also provide many less obvious outlets for practicing and improving communication skills. Association committees, panels, presentations, elections, receptions, and other occasions provide opportunities for skill development. Professional associations depend heavily on voluntary help and on new blood to conduct their activities. Some associations are desperate for help; most encourage wider involvement. For these reasons, many public administrators I know have held positions in associations that give them a level of authority and learning they would be unlikely to experience in their paid government job for another ten to twenty years. As discussed in Chapter Six, public administrators can benefit from experience gained via professional activity.

Skill Development from Reading

Reading can help administrators learn and apply communication principles. The professional literature on government communication is scant indeed compared to that for business communication. Much of the conceptual base for government communication is therefore derived from works on general communications theory and from research on business organizations. Nevertheless, in preparing this and other works on government administrative communication, I did uncover a limited but important body of literature that directly addresses government communication. Some works are descriptive research studies of communicating in public agencies. Others are primarily prescriptive textbooks or manuals such as the International City Management Association books cited above. To expand the pool of reading on government communication, I have deliberately drawn from a wide range of sources and literatures. Readers can consult the references at the end of this book to access this knowledge.

Tracking Communication Trends

Yet another key way to enhance communication skills is to keep track of trends in communication and communication technology. This can enable public administrators to take advantage of new trends or at least better understand them. The trends discussed below appear to be important for the rest of the 1990s.

Accelerating Communications Capability

During the Revolutionary War it took two days for General George Washington, commander-in-chief of the Continental Army, to communicate war results to the Continental Congress 100 miles away in Philadelphia. During the Persian Gulf War, cable and network television relayed coverage by satellite, showing battles as they occurred in a desert thousands of miles away. This is but one of many examples of how technological advances have reduced time and distance factors in communication.

Communication technology has been changing rapidly since 1876, when the first telegraph allowed people to communicate over long distances. The telegraph was a breakthrough and the basis for much of today's progress in the routing, transmission, and processing of information. Approximately forty years later, the telephone was conceived and developed as an extension of telegraphy. Radio came one generation after the telephone. In the 1930s television was developed to add an image to the voice transmission. Wartime needs during World War II inspired several different communication methods, among them electromechanical "Strowger" type switching relay, coaxial cable, the termionic valve, the transistor, and the computer. Since World War II, the integration of electronic circuitry into less space has progressed enormously.

The computer was born out of research for telephone switching techniques. The explosive growth in computer usage in telecommunications has been due to the advances in semiconductor technology and microelectronics, which have produced increasingly smaller and more powerful circuits and chips. Progress with parallel circuitry promises to make computers even smaller and more powerful. The development of computers led to the electronic information age, permitting teleconferences between groups in the United States, Europe, and the Far East, without leaving the office. One of the largest video conferences was held by Texas Instruments on November 13, 1985. It involved 20,000 people who participated in an artificial intelligence symposium. Governments also use teleconferencing for many purposes, including conducting trials when all participants cannot be at the same courtroom.

In 1960, the United States started launching communication satellites to develop communication capabilities beyond the connection of wires between two points. In 1965, *Early Bird,* the first commercial satellite was placed in service to handle 240 two-way telephone circuits between Europe and the United States. Radio Corporation of America's SATCOM I, launched in 1975, boosted the capability of cable television (Bozeman and Rahm, 1989). The two-way videotext capability of cable television can now enable interaction among governments and their citizenry, allowing viewers to respond to a local government survey, for example. Satellite networks will soon be as common as truck fleets that carry supplies. Government and corporate branch offices, schools, and businesses will increasingly have dish antennas to send and receive information. Two-way voice, image, and text communications are now available between offices and across continents. New technologies even enable users to record and play back sound at a local computer workstation and send that sound over a local area network, allowing voice mail and real-time voice conversations via computer. For less than $150, users can augment computer text and data communication with actual voice transmission via computer.

Futurist John Naisbitt notes that by 1992 more than sixteen million miles of fiber optic communications cable will be in place around the world. He observes that "we are laying the foundations for an international information highway system. In telecommunications we are moving to a single worldwide information network. . . . We are moving toward the capability to communicate anything to anyone, anywhere, by any form—voice, data, text, image—at the speed of light" (Naisbitt and Aburdene, 1990, p. 6). The proposed National Research and Education Network (NREN) being discussed in Congress in 1991 would upgrade fiber optics transmission capability by 1995 to sixty-six times the current capacity for carrying data, sounds, graphic images, and even video images. It would have the capacity to "transmit the entire *Encyclopaedia Britannica* in a second" (Karraker, 1991, p. 7).

The benefits and the challenges inherent in these and other advances in communications technology profoundly affect government management. The means exist to increase the capability of citizens to express their opinions and preferences to governments. Public officials and administrators would do well to enable and encourage citizen input and to be responsive to that input. Responsiveness to citizens' needs and demands can eliminate political and economic reaction problems resulting from going against citizen wishes, either deliberately or inadvertently. However, advances in technology may result in a widening disparity of citizen access unless governments guard against it. Despite the growing number of cable television hookups, public service viewing and interactive capability remain limited. Many more citizens own computers than have the knowledge and communication capability to interact directly with government officials. People who can afford to own computers, fax machines, and other technologies and know how to use them will have an advantage. Herein lies the danger of further empowering the already powerful without aiding the powerless. This issue lies at the heart of the current debate over a new national telecomputer network. Will the National Research and Education Network be accessible only to major government agencies, universities, and corporations, or will elementary and secondary schools, nonprofit organizations, and others have access?

Governments can guard against the widening inequality of information access by fostering the spread of technological devices and a knowledge of how to use them and by avoiding reliance on a few high-tech, high-cost media. By sending and receiving information through a broad range of media—including inexpensive, low-tech means such as neighborhood meetings and phone-in programs—governments broaden citizen access.

In the past, messages from citizens, news media, lobbyists, and other government actors came more slowly. To be sure, the slowness of messages often meant hearing about an event or action after the fact, complicating how to deal with it. Almost the opposite problem often occurs today. Getting information quickly and sometimes vividly can lead to overreacting and to overmanaging some situations. Managers have a bias for action that results from temperament and from following the admonitions of management scholars (Mintzberg, 1973; Peters and Waterman, 1982). Accordingly, many public (and business) managers sometimes act when action is counterproductive. Some situations work themselves out in due course if no precipitous action is taken to stir them up. One of the hardest lessons I had to learn early in my government career was to avoid overmanaging—constantly calling and writing about each small development without letting the situation settle and without letting my grasp of it mature. There were times when administrators and lobbyists gave me what I wanted just to be rid of me. In other situations, however, micromanaging probably complicated the issues. Communication today can be so quick and so easy that public administrators can send messages inappropriate to the audience and the situation and regret it later.

Personal, Informal Communication in a High-Tech Era

Despite all the technology available to aid communication, public administrators should remember that high-tech communication may be inappropriate to audience, purpose, and management situation. If fancy communicating tools are available, there is the feeling they should be used. If such tools are not available, many agencies have sought them even when unnecessary to their work and expensive on the budget. Kraemer (1989, p. 533) observes that "the research does not support slavish attempts to be at the leading edge of technology's applications." He notes that failures to develop leading-edge information system technologies often demoralize users and set progress back more than if more modest attempts had been made.

    Informal, personal, low-tech communication is more appropriate in many situations. The way to influence government decision making in many towns, counties, and states is to be at the coffee shop or restaurant that key officials and politicians frequent. Santa Monica, California, may hold some town meetings via computer bulletin board, but Santa Monica officials provide other opportunities for personal, face-to-face contact. Tom Peters and others advocate the need for simpler, more informal communicating in organizations at the same time that organizations rush to get telecommunications, fax, computer communications, and other technological capabilities. The key is to recognize the value of both high- and low-tech communicating, using each when it is appropriate to audience, purpose, and management situation. Even when high-tech communication is preferred, users should be aware of the need for human touches to compensate for the potential sterility of the high-tech approach. John Naisbitt (1984) claims that the trend is toward both high-tech and "high-touch," being responsive to human concerns. Failures to consider human feelings when introducing communication technology will likely scuttle that technology.

Decentralizing Power and Communications:
From Hierarchies to Networking

Networks, in Naisbitt's terms (1984), are people communicating with each other, sharing ideas, information, and resources. The communication may be via high-tech computer or satellite networks or via newsletters, telephone calls, neighborhood meetings, coalitions of organizations, and the like. Networks make it easier to get information, cutting across disciplines, organizations, and hierarchies. Networks tend to be more egalitarian, allowing access and participation based more on knowledge and information than on hierarchical status. Remember astronomer Clifford Stoll's success chasing a computer spy through networking when hierarchical channels were closed.

   I will avoid making the mistake that several noted management scholars have made of predicting the end of bureaucracy and hierarchy. These structures display time-tested hardiness and function well in many situations. What I am noting is that an increasing amount of government policy setting and implementation is being done by networks of administrators, scientists, lobbyists, academics, lawyers, and others. Such networks arise because government is buried in information. Networks allow participants to select and acquire the information they need more quickly and less expensively than through hierarchical channels. Networks also arise because of mutual interests and aims. Networks typically promote equal access by participants even if they do not always achieve it. This concept of equal access has been found to be important in St. Paul, Minnesota; Dayton, Ohio; and other places where strong efforts are under way to involve and empower citizens (Berry, Portney, and Thomson, 1989). The most far-reaching effect of networks is on power structure. Networks tend to disperse information and participation, making it more difficult to centralize authority.

Shortening of Attention Span and Messages

The public's desire for shorter, more visual, and more active messages is noted in Chapter Seven. This trend will probably intensify as the current generation of video-age youngsters enters the work force. As dependence on television and video increases, the ability to deal with the printed word decreases. Employers and educators bemoan the poor reading and writing skills of many students and graduates. Despite the growth in U.S. households from 64 million in 1970 to 91.1 million in 1988, daily newspaper circulation failed to grow, and the percentage of people who say they read a newspaper actually dropped from 73 percent to 50 percent (Kurtz, 1991). Even people who read newspapers tend to have a shorter attention span for hard news. As one newspaper publisher said, "For baby boomers who go to a lot of champagne parties, [the price of champagne] is more interesting than whatever Jack Kemp [secretary of the Department of Housing and Urban Development] had to say today" (Kurtz, 1991, p. 11).

Futurist Alvin Toffler (1980, p. 182) characterizes the trend toward message fragmentation this way: "Instead of receiving long, related 'strings' of ideas, organized or synthesized for us, we are increasingly exposed to short, modular blips of information—ads, commands, theories, shreds of news, truncated bits and blobs that refuse to fit nearly into our preexisting mental files." Toffler claims that "the new generation is more at ease in the midst of this bombardment of blips: the ninety-second newsclip with a thirty-second commercial, a fragment of a song or lyric, a headline, a cartoon, a collage, a newsletter item, and a computer printout." "Third Wave people," as Toffler calls them, take in vast quantities of apparently disjointed information but seek metaphors or constructs that help them organize these blips into meaningful wholes. Government communicators need to learn that many members of the new generation have different frames of reference and different preferences for communication media. They resist long, formal messages conveyed to them by traditional media.

Another futurist, John Naisbitt (1984, p. 19) also emphasizes the trend toward user-responsive information. He observes: "For hundreds of years, authors and editors have decided what to put in the packages they create for us—newspapers, magazines, television programs—and we pick among them, deciding what we want to read or watch. Now with the new technologies, we will create our own packages, experiencing sovereignty over text." Governments will need to be responsive to the ways citizens and employees prefer to communicate information. This does not mean a headlong rush to outdo MTV. It does mean that governments will need to recognize these trends without abandoning their responsibility to provide more than superficial, capsulized information. This may involve repackaging information into more digestible, more attractive bits that add up to overall understanding.

This chapter is intended to guide readers as they begin to apply their learning from this book and to supplement that learning. Learning opportunities for improving communication skills are numerous and varied. Yet public administrators can still miss opportunities or miss the value of the opportunities they take. The major purpose of this book is to provide a conceptual framework that can help public administrators think more strategically and situationally about communicating than they did before. Having a framework like this within which to view communication situations can also increase the value of the learning opportunities necessary to consolidate and extend learning gained here. Applying the strategic contingency model and utilizing the concepts, guidelines, and ideas advanced here will make public administrators better communicators. If elected officials and administrative superiors make effective communication a priority for themselves and for their staffs and if government professionals work diligently and intelligently to improve their skills, government communication and overall effectiveness will improve.

Communication: An Idea Whose Time Has Long Since Come

Leading thinkers in the classical school of public administration, prominent when the discipline was at its height of influence, recognized a role for communication within the field. Luther Gulick's formulation of the critical functions of public administration—planning, organizing, staffing, directing, coordinating, reporting, and budgeting (POSDCORB)—includes attention to communication. Gulick's function of directing embodies communicating "specific and general orders and directions" (1937, p. 13). Reporting involves "keeping those to whom the executive is responsible informed as to what is going on, which thus includes keeping himself and his subordinates informed through records, research, and inspection" (p. 13). The task of coordinating, in Gulick's thinking, primarily involves organization, dominance of an idea, habit, and time, but it also involves sharing information and understanding the "network" in which officials operate (p. 21). Gulick recognized the importance of communicating to breathe life into the skeleton of organization. His considerable success in influencing reorganizations in numerous states, cities, and the federal government stemmed in large part from his ability to persuade government officials, politicians, citizens, and academics. That Gulick was no stranger to communication strategy is evidenced by the fact that he deliberately couched his ideas for reorganization in terms of "principles" that he and other reformers thought would appeal to the strong interest at that time in anything scientific, rational, and businesslike (L. H. Gulick, interview with the author, Nov. 30, 1976; Garnett, 1980). Henri Fayol's highly influential general principles of management emphasize communication as part of the scalar (hierarchical) and esprit de corps principles. Lateral communication, what Fayol called the "gang plank," he stressed is essential to cut through the formal chain of command. Fayol also advocated the use of oral rather than written communications to "gain in speed, clarity, and harmony" (Fayol, [1916] 1949). Fayol applied his substantial ability to communicate during his successful career in business. Leonard D. White (1939), in his formative public administration text *Introduction to the Study of Public Administration*, notes the importance of communication to field office–headquarters relationships, intergovernmental relations, morale of the public service, and other matters.

These authors, prominent in increasing the status and influence of public administration, recognized the importance of communication in their writings and especially in their actions. They rarely used the term *communication*, however. More often, they used other terms such as *reporting*. Furthermore, communication was mostly subsumed under other functions or principles of administration. It therefore became easier for future readers to overlook the significance of communication within the classical paradigm. Because of this problem and perceptions that communicating is a routine function that virtually everyone can do, communication later became de-emphasized along with other practical, nuts-and-bolts functions in the field of public administration. Not enough writers heeded Chester Barnard's later emphasis on communication as the first function of the executive.

Few texts or readers have dealt directly or significantly with the topic of communication, few college and university public administration programs have emphasized administrative communication, and communication has no accepted home within the discipline. No specialty section exists within the American Society for Public Administration to address communication issues specifically, and communication is hardly a major focus of other sections. Conference tracks and panels rarely emphasize administrative communication except for an occasional panel on administrative writing or press relations. The classical paradigm emphasizing the principles of administration recognized the important place of communication. This strong role for communication must exist within any intellectual paradigm found to replace the classical one. Another principle of administration deserves emphasis—the communication principle: communicate strategically, as appropriate to purpose, audience, and management situation.

Some recent developments underscore the need for public administration and public administrators to emphasize communication more than they have in the past. First, more communicating now occurs on a greater variety of subjects, and with a broader range of technologies than ever before. Second, the National Commission on the Public Service has identified major goals that need to be achieved before government as an institution and public administration as a profession and discipline will be able to turn around their declining image and influence. These include such core goals as rebuilding the public's trust, rebuilding student interest in government, and establishing a culture of performance within government. These and other commission goals integrally involve communication—with the public and within government itself. Third, recent major events such as the *Challenger* explosion, the savings and loan bailout, and the Persian Gulf War have dramatized the human and monetary costs of poor communication. On the other hand, we have seen vivid examples of effective communication that have led to success and helped restore confidence in government. The extraordinary communication to coordinate allied efforts in the Gulf War and General Schwarzkopf's tour-de-force briefing explaining military strategy are but two examples.

Better communication is no panacea for improved government performance. Public administrators and other public servants must have the substantive and procedural knowledge worth communicating. Communication skills can be used to perverse ends by unethical administrators or elected officials. Controversies will still arise if inequalities persist in quality of life. If government service and public administration as a discipline are to regain their credibility and influence, however, communication must play a stronger role—in government priorities, in service to citizens, in government training and executive development, and in the intellectual core of public administration.

REFERENCES

Adams, B. "The Limitations of Muddling Through: Does Anyone in Washington Really Think Anymore." *Public Administration Review*, 1979, *39*(6), 545–552.

Adams, S. "Vietnam Cover-Up: Playing War with Numbers." In R. J. Stillman, II (ed.), *Public Administration Concepts and Cases*, pp. 262–277. Boston: Houghton Mifflin, 1988.

Allport, G. W., and Postman, L. J. *The Psychology of Rumor*. New York: Holt, Rinehart & Winston, 1947.

American Library Association Washington Office. *Less Access to Less Information by and About the U.S. Government: A 1981–1987 Chronology*. Washington, D.C.: American Library Association Washington Office, 1988.

Appleby, P. H. *Morality and Administration in Democratic Government*. Baton Rouge: Louisiana State University Press, 1952.

Argyris, C., and Schön, D., *Theory in Practice: Increasing Professional Effectiveness*. San Francisco: Jossey-Bass, 1974.

Arnold, C. C., and Bowers, J. W. (eds.). *Handbook of Rhetorical and Communication Theory*. Needham Heights, Mass.: Allyn & Bacon, 1984.

Arnold, D. S., Becker, C. S., and Kellar, E. K. (eds.). *Effective Communication: Getting the Message Across*. Washington, D.C.: International City Management Association, 1983.

Asch, S. E. "Studies of Independence and Conformity: A Minority of One Against a Unanimous Majority." *Psychological Monographs*, 1956, *70*.

Balz, D., and Devroy, A. "Bush Broke Deadlock with the Word 'Me,' not 'Taxes.'" *Philadelphia Inquirer*, July 2, 1990, p. 4A.

Bardach, E. *The Implementation Game: What Happens After a Bill Becomes a Law*. Cambridge, Mass.: MIT Press, 1977.

Barnard, C. *The Functions of the Executive*. Cambridge, Mass.: Harvard University Press, 1938.

Baumann, R. M. "The Administration of Access to Confidential Records in State Archives: Common Practices and the Need for a Model Law." *American Archivist*, 1986, *49*, 349–360.

Bennis, W. G., and Nanus, B. *Leaders: The Strategies for Taking Charge*. New York: Harper & Row, 1985.

Berelson, B., and Steiner, G. A. *Human Behavior: An Inventory of Scientific Findings*. Orlando, Fla.: Harcourt Brace Jovanovich, 1969.

Berger, C. R., and Chafee, S. H. (eds.). *Handbook of Communication Science*. Newbury Park, Calif.: Sage, 1987.

Berry, J. M., Portney, K. E., and Thomson, K. "Empowering and Involving Citizens." In J. L. Perry (ed.), *Handbook of Public Administration*, pp. 208–222. San Francisco: Jossey-Bass, 1989.

Boje, D. M., and Whetten, D. A. "Effects of Organizational Strategies and Contextual Constraints on Centrality and Attributions of Influence in Interorganizational Networks." *Administrative Science Quarterly*, 1981, *26*(3), 378–395.

Bolman, L. G., and Deal, T. E. *Reframing Organizations: Artistry, Choice, and Leadership*. San Francisco: Jossey-Bass, 1991.

Bozeman, B., and Rahm, D. "The Explosion of Technology." In J. L. Perry (ed.), *Handbook of Public Administration*. San Francisco: Jossey-Bass, 1989.

Bravo, N. "Under the Wheel of Bureaucracy, License to Shriek." *New York Times*, Feb. 23, 1990, p. B1.

Breasure, J.M.C. (ed.). *Nonverbal Communication Skills Handbook*. Tampa, Fla.: Advance Development Systems, 1982.

Brooks, E., and Odiorne, G. S. *Managing by Negotiations*. Malabar, Fla.: Krieger, 1990.

Bryson, J. M. *Strategic Planning for Public and Nonprofit Organizations*. San Francisco: Jossey-Bass, 1988.

Buchert, W. "Fibbers Often Betrayed by Body Language." *USA Today*, Nov. 14, 1989, p. 11A.

Burke, R. J., and Wilcox, D. S. "Effects of Different Patterns and Degrees of Openness in Superior-Subordinate Communication on Job Satisfaction." *Academy of Management Journal,* 1969, *12,* 319–326.

Burns, J. M. *Leadership.* New York: Harper & Row, 1978.

Cameron, K. S., and Whetten, D. "An Assessment of Salient Management Skills." Working paper. School of Business, University of Wisconsin, 1980.

Campbell, R. W., and Garnett, J. L. "Implementing Strategy: Models and Factors." In J. Rabin, G. J. Miller, and W. B. Hildreth (eds.), *Handbook of Strategic Management,* pp. 257–278. New York: Marcel Dekker, 1989.

Capers, R. J., and Lipton, E. "NASA and Firm Cited in Telescope Flaw." *Philadelphia Inquirer,* Nov. 26, 1990, p. 3A.

Caplow, T. "Rumors in War." In A. H. Rubenstein and C. J. Haberstroh (eds.), *Some Theories of Organization,* pp. 280–287. Homewood, Ill.: Irwin-Dorsey, 1960.

Caplow, T. *How to Run Any Organization.* New York: Holt, Rinehart & Winston, 1976.

Carroll, J. D., Fritschler, A. L., and Smith, B.L.R. "Supply-Side Management in the Reagan Administration." *Public Administration Review,* 1985, *45*(2), 805–814.

Carroll, J. R. "Iraq Traps Thousands of Americans." *Philadelphia Inquirer,* Aug. 10, 1990, pp. 1A, 14A.

Chartrand, R. L. "The Many Potentials of Information Technology for Emergency Management." *Information Society,* 1985, *3,* 275–289.

Cogan, E. *How to Hold Successful Public Meetings.* San Francisco: Jossey-Bass, 1992.

Cohen, H. *You Can Negotiate Anything.* New York: Bantam Books, 1983.

Cohen, M. *The Effective Public Manager.* San Francisco: Jossey-Bass, 1988.

Cohen, S., and Wills, T. A. "Stress, Social Support, and the Buffering Hypothesis." *Psychological Bulletin,* 1985, *98,* 310–357.

Conger, J. A. *The Charismatic Leader.* San Francisco: Jossey-Bass, 1989.

Converse, J. M., and Presser, S. *Survey Questions: Handcrafting the Standardized Questionnaire.* Newbury Park, Calif.: Sage, 1986.

Cooper, P. J. "Legal Tools for Accomplishing Administrative Responsibilities." In J. L. Perry (ed.), *Handbook of Public Administration,* pp. 97-113. San Francisco: Jossey-Bass, 1989.

Corson, J. J., and Paul, R. S. *Men Near the Top: Filling Key Posts in the Federal Service.* New York: Committee for Economic Development, 1966.

Cousins, N. "Editor's Odyssey." *Saturday Review,* Apr. 15, 1978, p. 13.

Cuccia, R. A. "Public Service Announcements as Free Advertising." In L. M. Helm and others (eds.), *Informing the People: A Public Affairs Handbook,* pp. 153-157. White Plains, N.Y.: Longman, 1981.

Curry, R. O. (ed.). *Freedom at Risk: Secrecy, Censorship, and Repression in the 1980's.* Philadelphia: Temple University Press, 1988.

Cushman, J. H. "Safety Board Cites Poor Communications in Avianca Crash." *New York Times,* Feb. 22, 1990, p. B3.

Daloz, L. A. *Effective Teaching and Mentoring.* San Francisco: Jossey-Bass, 1986.

Dearborn, D. C., and Simon, H. A. "Selective Perception: A Note on the Departmental Identification of Executives." *Sociometry,* 1958, *21,* 140-144.

Delbeca, A., Van De Ven, A., and Gustavson, D. *Group Techniques for Program Planning: A Guide to Nominal Group and Delphi Processes.* Glenview, Ill.: Scott, Foresman, 1975.

DeMaio, T. J. (ed.). *Approaches to Developing Questionnaires, Statistical Policy Working Paper 10.* Washington, D.C.: Office of Management and Budget, 1983.

Donovan, R. J. *Confidential Secretary: Ann Whitman's 20 Years with Eisenhower and Rockefeller.* New York: Dutton, 1988.

Downs, A. *Inside Bureaucracy.* Boston: Little, Brown, 1967.

Downs, C. W. *Communication Audits.* Glenview, Ill.: Scott, Foresman, 1988.

Dumaine, B. "Creating a New Company Culture." *Fortune,* Jan. 15, 1990, pp. 127-131.

Ekman, P. *Telling Lies: Clues to Deceit in the Marketplace, Politics, and Marriage.* New York: Norton, 1985.

Epstein, A. "Reagan Says No 'Inkling' of Contra Aid." *Philadelphia Inquirer,* Feb. 23, 1990. p. 10A.

Esposito, J. L., and Rosnow, R. L., "Corporate Rumors: How They Start and How to Stop Them." *Management Review,* 1983, *72,* 44–49.

Etzioni, A. "Mixed Scanning: A Third Approach to Decision Making." *Public Administration Review,* 1967, *27*(5), 385–392.

Falcione, R. *Guide to Better Communication in Government Service.* Glenview, Ill.: Scott, Foresman, 1984.

Fayol, H. *General and Industrial Management.* London: Pitman, 1949. (Originally published 1916.)

Feinsilber, M. "Ex-Ambassador Says He Warned U.S. About Ceausescu." *Philadelphia Inquirer,* Jan. 22, 1990, p. 4A.

Festinger, L. *Social Pressures in Informal Groups: A Study of Human Factors in Housing.* Stanford, Calif.: Stanford University Press, 1963.

Fiedler, F. E. *A Theory of Leadership Effectiveness.* New York: McGraw-Hill, 1967.

Fink, S. *Crisis Management: Planning for the Inevitable.* New York: AMACOM, 1986.

Fisher, A. B. *Perspectives on Human Communication.* New York: Macmillan, 1978.

Fitzgerald, S. "Workers Get Feel of the Real World." *Philadelphia Inquirer,* Apr. 11, 1990, pp. 1B, 8B.

Frandsen, K. D., and Clement, D. A. "The Functions of Human Communication in Informing: Communicating and Processing Information." In C. C. Arnold and J. W. Bowers (eds.), *Handbook of Rhetorical and Communication Theory.* Needham Heights, Mass.: Allyn & Bacon, 1984.

French, W. *Human Resources Management.* (2nd ed.) Boston: Houghton Mifflin, 1990.

Gair, R. B. "Back to the Future: Strategic Planning." *Bureaucrat,* 1987, *16*(1), 7–10.

Gardner, J. *On Leadership.* New York: Free Press, 1990.

Garnett, J. L. *Reorganizing State Government: The Executive Branch.* Boulder, Colo.: Westview Press, 1980.

Garnett, J. L. "Effective Communications in Government." In J. L. Perry, (ed.). *Handbook of Public Administration*, pp. 545–588. San Francisco: Jossey-Bass, 1989.

Garnett, J. L. (ed.). *Handbook of Administrative Communication.* New York: Marcel Dekker, forthcoming.

Gibson, J. W., and Hanna, M. S. *Audience Analysis: A Programmed Approach to Receiver Behavior.* Englewood Cliffs, N.J.: Prentice-Hall, 1976.

Gilbert, W. H. (ed.). *Public Relations in Local Government.* Washington, D.C.: International City Management Association, 1975.

Goldhaber, G. M. *Organizational Communication.* (4th ed.) Dubuque, Iowa: Brown, 1986.

Goldhaber, G. M., Yates, M. P., Porter, D. T., and Lesniak, R. "Organizational Communication: 1978." *Human Communication Research,* 1979, *5,* 76–96.

Goodsell, C. T. *The Case for Bureaucracy.* Chatham, N.J.: Chatham House, 1983.

Goodsell, C. T. "Balancing Competing Values." In J. L. Perry (ed.), *Handbook of Public Administration,* pp. 575–584. San Francisco: Jossey-Bass, 1989.

Gortner, H. F., Mahler, J., and Nicholson, J. B. *Organization Theory: A Public Perspective.* Belmont, Calif.: Dorsey Press, 1987.

Gulick, L. H. "Notes on the Theory of Organization." In L. H. Gulick and L. Urwick (eds.), *Papers on the Science of Administration.* New York: Institute of Public Administration, 1937.

Halberstam, D. *The Best and the Brightest.* Greenwich, Conn.: Fawcett Crest Books, 1969. As cited in G. Starling, *Managing the Public Sector* (3rd ed.), pp. 176–177. Belmont, Calif.: Dorsey Press, 1986.

Harper, R. G. *Nonverbal Communication: The State of the Art.* New York: Wiley-Interscience, 1982.

Heise, J. A. "Toward Closing the Confidence Gap: An Alternative Approach to Communication Between Public and Government." *Public Administration Quarterly,* Summer 1985, pp. 196–216.

Herold, D. "Historical Perspectives on Government Communication." In L. M. Helm, R. E. Hiebert, M. R. Naver, and K. Rabin (eds.), *Informing the People: A Public Affairs Handbook.* New York: Longman, 1981.

Hersey, P., and Blanchard, K. *Management of Organizational Behavior.* Englewood Cliffs, N.J.: Prentice-Hall, 1982.

Hershey, R. D., Jr. "Tax Sleuths Turn to Technology." *Philadelphia Inquirer,* Mar. 28, 1990, pp. D1, D4.

Hitler, A. *Mein Kampf.* Cambridge, Mass.: Riverside, 1933.

Hollman, L., and Tulsky, F. N. "SEPTA Missed Trouble Signs." *Philadelphia Inquirer,* Mar. 25, 1990, p. 1A.

Isaac, S., and Michael, W. B. *Handbook in Research and Evaluation.* (2nd ed.) San Diego: EDITS Publishers, 1981.

Jablin, F. M. "Superior-Subordinate Communication: The State of the Art." *Psychological Bulletin,* 1979, *86,* 1201-1222.

Janis, I. L. *Crucial Decisions: Leadership in Policy Making and Crisis Management.* New York: Free Press, 1989.

Johnston, W., and others. *Civil Service 2000.* Washington, D.C.: U.S. Government Printing Office, 1988.

Karraker, R. "Highways of the Mind or Toll Roads Between Information's Castles." *Whole Earth Review,* 1991, *70,* 4-11.

Katz, D., and Kahn, R. L. *The Social Psychology of Organizations.* New York: Wiley, 1966.

Katz, E., and Lazarsfeld, P. *Personal Influence.* New York: Free Press, 1955.

Kaufman, H., and Couzens, M. *Administrative Feedback: Monitoring Subordinates' Behavior.* Washington, D.C.: Brookings Institution, 1973.

"Keeping Secrets: Congress, the Courts, and National Security Information." *Harvard Law Review,* 1990, *103,* 906-925.

Kellar, E. K. "Communicating with Elected Officials." In D. S. Arnold, C. S. Becker, and E. K. Kellar (eds.), *Effective Communication: Getting the Message Across.* Washington, D.C.: International City Management Association, 1983.

Kiechel, W. "How to Spot an Empty Suit." *Fortune,* Nov. 20, 1989, pp. 227-229.

King, M. L., Jr. Address at Birmingham, Ala., Dec. 31, 1963.

Kirmeyer, S. L., and Lin, T. "Social Support: Its Relationship to Observed Communication with Peers and Superiors." *Academy of Management Journal,* 1987, *30*(1), 138-151.

Kirst, M. "Crafting Policy Analysis for Decision Makers: An Interview with Lawrence Lynn." *Educational Evaluation and Policy Analysis*, 1980, *2*, 86-87.

Kotter, J. P. *Organizational Dynamics: Diagnosis and Intervention.* Reading, Mass.: Addison-Wesley, 1978.

Kouzes, J. M., and Posner, B. Z. *The Leadership Challenge: How to Get Extraordinary Things Done in Organizations.* San Francisco: Jossey-Bass, 1987.

Kouzmin, A., and Jarman, A. "Crisis Decision Making: Towards a Contingent Decision Path Perspective." In U. Rosenthal, M. T. Charles, and P. 'T. Hart (eds.), *Coping with Crises: The Management of Disasters, Riots, and Terrorism.* Springfield, Ill.: Thomas, 1989.

Kraemer, K. L. "Managing Information Systems." In J. L. Perry (ed.), *Handbook of Public Administration.* San Francisco: Jossey-Bass, 1989.

Krone, K. J., Jablin, F. M., and Putnam, L. L. "Communication Theory and Organizational Communication: Multiple Perspectives." In R. D. McPhee and P. K. Tompkins (eds.), *Handbook of Organizational Communication.* Newbury Park, Calif.: Sage, 1987.

Kurtz, H. "Pink, Bright, and Brief All Over." *Washington Post National Weekly Edition*, Feb. 25-Mar. 3, 1991, pp. 11-12.

Lawler, E. E. *Pay and Organizational Effectiveness.* Reading, Mass.: Addison-Wesley, 1981.

Lawrence, P., and Lorsch, J. *Organization and Environment.* Boston: Graduate School of Business Administration, Harvard University, 1967.

Levine, C., Backoff, R., Cahoon, A., and Siffin, W. "Organizational Design: A Post Minnowbrook Perspective for the New Public Administration." *Public Administration Review*, 1975, *35*, 425-435.

Lewis, P. V. *Organizational Communication: The Essence of Effective Management.* (3rd ed.) New York: Wiley, 1987.

Lewis, R. *Challenger: The Final Voyage.* New York: Columbia University Press, 1988.

Lindblom, C. E. "The Science of Muddling Through." *Public Administration Review*, 1959, *19*, 79-88.

Linden, R. M. *From Vision to Reality: Strategies of Successful Innovators in Government.* Charlottesville, Va.: LEL Enterprises, 1990.

Lipsky, M. "Street Level Bureaucracy and the Analysis of Urban Reform." *Urban Affairs Quarterly,* 1971, *6,* 391–409.

Littlejohn, R. F. *Crisis Management: A Team Approach.* New York: American Management Association, 1983.

Littlejohn, S. W. *Theories of Human Communication.* Columbus, Ohio: Merrill, 1978.

Lorch, R. S. *Public Administration.* St. Paul, Minn.: West, 1978.

Lounsberry, E. "Fierce, Funny, FBI Chief Gets Reward." *Philadelphia Inquirer,* Mar. 20, 1991, pp. 1B, 4B.

Lutz, W. *Doublespeak.* New York: Harper & Row, 1989.

Macaulay, T. B. "Machiavelli." In G. M. Young (ed.), *Macaulay: Prose and Poetry.* Cambridge, Mass.: Harvard University Press, 1967.

March, J., and Olsen, J. (eds.). *Ambiguity and Choice in Organizations.* Bergen, Norway: Universitetsforlaget, 1979.

March, J. G. "Bounded Rationality, Ambiguity, and the Engineering of Choice." *Bell Journal of Economics,* Aug. 1978, pp. 587–608.

Martin, J. B. "The Blast in Centralia No. 5: A Mine Disaster No One Stopped." In R. J. Stillman, II (ed.), *Public Administration: Concepts and Cases* (4th ed.), pp. 17–31. Boston: Houghton Mifflin, 1988.

Marwick, C. M. *Your Right to Government Information.* New York: Bantam Books, 1985.

Mathes, J. C., and Stevenson, D. W. *Designing Technical Reports: Writing for Audiences in Organizations.* (2nd ed.) New York: Macmillan, 1991.

Maude, B. *Practical Communication for Managers.* White Plains, N.Y.: Longman, 1974.

Maykuth, A. "Pilot's Plea for 'Priority' Was Held Up." *Philadelphia Inquirer,* Jan. 29, 1990, pp. 1A, 4A.

Mendelsohn, H., and O'Keefe, G. "Social Psychological Grounding for Effective Communication on Behalf of Crime Prevention." Paper presented at the annual meeting of the American Psychological Association, Los Angeles, 1981.

Miller, G. R. "Persuasion." In C. R. Berger and S. H. Chafee (eds.), *Handbook of Communication Science.* Newbury Park, Calif.: Sage, 1987.

Mintzberg, H. *The Nature of Managerial Work.* New York: Harper & Row, 1973.

Mitroff, I. I. "Crisis Management: Cutting Through the Confusion." *Sloan Management Review,* 1988, *29,* 15-20.

Murray, M. A. "Education for Public Administrators." *Public Personnel Management,* 1976, *5,* 239-245, 248-249.

Naisbitt, J. *Megatrends: Ten New Directions Transforming Our Lives.* New York: Warner Books, 1984.

Naisbitt, J., and Aburdene, P. *Megatrends 2000: Ten New Directions for the 1990s.* New York: Avon, 1990.

National Association of Government Communicators. *Journal of Public Communication,* 1990, *13* (entire fall issue).

National Commission on the Public Service. *Leadership for America: Rebuilding the Public Service.* Washington, D.C.: National Commission on the Public Service, 1989.

National Commission on the Public Service. *Leadership for America: Rebuilding the Public Service. The Report of the National Commission on the Public Service and the Task Force Reports.* Lexington, Mass.: Lexington Books, 1990.

Nichols, R. "Listening Is a 10 Part Skill." *Nation's Business,* 1957, *45,* 56-60.

Nowak, K. L. "A State Agency Gets Spirit." *Journal of Public Communication,* 1990, *13,* 13-17.

Oberdorfer, D. "The War No One Saw Coming." *Washington Post National Weekly Edition,* Mar. 18-24, 1991, pp. 6-10.

O'Reilly, C. A., and Roberts, K. H. "Information Filtration in Organizations: Three Experiments." *Organizational Behavior and Human Performance,* 1974, *11,* 253-265.

Orwell, G. "Politics and the English Language." *A Collection of Essays.* New York: Doubleday, 1954.

"A Painful Choice: Why the West Isn't Rallying Behind Lithuania." *Philadelphia Inquirer,* Apr. 29, 1990, p. 6E.

Paolantonio, S. A. "Face to Face with Death, the Shock of Surviving." *Philadelphia Inquirer,* Mar. 8, 1990, p. 17A.

Perrow, C. *Organizational Analysis: A Sociological View*. Belmont, Calif.: Wadsworth, 1970.

Peters, T. *Thriving on Chaos: Handbook for a Management Revolution*. New York: Knopf, 1987.

Peters, T. J., and Austin, N. A. *A Passion for Excellence*. New York: Random House, 1985.

Peters, T. J., and Waterman, R. H. *In Search of Excellence: Lessons from America's Best-Run Companies*. New York: Harper & Row, 1982.

Peterson, N. "New Weapons in the War on Computers." *Parade*, Jan. 1979, p. 22.

Phillips, D. "Warning Lights Were Blinking for Years Before the L.A. Crash." *Washington Post National Weekly Edition*, Feb. 11-17, 1991, p. 35.

Porras, J. I., and Anderson, B. "Improving Managerial Effectiveness Through Modeling-Based Training." *Organizational Dynamics*, 1981, *9*, 60-77.

Porter, L. W., and Lawler, E. E. *Managerial Attitudes and Performance*. Homewood, Ill.: Irwin-Dorsey, 1968.

Purdy, M. "For Thornburgh, a Few Unwelcome Surprises." *Philadelphia Inquirer*, Sept. 17, 1989, pp. 1A, 10A.

Quinn, J. B. *Strategies for Change: Logical Incrementalism*. Homewood, Ill.: Irwin, 1980.

Rabin, J., Miller, G. J., and Hildreth, W. B. (eds.). *Handbook of Strategic Management*. New York: Marcel Dekker, 1989.

Rainey, H. G. *Understanding and Managing Public Organizations*. San Francisco: Jossey-Bass, 1991.

Raphael, B. *When Disaster Strikes: How Individuals and Communities Cope with Catastrophe*. New York: Basic Books, 1986.

Redfield, L. "Chief Uses Repertoire of Skills." *South Jersey Courier-Post*, Nov. 18, 1990, pp. 1B, 3B.

Reitman, V. "For Computer Users, It's Big Brother on the Party Line." *Philadelphia Inquirer*, Mar. 17, 1991, pp. 1D, 8D.

Rich, W. C. "Appraising Employee Performance." In J. L. Perry (ed.), *Handbook of Public Administration*, pp. 388-400. San Francisco: Jossey-Bass, 1989.

Robbin, A. "State Archives and Issues of Personal Privacy." *American Archivist*, 1986, *49*, 163-75.

Rogers, E. M., and Storey, J. D. "Communication Campaigns." In C. R. Berger and S. H. Chafee (eds.), *Handbook of Communication Science*. Newbury Park, Calif.: Sage, 1987.

Rosenthal, U., Charles, M. T., and 'T Hart, P. (eds.). *Coping with Crises: The Management of Disasters, Riots, and Terrorism*. Springfield, Ill.: Thomas, 1989.

Rothschild, M. A. "Marketing Communications in Nonbusiness Situations or Why It's So Hard to Sell Brotherhood Like Soap." *Journal of Marketing*, Spring 1979, pp. 11–20.

Ruesch, J., and Kees, W. *Nonverbal Communication: Notes on the Visual Perception of Human Relations*. Berkeley: University of California Press, 1956.

Samuelson, R. J. "The Culture of Competence (and Incompetence)." *Washington Post National Weekly Edition,* Mar. 11–17, 1991, p. 31.

Sayles, L. R., and Chandler, M. K. *Managing Large Systems: Organizations for the Future*. New York: Harper & Row, 1971.

Schachter, H. *Public Agency Communication*. Chicago: Nelson-Hall, 1983.

Schmitt, E. "Faulty Communication Hindered Flight 52 Rescue, a Report Says." *New York Times*, Feb. 12, 1990, p. B3.

Sciolino, E. "Guardian of Baker's Door at State: A Quick Study Who Rose Rapidly." *New York Times*, Feb. 23, 1990, p. A12.

Seidman, H., and Gilmour, R. *Politics, Position, and Power: From the Positive to the Regulatory State*. (4th ed.) New York: Oxford University Press, 1986.

Seitz, S. T. *Bureaucracy, Policy, and the Public*. St. Louis, Mo.: Mosby, 1978.

Sherman, H. *It All Depends: A Pragmatic Approach to Organization*. University, Ala.: University of Alabama Press, 1966.

Simon, H. A., Smithburg, D. W., and Thompson, V. A. *Public Administration*. New York: Knopf, 1950.

Sims, C. "AT&T to Expand Service for Foreign Language Translations." *New York Times*, Feb. 15, 1990, pp. D1, D11.

Sorensen, T. *Kennedy*. New York: Harper & Row, 1965.

Stecklow, S. "Evidently, the Whole System Failed." *Philadelphia Inquirer*, May 3, 1991, pp. 1A, 6A.

Steers, R. M., and Porter, L. W. *Motivation and Work Behavior.* (4th ed.) New York: McGraw-Hill, 1987.

Stillman, R. J. *The American Bureaucracy.* Chicago: Nelson-Hall, 1987.

Stilwell, E. "Teacher's Conduct Charge Dismissed." *South Jersey Courier-Post,* Feb. 24, 1990, p. B1.

Stoll, C. *The Cuckoo's Egg: Tracking a Spy Through the Maze of Computer Espionage.* New York: Doubleday, 1989.

Strauss, G., and Sayles, L. R. *Personnel: The Human Problems of Management.* Englewood Cliffs, N.J.: Prentice-Hall, 1972.

Sulzberger, A. H. "Without Fear or Favor." *Time,* May 8, 1980, p. 77.

Susskind, L. *Resolving Public Disputes: Interactive Teaching of Negotiation and Dispute Resolution in the Public Sector.* Cambridge, Mass.: MIT-Harvard Public Disputes Program, 1987.

Thompson, F. J. "Policy Implementation and Overhead Control." In G. C. Edwards, III (ed.), *Public Policy Implementation.* Greenwich, Conn.: JAI Press, 1984.

Thompson, J. D. *Organizations in Action.* New York: McGraw-Hill, 1967.

Thompson, J. D., and Tuden, A. "Strategies, Structures and Processes of Organizational Decision." In J. D. Thompson and others (eds.), *Comparative Studies in Administration.* Pittsburgh, Pa.: University of Pittsburgh Press, 1959.

Thompson, M. "Air Force Chief Fired for Talk of Targets in Iraq." *Philadelphia Inquirer,* Sept. 18, 1990, pp. A1, A12.

Toffler, A. *The Third Wave.* New York: Morrow, 1980.

Tompkins, P. K. "The Functions of Human Communication in Organization." In C. C. Arnold and J. W. Bowers (eds.), *Handbook of Rhetorical and Communication Theory.* Needham Heights, Mass.: Allyn & Bacon, 1984.

Tullock, G. *The Politics of Bureaucracy.* Washington, D.C.: Public Affairs Press, 1965.

"TV Crew Pre-empts Drug Raid: Cameras Cue Dealers Before Police Arrive." *Philadelphia Inquirer,* June 4, 1990, p. 8A.

Ulrich, D., Quinn, R., and Cameron, K. S. "Designing Effective Organizational Systems." In J. L. Perry (ed.), *Handbook of Pub-*

lic Administration, pp. 148–161. San Francisco: Jossey-Bass, 1989.

U.S. Air Force. *Air Force Guide to Effective Writing.* Washington, D.C.: U.S. Government Printing Office, 1963.

Uris, A. *The Executive Deskbook.* New York: Van Nostrand Reinhold, 1970.

Verderber, R. *Communicate.* Belmont, Calif.: Wadsworth, 1981.

Vroom, V. *Work and Motivation.* New York: Wiley, 1964.

Vroom, V., and Yetton, P. W. *Leadership and Decision Making.* Pittsburgh, Pa.: University of Pittsburgh Press, 1973.

Walton, E. *A Magnetic Theory of Organizational Communication.* China Lake, Calif.: U.S. Naval Ordnance Test Station, 1962.

Webb, K., and Hatry, H. *Obtaining Citizen Feedback: The Application of Citizen Surveys to Local Government.* Washington, D.C.: Urban Institute, 1973.

Weiss, W. "Effect on Social Judgment of Prior Nonjudgment Responses to Related Stimuli." *Psychology Report,* 1969, *24,* 19.

Whetten, D. A., and Cameron, K. S. *Developing Management Skills.* Glenview, Ill.: Scott, Foresman, 1984.

White, L. D. *Introduction to the Study of Public Administration.* (rev. ed.) New York: Macmillan, 1939.

White, T. H. *Breach of Faith.* New York: Atheneum, 1975.

Wilson, G. C., and Weisskopf, M. "Pentagon, Congress Seek Cure to Shortcomings Exposed in Grenada Invasion." *Washington Post,* Feb. 20, 1986, p. A24.

Wilson, J. Q. *Bureaucracy.* New York: Basic Books, 1989.

Woodward, B. *The Commanders.* New York: Simon & Schuster, 1991a.

Woodward, B. "The Road to the Gulf War." *Washington Post National Weekly Edition,* May 6–12, 1991b, p. 7.

Yarwood, D. L., and Enis, B. J. "Advertising and Publicity Programs in the Executive Branch of the National Government: Hustling or Helping the People?" *Public Administration Review,* 1982, *42*(1), 37–46.

Zander, A. *Making Groups Effective.* San Francisco: Jossey-Bass, 1982.

NAME INDEX

291

SUBJECT INDEX

A

Accuracy, issue of, 234–237
Actions: and downward communication, 105–106; ethical, 246–248; and public communication, 186
Administrative superiors. *See* Superiors and elected officials
Administrators: boundary spanning by, 158; at crisis scene, 208–210
Advisory Commission on Intergovernmental Relations, 89
Advisory Committee Act of 1972, 175
Aeromexico, 12
Age, in audience profile, 48
Agencies: boundary spanning among, 157–160; citizen contact with, 194; collegial communication among, 155–164; coordinating cooperation among, 160–163; and crises, 211; and ethical actions, 235–236, 246–247; lead, 161; news media policies of, 191–192; norms of, 156–157; support for, 89–91, 163–164; task coordination in, 141; training based in, 250–251; "universities" in, 106
Agenda strategy, for public hearings, 179–180

AIDS, objectives for communicating about, 39–40
Airline safety, and communication problems, 10–12
American Assembly of Collegiate Schools of Business, 252
American Library Association, Washington Office, 240, 241–242
American Society for Public Administration: code of ethics of, 229, 238, 240; and networks, 153; and training, 264, 274
American Telephone and Telegraph (AT&T): and Grenada invasion, 13; translation services of, 182
Analysis, as strategy design factor, 64, 82–84
Apollo project, 162–163
Argentina, and Falkland Islands, 210
Arizona, media use in, 62
Armed forces, and marketing, 169
Attention: selective, 10, 21–22; shortening span of, 271–272
Attica Prison riot, 53–54, 131, 208, 210–211
Audience profile: for agencies, 157; for agency support, 163–164; for delivering bad news, 224–225; format, 47; for publics, 177, 183; for subordinates, 101–102; for superiors, 72–76

Printed in the United States
135336LV00001B/1/A